The Southern Massacre

The Story of the 1979 Presbyterian College
Blue Hose Football Team

13 Weeks to Remember

Chip Porter

© 2023 Chip Porter

All rights reserved. No part of this publication may be reproduced, stored in a retrieval system or transmited in any form or by any means, electronic, mechanical, photocopying, recording or otherwise without the prior permision of the publisher or in accordance with the provisions of the Copyright, Designs and Patents Act 1988 or under the terms of any licence permitting limited copying issued by the Copyright Licensing Angency.

Cover Art: Savannah Raines

Paperback ISBN: 978-1-959563-19-8
eBook ISBN: 978-1-959563-20-4

Published by:
Maudlin Pond Press
P.O. Box 53
Tybee Island, GA 31328

www.maudlinpond.com

Prologue

As a former professional golfer, I can remember playing a tournament at Bay Hill in Orlando, Florida. On #18, my drive was dead center in the middle of the fairway. For my second shot, I had 198 yards to the pin. There was a slight breeze in my face and water in the front and to the right of the green. I decided to hit a 3 iron, moving the ball from left to right. I caught it perfectly, landing on the left side of the green. The ball worked its way towards the hole that was cut on the right center of the green. I had a putt of approximately 22 feet. I made the putt which moved 12 inches left to right towards the water. With a birdie at #18, I picked up, on average, 2 shots on the field. This happened over 40 years ago. I remember it like it happened yesterday.

The details we can remember seem to resurrect when something means so much to us. Throughout my interview process for The Southern Massacre, player after player and person after person had specific memories of the 1979 Presbyterian College football team. Bruce Ollis, 1979 PC OG and Co-Captain, told how he had a banner in his high school gym. Bruce, like many other Presbyterian College graduates, was part of PC's legendary Coach Cally Gault's coaching tree. The banner stated, "Football lasts 48 minutes. Memories are for a lifetime!"

In years to come, the Presbyterian College record books would include the 1979 Blue Hose football team with an overall record of 11-2. Many would look at the record and think "That was pretty good!" Success for the 1979 Blue Hose certainly did not come overnight. The blueprint for success began in the mid 1970's. I was afraid the significance and achievements of the 1979 Presbyterian College Blue Hose football team would be lost forever. I decided to document the season and The Southern Massacre was written.

Narratives of the games are captured by newspaper articles. The book reflects and reminds us of social, political and economic issues of 1979. Portions of the layout will be nostalgic to many. The format is different as I have emphasized the reflections from my interviews of the players, coaches and others associated with the team looking back years later. I have concentrated on the performance on the field in what I call "In between the lines."

The inspiration to document this story began in the spring of 2022. While searching Presbyterian College on eBay, I came across an auction for a football. Closer examination of the auction revealed that the football, which somehow got in the marketplace, was the most historical football in Presbyterian College football history. It was the game ball from the 1979 Bronze Derby game, signed by the team. I was a sophomore at PC in 1979. I witnessed this historical team. They were my classmates and friends. I was afraid that the ball would fall in the hands of a football autograph collector and the ball would never be seen again. I purchased and rescued the ball!

Historically in 1979, the 16-14 win over Newberry College was the 43rd win over the Indians (43-21-4) retaining the Bronze Derby for a third straight year. The team solidified both a SAC-8 Football Championship and a NAIA Division 1 quarter final home game against Saginaw Valley. For the first and only time in Presbyterian College football history, the team was ranked #1 in the NAIA Division 1 season ending national standings. A blueprint for success had been followed by the team and had succeeded.

In a perfect world, writing and reflecting on the 1979 Presbyterian College football team would include interviewing every player and anyone associated with the team. Unfortunately, some are no longer with us. Some do not want to participate, and I have great respect for that decision. Some cannot be found. Finally, some have not been heard from in years. They are missed by both their football family and college friends. I exceeded my expectations regarding the number of individuals I would make contact with. I experienced some surprises, but most of all, the enthusiasm has been overwhelming regarding documenting The Southern Massacre. Thank you to all that have participated.

Researching newspapers today is most simplistic. Specialized online sites have many newspapers online for informational research. But there are small and rural newspapers that have not downloaded their archives. I also discovered that smaller newspapers' archives were incomplete, damaged or even have been lost over the years. I reached out to all. When researching, it is a simple hit or miss. For example, I was disappointed to find that both "The Clinton Chronicle" and "The Newberry Observer" have no record of the 1979 Thanksgiving Day Bronze Derby game. The newspapers are missing and no microfilm is available. With all that said, I did my best to provide the most complete story available today.

In the early 1970's, the NCAA reduced Division 1 scholarships. Many refer to this rule as the Bear Bryant Rule. It simply eliminated big and perennial powerful football programs such as Alabama, Texas and the University of Southern California from stacking their teams with the best athletes in the country. As a result of the new scholarship football rule, athletes that may have gone and hoped to play at elite schools on scholarship looked to both smaller NCAA Division 1 schools and NAIA schools to continue their football careers. Presbyterian College had both a strong academic and football tradition. The coaching staff went to work. Recruiting efforts were exhausting. A culture was on the horizon.

In the mid 1970's, Presbyterian College Head Football Coach Cally Gault went through a coaching carousel. Coach Gault was already blessed with longtime Assistant Coach Bob Strock, and added former PC football student athletes Elliot Poss, John Perry and Wayne Renwick. The coaching foundation had been set. The coaches immediately started working on developing a winning tradition.

"Mid 70's were bad years for success" commented Presbyterian College Assistant Football Coach John Perry. In 1975 the Blue Hose joined the South Atlantic Conference finishing with a 3-6-1 record. In 1976, the Blue Hose went 3-7. The first freshman recruits were not "Cobs" anymore. They came from winning traditions in high school and dedicated themselves to developing a winning culture.

The 1977 Blue Hose football team went 7-3-1, tying for 2nd in the SAC-8. The team lost to The Citadel 7-13; Tied Furman 13-13; Beat Elon 45-6 and beat Newberry 3-0. The team demonstrated the commitment by senior leadership and finished #19 in the NAIA Division 1 national rankings.

The 1978 Blue Hose football team went 8-2-1, tying for first in the SAC-8. The team lost to Citadel 17-28; Tied Elon 21-21 and beat Newberry 26-0. Offensive lineman Roy Walker was a Kodak All American; Sophomore quarterback Jimmy Spence was SAC-8 player of the year and the Blue Hose defense allowed less than 12 points per game. Elon represented the SAC-8 in the NAIA playoffs and eventually lost to Angelo State in the NAIA Division 1 Championship game 24-14.

1979 began with a strong commitment to strength and conditioning. Fifth year seniors returned to campus. An optimistic group with promising freshmen and talented transfers had their sights on September. Football was a tremendous tradition at Presbyterian College. Beginning in 1913, Coach E L Booe guided the Garnet and Blue to a 5-3 record. Sixty-six years later, 1979 Presbyterian College Blue Hose football will be a year that will never be forgotten. They were the best collection of athletes to play football at Presbyterian College. They were the best football team to play at Presbyterian College. "They deserve the recognition that is long overdue," said Presbyterian College Assistant Football Coach John Perry. To my fellow classmates and friends, thank you for the memories. This is for you!

- Chip Porter '81

To Coach Bob Strock, who taught the Presbyterian Blue Hose student athletes and staff to live and serve as leaders and mentors in their community. Your lessons on the field and in life are most appreciated.

Foreword

I was humbled at Chip's request, and I take great pride penning a foreword to this remembrance of PC's special 1979 season. He has shared with me memories from several of the players and the remaining coaches that he has spoken with, and I cannot wait to read the many things these young men have shared about that season in retrospect. From the very hot days of preseason camp on the "Ponderosa" in August to the harsh, almost brutal winds to end the season in Oklahoma, the memories shared here are special. These young men played through injury and fatigue to perform at an extremely high level to which they can all be proud of achieving. Maybe more importantly is the team spirit they shared and the bond they developed during that season that they still share to this day!

A very special THANK YOU is sent to Chip for his foresight in putting this season in words to remember these young men and their tremendous efforts. We will always be proud to think about this milestone in PC's football history.

Coach Wayne Renwick

In 2017, Presbyterian College won the Fox Sports College Basketball Team Nickname Bracket Championship. How 'bout them Hose!

Living the Legacy: What the Hell is a Blue Hose?

By: Jacalin Shealy

One story is that the Presbyterian Scotch-Irish wore blue stockings in the early years of our country. Another is that a fierce, warlike band of Scotch-Irish named the Hose painted their entire bodies blue before going into battle. Yet another explanation came from a letter written in 1935 by athletic director Walter Johnson. Johnson changed uniform colors to blue, and a sports writer started calling the PC teams the Blue Stockings. Later, students abbreviated "Stockings" to "The Hose," which was eventually adopted by the student body in the '50s. Which is myth? Which is fact? Everyone has an opinion. What's yours?

Southern Massacre

Presbyterian College Blue Hose
1979 Football Schedule

September 8	at The Citadel Bulldogs	Charleston, SC	7:00
September 15	at Furman Paladins	Greenville, SC	1:30
September 22	at Lenoir Rhyne Bears*	Hickory, NC	7:30
September 29	vs Wofford Terriers	Clinton, SC	7:30
October 6	at Catawba Indians*	Salisbury, NC	2:00
October 13	vs Elon Fighting Christians*	Clinton, SC	7:30
October 20	vs Mars Hill Lions* Homecoming	Clinton, SC	3:00
October 27	vs UCF Knights Parents Night	Clinton, SC	7:30
November 3	at Gardner Webb Bulldogs*	Boiling Springs, NC	2:00
November 10	vs Carson Newman Eagles* Youth Day	Clinton, SC	2:00
November 22	at Newberry Indians* Bronze Derby	Newberry, SC	2:00

* Denotes SAC-8 Conference Game

A Look at a Decade of Presbyterian College Football

1978 8-2-1
1977 7-3-1
1976 3-7-0
1975 3-6-1
1974 6-5-0
1973 3-8-0
1972 7-2-1
1971 8-3-0
1970 8-3-0

Preseason

January 1979

- The United Nations designates 1979 as the International Year of the Child.
- Drew Brees, National Football League quarterback, was born.
- The United States and China establish full diplomatic relations.
- John Mitchell is released on parole from Federal prison in Alabama serving 19 months for his role in Watergate.
- Pope John Paul II visits Mexico.
- The top songs included "Too Much Heaven" by the Bee Gees and "Le Freak" by Chic.
- Founder of the Hilton Hotels, Conrad Hilton passed away at 91 years old.
- Ted Cassidy, the actor who played Lurch on *The Adams Family*, passed away at 46 years old.
- United States Vice President Nelson Rockefeller passed away at 70 years old.
- The TV series *The Dukes of Hazzard* debuted.

February 1979

- Religious leader Ayatollah Khomeini begins the Iranian Revolution.
- Actress Jennifer Love Hewitt was born.
- Richard Petty wins the Daytona 500, the first ever televised 500 mile race on television.
- The top song was "Da Ya Think I'm Sexy" by Rod Stewart.
- The 1979 Super Bowl played in Miami was won by the Pittsburgh Steelers over the Dallas Cowboys 35-31.
- Sid Vicious of the Sex Pistols passed away at 21 of a drug overdose.
- Mr. Ed, the talking horse on TVs "Mr. Ed" passed away from an inadvertent tranquilizer while he was in his California retirement stable.

Dr. Kenneth B. Orr

March 1979

- Spaceprobe Voyager sends pictures of exploration from Jupiter.
- Pornographic actress Stormy Daniels is born.
- Singer Adam Levine was born.
- Phillips reveals the compact disk for the first time.
- American television channel C-SPAN, focusing on the United States government, debuts.
- The movie *China Syndrome* is released.
- The National Hockey League approves a merger with the World Hockey Association.
- Columbia, the first United States space shuttle is delivered to Kennedy Space Center in Florida.
- President Jimmy Carter, Anwar Sadat of Egypt and Menachem Begin of Israel signed an Egypt Israel peace treaty.
- Michigan State with Magic Johnson defeated Indiana State and Larry Bird 75-64 in the NCAA Basketball Championship finals.
- The top Songs included "I Will Survive" by Gloria Gaynor and "Tragedy" by the Bee Gees.

April 1979

- Nickelodeon debuts on Warner Cable systems.
- Actor Heath Ledger was born.
- Reality TV star Kourtney Kardashian was born.
- Actress Kate Hudson was born.
- Dale Earnhardt Sr. wins his first career NASCAR race, the Southeastern 500 at Bristol Motor Speedway.
- The top Songs included "What a Fool Believes" by the Doobie Brothers, "Knock on Wood" by Amii Stewart and "Heart of Glass" by Blondie.
- The Masters golf tournament was won by Fuzzy Zoeller, his first time playing at Augusta National Golf Club in Augusta, Georgia.

CHRONICLE PUBLISHING CO.

Publishers—Printers—Stationers

Your Every Printing Need Can Be Supplied Here

Subscribe To The Chronicle For Complete Coverage of The Blue Hose

Clinton's Newspaper Since 1900

TELEPHONE 833-0541

May 1979

- Margaret Thatcher becomes the United Kingdom's first woman Prime Minister.
- Singer Lance Bass of NSYNC was born.
- The Unabomber Ted Kaczynski injures Northwestern University graduate student John Harris. Minor injuries were sustained by the detonation of a bomb.
- The Montreal Canadiens defeat the New York Rangers four games to one to win their fourth consecutive National Hockey League Stanley Cup.
- The movies *Battlestar Galactica* and *Alien* are released.
- Spectacular Bid wins the 105th running of the Kentucky Derby.
- American Airlines flight 191 in Chicago crashes, killing all 271 on board and 2 on the ground becoming the deadliest aviation accident in US aviation history.
- The top song was" Reunited" by Peaches and Herb.
- The French Open tennis tournament singles was won by Bjorn Borg and Chris Evert Lloyd.
- Rick Mears wins the Indianapolis 500.
- Mary Pickford, American film star passed away at 87 years old.

SUNSHINE CLEANERS

Quality Work - Quick Service

Shirt Specialists

Phone 833-1492 Clinton, S.C.

Self-Service Laundry

June 1979

- Pope John Paul II visits his native Poland becoming the first Pope to visit a communist country.
- Actor Chris Pratt was born.
- The Seattle Supersonics defeat the Washington Bullets four games to one to win the National Basketball League Championship.
- McDonalds introduces the Happy Meal.
- President Jimmy Carter and Soviet Leader Leonid Brezhnev sign the SALT II agreement in Vienna, Austria.
- The movies *Rocky 2* and *The Muppet Movie* are released.
- NATO Supreme Allied Commander Alexander Haig escapes an assassination attempt in Belgium.
- The top songs included "Hot Stuff" by Donna Summer and "Love You Inside Out" by the Bee Gees.
- The United States Open golf tournament was won by Hale Irwin.
- Jack Haley, the actor who played the Tin Man on *The Wizard of Oz* passed away at 81.
- Actor John Wayne passed away at 72.

July 1979

- The Sony Walkman debuts in Japan.
- Comedian and Actor Kevin Hart was born.
- Los Angeles passes its gay and lesbian civil rights bill.
- NASA's first orbiting space station Skylab begins falling back to earth.
- The Chicago White Sox were forced to forfeit the second game of a double header versus the Detroit Tigers at Comiskey Park as the Disco Demolition night did not go as expected.
- Disco music dominated the Billboard top 100.
- The top songs included "Ring My Bell" by Anita Ward and "Bad Girls" by Donna Summer.
- The Wimbledon Tennis Tournament singles was won by Bjorn Borg and Martina Navratilova.
- The British Open and United States Open golf tournaments were won by Seve Ballesteros.
- Singer Minnie Ripperton passed away at 31 from breast cancer.
- Both TV series *Hart to Hart* and *The Facts* of Life debut.
- Jerilyn Britz wins the women's United States Open Golf Championship.
- The Presbyterian College Blue Hose Football team reports to school in preparation of the 1979 season.

WHITEFORD'S DRIVE-IN

S. Broad St.   Clinton, S.C.

FINE FOODS

Bring Your Family

Telephone 833-0193

August 1979

- The first ever German league game of American football debuted. The Frankfurter Lowen defeated the Dusseldorf Panther.
- Actor Jason Momoa was born.
- National Football League player Jamal Lewis was born.
- Micheal Jackson releases the album *Off the Wall*.
- The *Amityville Horror*, *North Dallas Forty* and *Apocalypse Now* movies are released,
- The top songs included "Good Times" by Chic and "My Sharona" by the Knack.
- The PGA golf Championship was won by David Graham.
- Sam Snead, at age 67, sets the record as the oldest player to make the cut in a major golf championship in the PGA Championship at Oakland Hills Country Club.
- Walter O'Malley, owner of the LA Dodgers passed away at 75.
- Actress Vivian Vance, known for her character Ethel Mertz on Lucy, passed away at 70.
- The Presbyterian College Blue Hose Football team prepares for their opening game at The Citadel on Saturday, September 8, 1979.

BEST WISHES TO THE "BLUE HOSE"

GRAY FUNERAL HOME

Ralph F. Patterson, Owner

CLINTON, LAURENS AND WHITMIRE

An optimistic Presbyterian College Head Football Coach Cally Gault reflects on the upcoming 1979 football season.

The 1979 Presbyterian Blue Hose Football Team

10 The Laurens County Advertiser August 22, 1979

Gault enthusiastic

PC picked to win SAC-8

Optimism abounds at Presbyterian College where the football team, coming off their best season in 20 years with an 8-2-1 mark, is returning all but one starter on a potent offense.

The Blue Hose, co-South Atlantic Conference champions along with Elon last season, have been picked by SAC-Eight coaches to finish first, despite the Fighting Christians' number two national ranking last season.

"I've never been so enthusiastic in my 31 years of coaching," said Coach Cally Gault, who is entering his 17th year at Presbyterian with a 89-73-6 mark. "I voted for Presbyterian College to win the conference championship this season just like I did last year."

Gault is being perfectly honest in assessing his team's superiority. Returning from last year's offense which averaged 22.5 points per contest is tackle Roy Walker, a Kodak All-American and quarterback Jimmy Spence. Walker, a former Clinton High School standout, was also named to the third team of the Coaches All-America squad.

Spence, last year's SAC-Eight Offensive Player of the Year, suffered a knee injury during the last day of spring practice but is expected to be fully recovered from surgery. The 6-2, 185-pound Lexington native hit on 88 of 159 attempts passing for 1,032 yards and rushed for 594 more.

Adding to Gault's excitement over the upcoming season is the chance of a 200-pound backfield. Joining Spence will be senior halfback Clayto Burke, who rushed for 921 yards and nine touchdowns last season. Burke, a combination of speed and balance, is also an excellent receiver. Rounding out the backfield should be Ben Hood (6-0, 207), sophomore Walter Atkins, or freshman Chris Fowler.

Expected to fill the shoes of NAIA All-American center pound sophomore Frank Kube or Jarrold Reevis. The rest of the line is set, with tri-captain Bruce Ollis and Barry Taylor at guards and 255 pound Gene Harper at right tackle. Jesse Cason, who burned defensive backs with 46 receptions for 552 yards last season will be at split end with Danny Thornton, second to Cason in receiving, starting at tight end. At flanker will be senior Jay Byars.

Anchoring the defense will be tri-captain and All-Conference defensive end Jim McCoun and Joe Grant, a junior guard. The other two returnees from last year's defensive squad are Erskine Reed and Haywood Hinton, who defensive secondary coach Bob Strock says could play anywhere. Also expected to see a great deal of playing time is Steve Stalvey, a sophomore linebacker.

All the assistant coaches but Strock, who has logged 10 years at PC, are products of Gault's previous Blue Hose teams and when asked about his team's strengths he never fails to mention his coaching staff.

But when Gault talks about concerns he notes the cheerleading squad and their lack of a squad member with red hair. "I've never seen a cheerleading squad without a redhead that was worth a hoot," he said jokingly.

It should be a good year for

> "I voted for PC to win the conference championship."
>
> --Coach Gault

Cally Gault

Presbyterian College Head Coach Cally Gault, speaking at a local Rotary event, is pleased with the addition of a redhead to the Presbyterian College cheerleading squad. The 1979 team is "Now fixed up!"

Cally Gault— good humor man

By JIM KLUTTZ

Football prospects for the Presbyterian College Blue Hose this fall are bright.

And that statement is coming right from the horse's mouth.

THAT IS, it comes from none other than Head Coach and Athletic Director Cally Gault.

This optimism is also seconded by his assistants.

COACH GAULT, Defensive Coach Bob Strock and Wayne Renwick, coach of the offensive backfield and receivers, were guests of the Laurens Rotary Club Thursday at a luncheon meeting that has become an annual affair when the Blue Hose coaches give Rotarians a report of what to expect from the Blue Hose in the upcoming season.

"In the 17 years I have been at Presbyterian College," Coach Gault said, "we've always tried to be optimistic.

"I CAN say that this year I'm more optimistic than I've ever been."

One of the outstanding qualities of this year's squad, Coach Gault pointed out, has been the spirit shown by the entire squad. They are, he said, fired up and anxious to play ball.

PC COACHES—Presbyterian College Head Football Coach Cally Gault (center) and assistant Wayne Renwick (left) discuss PC football with Rotarian Frank Roper at the Laurens Rotary Club following its luncheon meeting at the YMCA Thursday.

COACH Gault went on to praise the calibre of football, both from the standpoint of the players, and the coaches, to be found in Laurens County and the state of South Carolina as a whole.

"One of the things I like about South Carolina is that we have some of the finest coaches at all levels that you will find anywhere.

"COACH Jim Carlen at the University of South Carolina is forthright and honest, a gentleman and a fine person, and he has a good Christian staff. This same thing is true of Coach Danny Ford and his staff at Clemson. You won't find better people anywhere."

Getting around to the PC schedule, which he said was as difficult as that of any school in the area, he explained the reason why he scheduled teams like Furman and The Citadel.

"I'M NOT going to load up our schedule with schools we don't know just in order to roll up a lot of wins," he said.

Coach Gault, who always laces his talks with a lot of good humor, said that a sportswriter asked him what were the weaknesses of Presbyterian College football this year.

"I TOLD him that our biggest weakness was that we had a cheering squad with six cheerleaders—three blondes and three brunettes—and I've never seen a good cheerleading squad without a red head. So we got one and now we're fixed up!"

Defensive Coach Bob Strock told the Rotarians that he saw Clemson play Ohio State in the Orange Bowl, and that the Tigers were terrific. "With all due respect to the Tigers," Strock said, "if they had had two of our players, there were two of their defensive backs who wouldn't have started. Our two men are better," he said.

HE REFERRED to Heyward Hinton, a 199-pound junior and Erskine Reed, a 185-pound senior, who will lead the PC defense.

Coach Renwick then spoke highly of flanker Jay Byars, a 172-pound senior from Cayce. "He's the greatest blocker in the open field I have ever seen," Renwick said.

IN WINDING up the meeting, Coach Gault said that Roy Walker, a 232-pound offensive tackle and a tri-captain, was the best offensive lineman he had coached in his 16 years at PC. Walker was a first team All American on the prestigious American Football Coaches Association-Kodak organizations.

Another standout is Jim McCoun, a 209-pound senior defensive end who was all SAC-8 both as a sophomore and a junior, is an All-American candidate and is one of the Tri-Captains.

THE THIRD of the three truly outstanding players is quarterback Jimmy Spence, a 185-pound junior who last year was overwhelmingly voted by teammates as the team's most valuable player—the first time this honor has ever been won by a sophomore at PC. He is a PC record holder for passing accuracy and fewest interceptions, and is also an outstanding candidate for All-American honors.

The PC coaches were introduced by Frank Roper, who annually is in charge of this program.

The 1979 Presbyterian Blue Hose Football Team

Presbyterian College Head Coach Cally Gault tries to hold back the optimism regarding the 1979 Presbyterian College football team. Coach Gault had tremendous success in 1977 and 1978.

Offensive guns stronger for '79 Blue Hose

Passes by Jimmy Spence to augment the power running of Clayto Burke.

Cally Gault faces a good kind of problem trying to hold back the optimism over his 1979 football prospects.

If this has a familiar ring, past records prove the positive-thinking head coach an accurate prognosticator.

"Everything points to the fact we will have another fine team," he said, "but we don't want to get over-exuberant. After all, it will be difficult to repeat the last two seasons in terms of record."

Those statistics read 7-3-1 for 1977 and 8-2-1 for 1978. The latter included co-championship (with Elon) of the South Atlantic Conference, perhaps the NAIA's fastest league.

Gault believes the same successful ingredients of the last two years are present in abundant supply as the Blue Hose prepare for the next campaign. These include some excellent individual performers, outstanding leadership from the captains and senior players, and a fierce team spirit to keep the Presbyterian College banner flying high.

He also points to a football-smart, closely-knit staff comprised of Bob Strock (defensive backs), John Perry '72 (offensive line), Elliott Poss '71 (defensive line) and Wayne Renwick '73 (receivers).

Two all-time great linemen

Heading the individual stars, offensive tackle Roy Walker of Clinton and defensive end Jim McCoin of Decatur, Ga., just may be the best two at their positions ever to wear the PC uniform.

The 6-3, 225-pound Walker last year as a junior made All-American on the prestigious American Football Coaches Association-Kodak team. He should pick up even more honors this season as he guns for a pro career.

The aggressive defensive play of McCoin already has earned this 6-2, 210-pound senior all-conference selection the last two years. He can simply dominate the line of scrimmage. He and Walker and offensive guard Bruce Ollis were chosen by their teammates to be the 1979 captains.

Quarterback Jimmy Spence of Lexington, S. C., as a sophomore last year, set a PC passing accuracy record (58.7%) and earned the conference "offensive player-of-the-year" award. But he suffered a spring practice knee injury that required surgery.

If, as now diagnosed, Spence is back in top shape, he will key the attack with a deceptive mixture of running and passing.

Another record-setter on the receiving end of Spence aerials is split-end Jesse Cason of Orlando, Fla. This leaping, soft-handed junior put the new mark of 46 receptions into the PC book last year.

Workhorse of the running game will be tailback Clayto Burke, 195-pound three-year letterman from Macon, Ga. A combination of elusive speed and power, he churned up 921 rushing yards last year for a 3.8 per-carry average.

On paper the Blue Hose offense looks especially strong, with most of the 1979 starters returning. Gault said:

"This backfield overall may be our fastest and largest. And, certainly, it has the best depth of any in my 16 years at PC. Although we will still throw the football a lot, we do have the kind of big backs and solid line that should enable us to establish the ground game first."

Besides Spence and Burke, the backfield will see both Wade Atkins of Greenville and Ben Hood of Greensboro, Ga., getting action at fullback—along with Jimmy Chupp of Doraville, Ga.—and Jay Byars of Cayce earning his fourth letter as a flanker. Ready to relieve Spence at quarterback are Ward Gatlin of Conway and Donald Porter of Washington, D. C., who is also a capable flanker and punt-returner.

Coach Gault also takes special pride in the offensive line, where all positions except center are secured by experienced men. Paired opposite Roy Walker at the other tackle is Gene Harper of Eatonton, Ga., PC's biggest ever at 255 pounds. And opposite split end Cason is tight end Danny Thornton of Washington, Ga., a veteran with sure blocking skill. Of the guards, Gault said:

"PC has always had quick, fast guards. They make our team plays work, and they have the speed to pull in front of the ball-carrier on wide plays. This year, our guards will be somewhat bigger and more experienced, with Bruce Ollis and Barry Taylor of Durham, N. C., back as starters."

What about the question mark at offensive center? Right now, Frank Kube of Orlando, Fla., and Jarrold Reeves of Avondale Estates, Ga., battle to fill the hole. They have promise but lack experience.

By pre-season calculations, much of the Blue Hose defense would seem cause for worry with just four returning starters of last year. Even so, Cally Gault views the situation with confidence:

"We lost some good ones to graduation, but we also had a very fine spring practice. Although few of our defensive people have even played in college competition, they showed up well against the PC offense last spring—and that's saying something. We believe they will stand up, will maintain our tradition of strong defense."

This could be Mark Kay's year

Besides end Jim McCoin, the key veterans returning to the defensive front line are: defensive tackle Mark Kay, strong 245-pounder from Anderson who alternated as a third tackle the past two years, and middle guard Joe Grant of Charleston, quick and aggressive starter as a sophomore last season. Senior Leonard Howard of Doraville, Ga., backs up Grant.

What about the other end and tackle? Competing for the flank position opposite McCoin are Joe Lane of Tallahassee, Hugh Bailey of Liberty and Mark Wheless of Clearwater, Fla. Chris Williams of Lawrenceville, Ga., or transfer Reeve Ammons of Darlington should handle the other defensive tackle slot.

With both linebacker positions emptied by graduation, experience here is limited to Steve Stalvey of Waycross, Ga., a letter-man substitute, and Greenville's Larry Bridges, who has functioned mainly as a place-kicker in the past.

PC's defensive secondary has two outstanding returnees in strong safety Erskine Reed of Orangeburg and Columbia's Heyward Hinton at corner back. Both are large and fast, mixing good pass coverage with the ability to move up quickly and tackle well on running plays.

The quest for the other cornerback points mainly to sophomore Joe Mooneyham of Pauline and Hal Brannon of Unadilla, Ga., while the free safety assignment seems to be a tossup between Willie Cooper of Gable and Alan Gaston of Carrolton, Ga.

Last year, the strength was at defense. The offense replaced its pre-season question mark with a big exclamation point. Optimistic Cally Gault believes the opposite will be true this year.

As he did last year, he predicts a conference championship in 1979. Other coaches seem to agree, giving PC a slight edge over Elon, with whom the Blue Hose shared the crown last year.

It will be a perilous way, since each team anticipates improvement. But before the conference competition even gets underway, Presbyterian will face its two toughest opponents of the year on their home fields: opening with The Citadel and then tackling Furman the next weekend. Both rate as strong contenders for the Southern Conference title.

McCoin, Walker, Ollis with SAC-8 trophy

Southern Massacre

The Presbyterian College 1979 football team preseason Media Guide.

1979 PRESBYTERIAN UPPERCLASSMEN FOOTBALL ROSTER

NO.	NAME	POS.	HT.	WT.	YR.	LET.	HIGH SCHOOL	HOMETOWN
1	Bishop, Chuck	K	5-11	148	3	1	Andrew Jackson Ac.	Lodge, S.C.
10	Gatlin, Ward	QB	6-3	180	4	0	Conway	Conway, S.C.
11	Porter, Donald	QB	6-0	186	3	1	Eastern	Washington, D.C.
12	Byars, Jay	FLK-SE	6-1	172	4	3	Airport	Cayce, S.C.
14	Scott, Paul	QB	5-10	180	2	0	Chamblee	Chamblee, Ga.
15	Spence, James	QB	6-2	185	3	1	Lexington	Lexington, S.C.
17	Hollier, Ronnie	QB	6-2	185	2	0	Cardinal Newman	Columbia, S.C.
20	Barker, Mike	QB	5-10	185	2	0	Episcopal	Jacksonville, Fla.
22	Neisler, David	LB	5-11	187	2	0	Oak Ridge	Orlando, Fla.
23	Morris, Randy	SE	5-9	143	2	0	Osborne	Marietta, Ga.
24	Chupp, Jimmy	QB	6-½	172	3	1	Sequoyah	Doraville, Ga.
26	Gaston, Allan	QB	5-10	158	4	2	Carrollton	Carrollton, Ga.
27	Grove, Tony	FLK	6-2	187	3	1	Warwick	Lititz, Pa.
28	Reed, Erskine	CB	5-10	185	4	2	Wilkinson	Orangeburg, S.C.
29	Leverette, Mark	DB	5-11	170	2	0	Hillcrest	Simpsonville, S.C.
30	Price, Dean	TE-FB	6-2	234	3	1	Hanna	Anderson, S.C.
31	Nell, Jo	QB	5-9	180	1	0	Bishop England	Charleston, S.C.
32	Hood, Ben	QB	6-0	202	3	1	Green County	Greensboro, Ga.
33	Mooneyham, Joe	DB	5-10	177	2	0	Dorman	Pauline, S.C.
34	Hinton, Heyward	DB	5-11	199	3	2	Columbia	Columbia, S.C.
36	Cooper, Willie	DB	5-8	168	3	0	Mayewood	Gable, S.C.
37	Kirkpatrick, Ricky	DB	5-9	149	2	0	Gatewood	Milledgeville, Ga.
40	Burke, Clayto	QB	5-11	194	4	3	Southwest	Macon, Ga.
42	Howard, Anthony	TB	6-0	185	2	1	Christ School	Winston-Salem, N.C.
44	Owens, Mike	DB	5-11	170	2	0	Liberty	Spartanburg, S.C.
45	Goolsby, Burt	DB	5-9	165	2	0	Wilks Ac.	Washington, Ga.
46	Atkins, Walter	RB	5-11	200	2	1	Southside	Greenville, S.C.
47	Brannen, Hal	DB	6-1	188	3	1	Fullington Ac.	Unadilla, Ga.
50	Howard, Leonard	MG	6-2	219	4	2	Sequoyah	Doraville, Ga.
51	Roberts, Rob	LB	5-10	197	3	0	Southside	Greenville, S.C.
52	Owens, Larry	LB	6	198	3	1	Carolina	Greenville, S.C.
53	Stalvey, Steve	LB	5-10	192	2	1	Ware County	Waycross, Ga.
54	Shamrock, Greg	C	6-0	190	2	0	Eustis	Eustis, Fla.
55	Hannah, Robert	LB	5-11	210	4	0	Campbell	Fairburn, Ga.
56	Reeves, Jarrold	OG	6-¾	204	3	0	Avondale	Avondale Estates
57	Kube, Frank	C	6-0	205	2	0	Edgewater	Orlando, Fla.
58	Godley, Tommy	MG	5-11	218	2	0	And. Jackson Ac.	Islandton, S.C.
59	Riner, Garland	C	6-2	222	2	0	Baldwin	Milledgeville, Ga.
60	Bowen, Johnny	OG	5-9	227	4	0	Dodge County	Chester, Ga.
61	Bridges, Larry	LB	5-11	187	4	2	Carolina	Greenville, S.C.
62	Cross, Chip	LB	5-10	188	3	0	McDowell	Marion, N.C.
63	D'Andrea, John	OG	6-0	225	3	1	Westwood	Fairburn, Ga.
64	Ollis, Bruce	DE	5-11	206	4	2	Scotland	Laurinburg, N.C.
65	Forrest, Andy	OG	5-9	182	3	0	Mauldin	Mauldin, S.C.
66	Taylor, Barry	OG	5-11	212	4	2	N. Durham	Durham, N.C.
67	Wheless, Mark	DE	6-1	205	2	0	Clearwater	Clearwater, Fla.
69	Cann, John	OG	6-1	210	2	0	Chester	Chester, S.C.
70	Yarborough, Charles	OT	6-0	201	2	0	Clinton	Clinton, S.C.
71	Peterson, Robert	DT	6-1	218	3	0	Duluth	Duluth, Ga.
72	Finley, Hank	OT	6-2	220	2	0	Laurens	Laurens, S.C.
73	Martin, George	DT	6-0	224	2	0	Pickens	Pickens, S.C.
74	Way, Robbie	OG	6-2	225	1	0	Lugoff-Elgin	Lugoff, S.C.
75	Grant, Joe	MG	6-0	226	3	1	James Island	Charleston, S.C.
76	Harper, Gene	OT	6-4½	255	3	1	Gatewood	Eatonton, Ga.
77	Walker, Roy	OT	6-3¼	226	4	3	Clinton	Clinton, S.C.
78	Williams, Chris	DT	6-2	210	3	0	Central Gwinnett	Lawrenceville, Ga.
79	Ammons, Reese	DT	6-1	232	2	0	St. Johns	Darlington, S.C.
80	Cason, Jesse	SE	5-9	155	3	2	Oak Ridge	Orlando, Fla.
81	Thornton, Danny	TE	6-0	210	3	2	Washington-Wilkes	Washington, Ga.
82	Hobby, Rob	TE	6-¾	210	3	0	Tift County	Tifton, Ga.
83	Reeves, Cliff	TE	6-2	205	2	0	Riverview	Arlington, Ga.
84	Hosch, Scott	DE	6-0	202	1	0	N. Gwinnett	Buford, Ga.
85	Rabun, Dan	DT	6-2	200	2	0	Thomson	Thomson, Ga.
86	Bailey, Hugh	DE	5-11	204	3	0	Liberty	Liberty, S.C.
87	Gruber, Richard	DE	6-0	176	2	0	Dorchester Ac.	St. George, S.C.
88	Mason, Willie	SE	5-9	158	3	1	Laurens	Laurens, S.C.
89	D'Andrea, Chris	DE	6-2	190	2	0	Westwood	Fairburn, Ga.
90	Kay, Mark	DT	6-2	248	4	2	Hanna	Anderson, S.C.
91	Steele, Tommy	TE	6-1	190	2	0	Buford	Lancaster, S.C.
92	Bowles, Ralph	OT	6-0	200	2	0	Aquinas	Augusta, Ga.
93	Addison, Eddie	DT	6-1	215	2	0	Stevens Co.	Toccoa, Ga.
95	Lane, Joseph	DE	6-0	187	3	0	Rikards	Tallahassee, Fla.
99	McCoun, Jim	DE	6-2	209	4	3	Lakeside	Decatur, Ga.

PRESBYTERIAN COLLEGE FOOTBALL BROCHURE 1979

P.C CAPTAINS:
Jim McCoun
Roy Walker
Bruce Ollis

SCHOOL DATA:
President: Dr. Kenneth Orr
Enrollment: 500 Men, 400 Women
Faculty Athletic Chairman: Dr. Foard Tarbert (803 833-2820, ext. 258)
Athletic Director: Calhoun F. "Cally" Gault
Stadium and Capacity - Bailey memorial (5,000), Johnson Field
Athletic Offices: Ross E. Templeton Physical Education Center
Gym and Capacity: Furman Pinson - 3,000
Nickname of Athletic Teams: Blue Hose
School Colors: Garnet and Blue
Mascot: Scottish Highland Fighter
Denomination: Presbyterian
Year School Founded: 1880
Sports Information Director: TBA (803 833-0705) or 833-2820, ext. 309)

Mailing Address: Athletic Department, Presbyterian College, Clinton, S.C. 29325
National Affiliation: National Association of Intercollegiate Athletics (NAIA)

The 1979 Presbyterian Blue Hose Football Team

The Presbyterian College 1979 football team preseason Media Guide.

JESSE CASON'S record catch.

BLUE HOSE CANDIDATES
FOR POST SEASON HONORS

ROY WALKER: OT, 6'3¼", 226, Junior
True All American performer. First Team All American on prestigious American Football Coaches Association-Kodak organizations. Called by Coach Gault, "The best offensive lineman I have coached in 16 years at PC" - extremely quick - coaches assign him blocks others not expected to make. Pro prospect - Called "Pride", everybody's friend-PC's candidate for All-Everything.

JIM McCOUN: DE, 6'2", 209, Senior
All SAC-8 as both sophomore and junior. Called by coaches "PC's best ever at DE" - All American candidate - often dominates line play defensively - great football sense, tremendous aggressiveness - outstanding leader.

CLAYTO BURKE: RB, 5'11", 194, Senior
All SAC-8 - leading rusher and scorer - excellent speed - runs tough and elusively - outstanding receiver and blocker - Pro prospect.

JESSE CASON: SE, 5'9", 155, Junior
PC record holder with 46 season receptions makes the circus catch - great leaper with soft hands - always a threat - highly maneuverable.

DANNY THORNTON: TE, 6', 210, Junior
Third year starter - outstanding blocker - good hands - underated but recognized by team mates and coaches as tough blocker and dependable performer - hard worker - improves each game.

JIMMY SPENCE: QB, 6'1", 185, Junior
1978 SAC-8 Offensive Player of the Year. Overwhelmingly selected by team mates as PC's most valuable player to become first sophomore ever selected - PC record holder for passing accuracy and fewest interceptions - excellent student and leader - another candidate for All-Everything.

JOE GRANT: MG, 6', 237, Junior
Quick, strong, aggressive - developed into excellent performer in first year as starter last fall - should be one of PC's best ever as career progresses.

MARK KAY: DT, 6'2", 248, Senior
Alternated at both tackles last fall - had excellent spring - moves well for size - strong, aggressive, tough - "Big K" could be the Key to PC '79 defensive line.

HEYWARD HINTON: DB, 5'11", 199, Junior
Strong, hard hitter, who reacts fast to run or pass - good speed and maneuverability - dependable.

GENE HARPER: OT, 6'4½", 255, Junior
Teams well with Walker and the two could easily become PC's best ever duo at OT - improving in strength and speed.

ERSKINE REED: DB, 5'10", 185, Senior
Leads team in interceptions - good speed - 52 yard TD interception vs Carson-Newman - steady silent type who leads by example - makes the key play.

1979 TENTATIVE DEPTH CHART (SPRING PRACTICE)

OFFENSE								DEFENSE				
SE	LT	LG	C	RG	RT	TE	LE	LT	MG	RT	RE	
80 Cason	77 Walker	64 Ollis	57 Kube	66 Taylor	76 Harper	82 Thornton	99 McCoun	Williams	75 Grant	90 Kaye	95 Lane	
27 Grove	70 Yarborough	74 Way	or	52 L. Owens	63 J. D'Andrea	30 Price	84 Hosch	Ammons	50 L. Howard	75 Martin	or	
	or		56 Reeves							or	86 Bailey	
	72 Finley									71 Peterson	or	
											67 Wheless	
FLK			QB				LCB		LB	LB	RCB	
12 Byars			15 Spence				47 Brannen		53 Stalvey	61 Bridges	Hinton	
11 Porter			10 Gatlin				45 Goolsby		55 Hannah	62 Cross	Mooneyham	
			17 Hollier or 14 Scott							22 Neisler		
			FB	TB				FS			SS	
			46 Atkins	40 Burke				36 Cooper			28 Reed	
			or	24 Chupp				26 Gaston				

15

Southern Massacre

The Presbyterian College Blue Hose prepare for the season opener against The Citadel.

PC travels to Charleston

Fans in Charleston will get to see what Presbyterian Coach Cally Gault is so excited about this season when he takes his team there to face the Bulldogs of The Citadel this Saturday at 7 p.m.

Presbyterian, picked by SAC-Eight coaches to win their conference, lost to The Citadel 28-17 last year in a game that was closer than the score indicates.

But with 18 of 22 starters returning from last year's 5-6 squad, Art Baker, who will be in his second as Bulldog coach, is comparing this year's team to his senior-laden team at Furman a few years back, which was quarterbacked by David Whitehurst.

The only question mark on offense is at the quarterback position where Marty Crosby is a good passer and senior Tim Russel is a good runner but unproven as a passer. In the backfield with one of them will be Lyvonia Mitchell, who led the conference in rushing last season. In front of him will be one of the few veteran lines in the conference.

When one of these two quarterbacks do decide to go to the air, they should have no trouble locating tight end Orion Rust (6-4, 225) and flanker Mark Slawson (6-3, 185). On defense everyone is back, with the exception of two outstanding linebackers, Kenny Caldwell and Keith Allen.

"I think the secret will be in the kicking game," said coach Gault. "Neither of us has a returning punter." PC lost its punter in a weightroom accident. Most crucial for The Citadel will be the kicking game where the team hit only 4 of 11 field goals. Ermmer Chavez did much of last year's kicking.

The good news at Presbyterian is that last year's SAC-Eight offensive Player of the Year, Jimmy Spence, will be at the helm of the offense after undergoing knee surgery. Last year Spence set the school record for passing accuracy and fewest interceptions and barring injury, the 6-2 185-pound junior should be in for another sparkling year.

However, he hasn't been involved in any real contact thus far in practice, but Gault seems optimistic. "We kept him out of all real contact so far," said Gault. "But he's moving well and seems to be 100 percent.

"We expect them to be a tough defensive team but we feel like we can throw on them in certain areas," he said. "We know they throw the ball well and use an option-type offense."

If this week's weather is any indication of what's in store for this weekend, both teams could have a change in game plan. Gault, whose team practiced in the gym during the first half of practice and outdoors during the last half, worked on their goal line offense, which is where The Citadel ended it's 1978 season against Furman.

"We're not really worried about the weather," said Gault. "We were successful attacking them last year. We can throw and we are quick. We've had some big wins in bad weather."

Joining Spence in the Blue Hose backfield will be Clayto Burke, who was named All-SAC-Eight and was the conference's leading rusher and scorer. In front of them, anchoring down a veteran offensive line, will be Roy Walker, a Kodak All-America last season and pro-prospect. He is blessed with size (6-3½, 226 pounds) and speed.

Leading the defense will be one of the team's tri-captains, along with Walker and offensive guard Bruce Ollis, defensive end Jim McCoun. He was named to the All SAC-Eight team during his sophomore and junior year and is a candidate for All-American honors this season.

Holding down the secondary will be two returnees, Heywood Hinton and Erskine Reed. Hinton is one of the hardest hitters on the team while Reed goes for the ball, having led the team in interceptions last season.

This will be the 50th meeting between the two teams, The Bulldogs hold an 10-38-1 edge.

Jim McCoun

Roy Walker

Jimmy Spence

Week 1

- September 2, 1979, Mark O'Meara wins 8-7 over John Cook to win the US Amateur Golf Championship.
- September 3, 1979, *Benson* debuted on TV.
- September 5, 1979, Hurricane David moves towards the South Carolina coast.
- September 7, 1979, The television network *ESPN* debuts.
- September 8, 1979, Cheryl Prewitt of Mississippi was crowned the 52nd Miss America.
- Tracy Austin at 16 years old became the youngest US Open Tennis Champion defeating Chris Evert 6-4 6-3.
- September 8, 1979, The Presbyterian College Blue Hose football team defeated The Citadel Bulldogs 21-13 at Johnson Hagood Memorial Stadium in Charleston, South Carolina. Kickoff was at 7:00PM.

Citadel Head Coach Art Baker was a 1953 graduate of Presbyterian College. A member of Pi Kappa Alpha fraternity, he was also a Blue Hose quarterback and halfback from 1950-1953. Coach Baker lettered 3 years at Presbyterian College. The Citadel, a member of the Southern Conference, posted a 6-5 record in 1979 and boasted a 27-14 win over Vanderbilt University.

Citadel running back Stump Mitchell ran for 925 yards in 1979. In 1980, he rushed for 1647 yards, second in the nation to Heisman Trophy winner George Rogers of South Carolina. In 1981, he was drafted by the NFL's St. Louis Cardinals. He played for the Cardinals from 1981-1989. He also played for the Kansas City Chiefs in 1990. He was primarily a running back and kick return specialist. In 1981, his 1292 yards led the NFL in kick return yardage. After playing in the NFL, he coached in both college and the NFL.

I had the pleasure of speaking with Stump Mitchell in the Spring of 2023. He is currently the running backs coach for the NFL Cleveland Browns.

"I do remember the 1980 season. I don't remember much about the 1979 season. I do remember Presbyterian came down to Charleston and beat us. We always opened with Presbyterian. It was always a battle. The team was always a formidable opponent for The Citadel."
- Stump Mitchell, 1979 Citadel Running Back, 2023

The 1979 Presbyterian Blue Hose Football Team

THE CITADEL

PRESBYTERIAN

Southern Massacre

Week 1

Presbyterian College   21   The Citadel   13
Blue Hose   Bulldogs

Charleston, South Carolina   September 8, 1979   7:00 PM
Presbyterian Overall Record   1-0   SAC-8 Record   0-0
NAIA Division 1 Ranking #9

Statistics	PC	The Citadel
First Downs	25	16
Rushes / yards	59 - 210	46 / 212
Passing yards	199	88
Passes	11-16-0	7-21-0
Fumbles / lost	3-2	5-1
Penalties / yards	5-51	8-97
Punts / average	5-30	6-41

Scoring Summary

Q1   PC….PC 7 – The Citadel 0….73 yard drive….Burke 4 yard run….Bishop PAT….5:27 remaining

Q2   The Citadel….PC 7 – The Citadel 7….77 yard drive….Miller 5 yard run….Chavez PAT….8:46 remaining

Q2   PC….PC 14 – The Citadel 7…. 83 yard drive….Atkins 4 yard run….Bishop PAT…3:16 remaining

Q4   The Citadel….PC 14 – The Citadel 13….80 yard drive….Scadlock 3 yard run….2 point attempt unsuccessful….12:02 remaining

Q4   PC….PC 21 – The Citadel 13….77 yard drive….Spence 30 yard pass to Thornton….Bishop PAT….8:51 remaining

Highlights

Presbyterian College Blue Hose vs The Citadel Bulldogs

- This was the first Presbyterian College Blue Hose win over The Citadel since 1971.
- The Presbyterian College Blue Hose have played The Citadel 50 times in their history, and this was their 11th win.
- The Presbyterian College Blue Hose defense showed up in Charleston. In the second quarter, The Citadel had to convert 2 fourth downs in their first scoring drive.
- On a wet field, The Presbyterian College Blue Hose offense not only managed 210 yards rushing, but Presbyterian College Blue Hose QB Jimmy Spence also threw 199 yards and 1 touchdown.
- The Presbyterian College Blue Hose had a total of 409 yards from scrimmage.
- Presbyterian College Blue Hose receiver Danny Thornton had 5 receptions for 117 yards, which included a 30 yard touchdown pass from PC QB Jimmy Spence.
- The Presbyterian College Blue Hose overcame a third quarter turnover after driving 77 yards to The Citadel 3. The Citadel recovered a fumble by Presbyterian College running back Walter Atkins in the endzone and went on to score early in the fourth quarter.
- The Presbyterian College Blue Hose defense did not allow any points to The Citadel in the final 12 minutes of the game.
- The Presbyterian College Blue Hose defense had prepared for RB Stump Mitchell of The Citadel. He was not a factor in The Citadel offense, a credit to the preparation by the Blue Hose.

Presbyterian upsets Citadel, 21-13

	PC	Citadel
First downs	25	16
Rushes-yards	59-210	46-212
Passing-yards	199	86
Return yards	49	59
Passes	11-16-0	7-21-0
Punts	5-30-2	6-41-7
Fumbles-lost	3-2	5-1
Penalties-yards	5-51	8-97

Quarterback Jimmy Spence hit on 11 of 16 passes for 199 yards as Presbyterian College upset The Citadel 21-13 at Charleston Saturday.

The Blue Hose had a 14-13 lead in the fourth quarter when Spence hit tight end Danny Thornton on a 30-yard pass play. Chuck Bishop's point after was good, nailing down the win for the Blue Hose.

"I'm just glad the team backed up all I've been saying," said Coach Cally Gault. "Our defense was tough when it had to be and we had an extremely effective offense. We had a few mistakes but we hope to iron those out by next Saturday."

With 12 minutes left, The Citadel pulled within one point on an 80-yard scoring drive. Coach Art Baker decided to go for the lead with a two-point conversion but it failed.

Runningback Clayto Burke scored the opening touchdown on a four-yard run and rushed for 108 yards. Fullback Walter Atkins, who also scored on a four-yard scamper, rushed for 42 yards.

But what made the win that much sweeter was the performance of Spence, who underwent knee surgery during the off-season.

"It was a tribute to him and the hard work he put in during his rehabilitation," said Gault.

Walt Atkins ran for 42 yards and scored a late 2nd quarter touchdown enroute to a 21-13 Blue Hose victory over The Citadel.

Notable Quotes Regarding The Citadel

"I didn't plan for this to happen. We just got beat by a football team that wanted to win more than we did."
    - Art Baker, Head Football Coach, The Citadel, 1979

"We knew we had a good offensive football team and we knew we would be able to move the ball on The Citadel. What we didn't know was how our defense would hold up. They're young, and they made some mistakes. But when we needed them the most, that's when they were there."
    - Cally Gault, Presbyterian College Head Football Coach, 1979

"I was Cob (practice team) player of the week for The Citadel game. I take credit for our victory. I didn't understand why I didn't get the game ball! We were concerned about stopping Stump Mitchell. We played a fantastic game and the defense played great! I did (somehow) get on the field after the game to celebrate with the travel team."
    - Tom Steele TE, 2023

"I was fired up to return to The Citadel. I wore Sam Cunningham's ass out!"
    - Robbie Way OG, 2023

"Stop Stump period."
    - Jeff South DB, 2023

"Win over The Citadel is easy to see 40+ years later. The victory was big. The game set the tone that we could compete."
    - Chip Cross OG, 2023

"The defense played great. The wet field played to our advantage against running back Stump Mitchell."
    - Bob Peterson DT, 2023

"It was a homecoming for me as I was from Charleston. I remember after the win the kids asking for chin straps and autographs."
- Jo Nell RB, 2023

"In practice prior to The Citadel game, we worked on defending Stump Mitchell's spin move. It paid off."
- Leonard Howard MG, 2023

"We were confident going to The Citadel. Our expectation was to win."
- Bruce Ollis OG, 2023

"We were ready to play. We were confident we could win."
- Jesse Cason WR, 2023

"We knew we could compete."
- John Cann OG, 2023

"We anticipated a win, so we weren't so excited. We felt like we should have beat them the past two years."
- Presbyterian College Head Football Coach Cally Gault, 1979

"This is my biggest win since I've been at PC, especially since I did so well. Who knows, maybe next week I won't touch the ball all game!"
- Danny Thornton TE, 1979

"It was hot and humid."
- John D'Andrea OG, 2023

"I was happy for Coach Gault as it was his first victory over Art Baker."
- Presbyterian College Assistant Football Coach John Perry, 2023

"We always played well against The Citadel."
- Presbyterian College Assistant Coach Wayne Renwick, 2023

"I had great respect for The Citadel Head Coach Art Baker. Before I left The Citadel for Presbyterian, he pulled me aside and stressed the importance of learning about how to not quit schools. He had contacted Coach Gault and I was recruited to Presbyterian by Coach Strock."
 - Ronnie Hollier WR, 2023

"It's no fluke that they beat The Citadel. PC is a team like Wofford, an NAIA school with a good program. When they have a peak team, they are as good as any team that is in the Southern Conference."
 - Furman University Head Football Coach Dick Sheridan, 1979

"Playing The Citadel in Charleston was always something special."
 - Bentley Anderson Athletic Training Staff, 2023

"We had great tremendous respect for The Citadel. Both Presbyterian College and The Citadel have great military traditions. When we arrived in the locker room, there were galvanized buckets of Coca Cola on ice. When we went on the field, I remember looking at their sidelines and seeing them drinking Gatorade. Years later, I ran into an Athletic Trainer who was at The Citadel during our era. I asked him about the iced down beverages in our locker room. Their (The Citadel) hydration simply did not include caffeine."
 - Jimmy Spence QB, 2023

"I remember the sand gnats and how hot and humid it was."
 - Chris D'Andrea DE, 2023

"Stump Mitchell had Gale Sayers-like cuts. He was slippery."
 - David Neisler LB, 2023

Southern Massacre

Blue Hose Outlast the Citadel

Last week the Blue Hose surprised everyone but themselves by manhandling the Bulldogs of Citadel 21-13. PC's offense dominated the game almost completely, seemingly able to move at will against the porous Citadel defense. Jimmy Spence passed for 199 yards completing 11 of 16 passes. Clayton Burke led the PC ground attack rushing for 108 yards and one touchdown in 31 carries for a 3.5 yard average. Danny Thornton brought down five of Spence's tosses for 117 yards including a 30 yard scoring strike late in the game to ice the victory.

PC opened the scoring when Burke bulled four yards for a score capping 73 yard drive, highlighted by a 41 yard bomb to Danny Thornton. The Citadel reciprocated knotting the score at 7-7, but the Hose went ahead to stay when Walter Atkins scored from four yards out to put PC in front 14-7. The Citadel pulled within one of PC, but the Bulldogs muffed an attempt at a two point conversion, and the Hose held a lead they never relinquished. Spence's 30 yard scoring play to Thornton completed the scoring.

Quarterback Jimmy Spence calls the signals as PC mounts a drive against the Bulldogs.

The Blue Stocking
PRESBYTERIAN COLLEGE
VOL. LXII-NO. 13   CLINTON, S.C. 29325   SEPTEMBER 14, 1979

Week 2

- September 9, 1979, John McEnroe wins his first Grand Slam tennis title defeating Vitus Gerulaitis 7-5 6-3 6-3 in the US Open.
- September 15, 1979, Major League baseball player Bob Watson of the Boston Red Sox is the first to hit for the cycle in both the American and the National League. He was a member of the Houston Astros in the National League when he hit for the cycle.
- September 15, 1979, The Presbyterian College Blue Hose football team defeated the Furman Paladins 17-10 at Sirrine Stadium in Greenville, South Carolina. Kickoff was at 1:30 PM.

Furman and their head coach Dick Sheridan were 5-6 in 1979. Sheridan was a quarterback at North Augusta High School in the late 1950's, coached by Presbyterian College Head Coach Cally Gault. He coached Furman from 1978-1985 with a 69-23-2 record. As a head coach at North Carolina State from 1986-1992, he had a record of 52-29-3 for a college career record of 121-52-5. Coach Sheridan was inducted to the College Football Hall of Fame in 2020.

Can Blue Hose knock off another giant?

The Laurens County Advertiser, September 12, 1979

Clayto Burke   Danny Thornton

By SAM REGISTER

For the second time in two weeks Cally Gault's Presbyterian Blue Hose will face a Southern Conference opponent. Last week Presbyterian pulled what most folks thought was an upset with a 21-13 win over The Citadel in Charleston.

Gault admittedly anticipated a win against Citadel, but is he as confident against Furman, which the Blue Hose will face this Saturday in Greenville?

"They didn't ask David to kill Goliath twice," said Gault. Now that doesn't mean that Gault is expecting to come out on the short end of the score, just that he isn't as confident against the Paladins as he was against The Citadel.

"They're physically stronger than The Citadel," he said. "I was impressed with their game against Clemson. They've got a passing quarterback where Citadel's quarterback was a better runner. They've got a good backfield and a fine offensive line. But they know they're in for a dogfight."

The PC coach said his team had little trouble coming down after Saturday's win, despite the fact they went into the game as underdogs and came out on top by eight points.

"We anticipated a win, so we weren't so excited," said Gault. "We felt like we should have beat them the past two years."

Dick Sheridan is in his second season at Furman. Last season he walked into a situation that any coach would have envied, a team composed mostly of seniors. As a result, the Paladins went 8-3 and shared the Southern Conference championship for the first time in the school's history.

But at the end of the season, Sheridan had to say good-bye to seven offensive and four defensive starters including six all-conference performers and three players who signed free agent contracts in the National Football League.

Last season quarterback David Henderson, a 6-2 senior from Atlanta, hit on 60 percent of his passes and threw for 1,732 yards and was named Southern Conference co-player of the year. He'll be joined in the backfield by Mike Glenn (over 700 yards last year), and fullbacks Sandy Davis and Steve Bishop. However, Paladin backs managed only 82 yards in 41 carries against Clemson last Saturday.

Henderson has a whole new bunch of receivers this season. He connected on 14 of 27 for 179 yards Saturday against the Tigers, but about half of those were thrown to backs.

Presbyterian's win over The Citadel Saturday was their first since 1971 and only their 11th in the 50 game series. Quarterback Jimmy Spence had a banner day, completing 11 of 16 passes for 199 yards and most of all showing no evidence of a knee injury during the off-season.

Five of his 11 completions were to junior tight end Jimmy Thornton who scored the winning touchdown on a 30-yard pass with 8:51 remaining in the fourth quarter. Thornton netted 117 yards on his five receptions.

Running back Clayto Burke opened the scoring on a four-yard run with 5:27 remaining in the first quarter. Burke rushed for 120 yards.

But despite the fact that his team beat a squad that is in the running for the Southern Conference Championship, Gault expects, as he said, "a dogfight" this Saturday in Greenville.

"We were bridesmaids before, but we finally got to the altar," he said of the

> "We were bridesmaids before but we finally got to the altar. But we know the honeymoon's over."
> —Cally Gault

The 1979 Presbyterian Blue Hose Football Team

FURMAN

PRESBYTERIAN
September 15 at Greenville, SC - 1:30 p.m.

Week 2

Presbyterian College   **17**   **Furman**   **10**
Blue Hose   Paladins

Greenville, South Carolina   September 15, 1979   1:30 PM
Presbyterian Overall Record   2-0   SAC-8 Record   0-0
NAIA Division 1 Ranking #6

Statistics	PC	Furman
First Downs	16	15
Rushes / yards	56 /182	41 / 143
Passing yards	111	131
Passes	10-16-1	10-25-5
Fumbles / lost	2-2	3-38
Penalties / yards	4-40	1-5
Punts / average	6-28	6-41

Scoring Summary

Q1 PC….PC 7 – Furman 0….50 yard drive….Burke 2 yard run….Bishop PAT

Q2 Furman….PC 7 – Furman 7….Snipes recovered QB Spense fumble in end zone…Potter PAT

Q2 PC….PC 14 – Furman 7….Mason 98 yard kickoff return….Bishop PAT

Q3 Furman….PC 14 – Furman 10….Potter 38 yard field goal

Q4 PC….PC 17 – Furman 10….Bishop 32 yard field goal

Highlights
Presbyterian College Blue Hose vs Furman Paladins

- The Presbyterian College Blue Hose win over The Citadel and Furman in the same season was the second time for Head Football Coach Cally Gault. In 1971, Coach Gault beat these 2 Southern Conference teams in the same season.
- Presbyterian Head Football Coach Cally Gault beat Dick Sheridan for the first time. Sheridan was a former player for Coach Gault at North Augusta High School in Augusta, GA.
- Presbyterian College Blue Hose running back Clayto Burke rushed for 100 yards.
- Willie Mason solidified the lead for the Blue Hose with a second quarter 98 yard kickoff return for a touchdown.
- Presbyterian College Blue Hose wide receiver Jesse Cason had 6 receptions for 84 yards.
- Furman quarterback David Henderson threw 5 interceptions. In his 1978 season, he only threw 6 interceptions.
- The 1979 Furman Paladins were the defending NCAA Division 1 Southern Conference Champions.
- Presbyterian College Blue Hose defensive back Heyward Hinton recovered a fumble and had an interception.
- The Presbyterian College Blue Hose offense was aggressive throughout the game. In the fourth quarter, PC had a fourth and four on the Furman 35 yard line. PC went for the first down and failed on the attempt. The defense, once again, stepped up.
- Presbyterian College Blue Hose defensive back Willie Cooper had 2 interceptions with a broken hand he had sustained against The Citadel.
- Media throughout the state of South Carolina marveled at the win by the Presbyterian College Blue Hose and Head Coach Cally Gault.

Southern Massacre

Presbyterian College Blue Hose Quarterback Jimmy Spence signals touchdown as Blue Hose Running Back Clayto Burke scores the first touchdown of the game in Greenville, South Carolina. The first quarter touchdown, a 2 yard run, helped Presbyterian beat Furman 17-10 on September 15, 1979.

The 1979 Presbyterian Blue Hose Football Team

Willie Mason returns a kickoff 98 yards against the Furman Paladins to spark a 17-10 upset win for the Presbyterian College Blue Hose.

Presbyterian stuns Paladins, 17-10

The Laurens County Advertiser, September 17, 1979

	Furman	Presbyterian
First downs	15	16
Rushes-yards	41-143	56-182
Passing yards	131	111
Passes	10-25-5	10-16-1
Punts	3-37.7	6-28.1
Fumbles-lost	3-2	2-2
Penalties-yards	1-5	4-40

By SAM REGISTER

Cally Gault stood at midfield of Sirrine Stadium Saturday, surrounded by a horde of admirers and sportswriters. His Presbyterian team had just knocked off its second Southern Conference team in two weeks and he was anything but speechless.

"I'll be frank. This game today was gravy," he said between handshakes and kisses. "Next week we have to get back to the lathack and turnip greens." He was referring to next week's return to SAC-eight competition.

Presbyterian's 17-10 victory over Furman marked only the third time that the Blue Hose have beaten The Citadel and Furman in the same year. It last occurred in 1971. The first time was in 1917.

Despite the fact that he reached the 3,000 yard plateau for total offense Saturday, the Blue Hose secondary managed to dampen Furman quarterback David Henderson's day. He threw five interceptions, only one less than he threw all of last year, and four of those came in the first half.

The first half was not void of action. After Brothel Cole took the kickoff at his three and returned it to the 16, Furman moved to their 43 in six plays before PC cornerback Hal Brannon made a diving interception of a Henderson pass.

The Blue Hose failed to capitalize on that possession but after running back Clayto Burke was stacked up after trying to go over the right side of the Palladin defensive line, he found a hole on the left side where he went in from the two yard line with 3:24 remaining in the first quarter.

Again Henderson began driving his team downfield where they reached their 37 under a hard rush from Steve Stalvey, he threw to the right side of the field where safety Willie Cooper was waiting. Despite a broken hand, Cooper made the interception at the four yard line and returned it to the 19.

Only five minutes later Heywood Hinton intercepted another Henderson pass. It appeared that Hinton's momentum carried him into the end zone and that the ball might be brought out to the 20. But the ball was spotted on the Blue Hose one and on the first play quarterback Jimmy Spence bobbled the snap from center and end Jeff Snipes fell on the ball in the end zone for a Paladin touchdown.

But even Gault couldn't explain what happened on the following kickoff.

Laurens junior Willie Mason took the kick on his two and raced up the PC side of the field. It appeared he would be pinned in at the 20 but a block by Jay Byars sprung Mason and he outran everyone else for a 98-yard TD return.

"That's the kind of thing only the Lord can explain," said Gault. "Only he knows why you lose fumbles on the one and then get 98-yard returns. I think we got a little anxious when we were pinned in at the one yard line. The quarterback never received the ball."

With a little over a minute left in the half Furman was on the PC 24 with a first down. But a pass to Terry Clarke fell incomplete and on the following play tailback Mike Glenn, who carried for 86 yards and had to be helped from the field following the game, was stopped when end Jim McCoun fought off a block and upended him for a two yard loss. Henderson's next pass was also incomplete and a 37-yard field goal by Keith Potter was wide and the Blue Hose held a 14-7 half time lead.

However, PC had only 76 yards total offense in the first half. Clayto Burke, who led all rushers with 100 yards in 24 carries, managed only four yards in the first half. The key was Henderson's four interceptions.

With 8:07 remaining in the third quarter, Potter's field goal from the 38 was good and the Presbyterian lead was cut to four. But Gault elected not to sit on the ball.

"We knew we couldn't get in a punting game with them," he said. "They've got a great punter. That's why we kept throwing the ball—to keep possession. That's what impressed me about us. We didn't play it close to the vest. We got stronger in the fourth quarter." Furman ventured within the Presbyterian 45 four times in the final half, but had only three points to show for it.

"It's hard to sort out anybody," said Gault, "but Jim McCoun (eight tackles) had a great game. Jesse Cason (six receptions) was magnificent. (Clayto) Burke had a great game, but he had some great blocking.

"We got frustrated but we never lost our cool," he said. "We told the defense to hang in there and we'd try to get it (the ball) back. We got it back and straightened things out."

But as he stood at midfield following the game Saturday, Gault was already looking forward to next Saturday. "We've won the Southern Conference championship. Now it's time to get back where it's tough."

Presbyterian 7 7 0 3 -17
Furman 0 7 3 0 -10

INDIVIDUAL STATISTICS

Rushing-PC: Burke 24-100, Atkins 12-37; Hood 4-13; Spence 14-(-3). Furman: Glenn 28-86; Bishop 8-15; Taylor 2-6; Henderson 2-6.

Passing-PC: Spence 10-16-1, for 111 yards. Furman: Henderson 10-25-5, for 131 yards

Receiving-PC: Cason 6-84, Thornton 2-16, Burke 1-8, Walker 1-3. Furman: Lee 3-39, Grainger 3-38, Rhsher 1-16, McDougall 1-16, Clark 1-13, Bishop 1-9.

SPENCE GOES TO THE AIR—Presbyterian quarterback Jimmy Spence fires this pass over the Furman defense. The 6-2 junior burnt the Furman defense for 111 yards passing, hitting on 10 of 16 passes

HANDOFF—Spence hands off to Greenville sophomore Walter Atkins. Atkins, a 5-1, 200-pound fullback picked up 37 yards rushing against the Paladin defense.

GOING OUTSIDE—Senior tailback Clayto Burke comes around the left side against Furman Saturday. Burke rushed for 100 yards in 24 carries. He was the game's leading rusher.

Southern Massacre

Face Lenoir Rhyne
Blue Hose Stop the Paladins, 17-10

The Blue Hose entered Saturday's game with Furman as a 15 point underdog, but that didn't bother the Hose, who the week before were 17 point underdogs to The Citadel, as they shocked the Furman Paladins 17-10. The last time PC knocked off The Citadel and the Paladins in the same year was in 1971, before that it was 1917.

The game started like the Paladins were going to make it a long day for PC; but the tone of the game was set when Hal Brennen picked off a David Henderson pass to stop a Furman drive early in the first quarter. Throughout the game, PC's secondary shined as they intercepted five Henderson passes to slow down the Paladin offensive attack. (Henderson had only six passes intercepted last year.) On P.C.'s first possession the Paladins showed how stubborn their defense was as they stopped the run cold and applied a fierce pass rush on Jimmy Spence. However, the Hose's offense did what it needed to put points on the board. Late in the first quarter, Spence engineered a 50 yard drive, highlighted by a long toss to Jesse Cason, to set up the first score of the game. Clayto Burke then burst over from two yards out to put P.C. in front 7-0 with Bishop's PAT. Furman used running back Mike Glenn to dash and dart for yardage against the pliable P.C. defense, but the Hose's defense never broke. Paladin quarterback David Henderson had good protection all day long; but he was obviously inconsistne with his tosses. Henderson occasionally showed his accurate arm by "threading the needle" on numerous passes. Whenever the Paladins seemed to move the ball, the PC defense would rise up and stall the drive by forcing a turnover. Willie Cooper, playing with a broken hand, intercepted 2 passes and recovered a fumble to stop three Paladin drives.

Furman's only touchdown, ironically, was the indirect result of one of their own turnovers. Heyward Hington intercepted a Paladin pass on the goal line and on the following play Jimmy Spence fumbled the ball in the end zone and Furman's defense jumped on it for their only touchdown. Furman appeared to have let the air out of PC's balloon at this point; but Willie Mason had other plans. On the ensuing kickoff, Willie Mason caught the ball, hesitated briefly and then simply outran everybody 98 yards for the eventual game winning score. The Hose led at the half 14-7.

Early in the third, Furman had a great chance to tie the score when Spence, hit from behind, fumbled and the Paladins recovered. They then drove to the PC 11 when the Hose's defense forced a fumble, recovered by Hinton, to delay Furman's next score. The Paladins intercepted on PC's possession and converted it into a 38 yard field goal.

The PC offense began to move with some consistency early in the fourth quarter as Clayto Burke, 24 carries for 100 yards, and Jesse Cason led the attack which ended when the Hose couldn't convert a fourth and four play. Furman took over at their own 35 and marched to the PC 34 until Willie Cooper recovered a Paladin fumble to stop the drive. Midway through the fourth quarter, Heyward Hington intercepted his second pass of the day to set up Chuck Bishop's 32 yard field goal to extend PC's lead to 17-10. Late in the game, the Paladins were moving steadily against the Hose; but when Furman failed to convert a fourth down and four play, it was all she wrote. Roy Walker even got into the passing game as he hauled in a tipped pass and rambled for three yards. In the battle of Conference Player of the Year, Spence, the SAC-8's Player of the Year, outdueled Henderson, the Southern Conference's Co-Player of the Year; as Spence completed 10 of 16 passes for 111 yards with only one interception while Henderson completed 10 for 131 yards with 5 interceptions.

This Saturday the Blue Hose will take on their first SAC-8 opponent of the year in Hickory, N.C. against the Lenoir Rhyne Bears. PC leads the lifetime series against the Bears with 12 wins, 9 defeats and 3 ties. The last time these two teams met the Hose were victorious by a 14-7 score; but this year's game should be a lot closer because of the improvement in Lenoir Rhyne's team from last year. The Bears main asset as a football club lies in their overall team speed. They have fast tailbacks and a quick defense, especially in the secondary. However, last week against Wofford, the Lenoir Rhyne defense allowed Wofford to run everywhere on the field but in the end zone. Wofford gained 357 yards against the Bear's defense, 208 yards by one runningback; but Wofford could only score 10 points. Another advantage possessed by Lenoir Rhyne is that they are a big veteran football team. Coach Gault was impressed with their ability to execute plays consistently well.

The punting game could prove to be a factor in this contest. PC's punting this year has not been spectacular, due to the loss of starting punter Tony Grove, but it has been adequate. Although the punts are not long (23.1 yard avg. last week), they are gotten off quickly, and the coverage on the punts has been super: zero return yardage. Lenoir Rhyne's punting is one of their strong points. Last week their punter had a 47 yard average on four punts. If this game turns out to be a defensive struggle, the contest could be decided by the effectiveness of the punting game.

Jim McCoun (99) stops a Paladin back behind the line.

CONFERENCE STANDINGS

	Conference W	L	T	Overall W	L	T
Gardner-Webb	1	0	0	1	0	0
Mars Hill	1	0	0	1	0	1
Lenoir Rhyne	0	0	0	2	0	0
Presbyterian	0	0	0	2	0	0
Carson Newman	0	0	0	0	1	0
Catawba	0	0	0	0	2	0
Elon	0	1	0	1	1	0
Newberry	0	1	0	0	1	0

LAST WEEK'S GAMES
Maryville 15, Carson Newman 7
Liberty Baptist 21, Catawba 14
Mars Hill 10, Elon 9
Gardner Webb 24, Newberry 13
Lenoir Rhyne 13, Wofford 10
Presbyterian 17, Furman 10

NEXT WEEK'S GAMES
Wofford at Carson Newman
Catawba at Newberry
Presbyterian at Lenoir Rhyne
NC Central at Elon
Gardner-Webb at Mars Hill

Clayto Burke (40) runs against the Paladin defenders with the help of Walter Atkins (46) blocking.

The 1979 Presbyterian Blue Hose Football Team

As a result of two wins over NCAA Division 1 teams, the Presbyterian College Blue Hose football team find themselves ranked #6 in the NAIA Division 1 poll.

Circus catches are routine for Jesse Cason, who already is off to a fast start after setting a new team record for receptions in his first season last year.

Ranked 6th nationally:

Blue Hose open with two major upsets

Sports writers termed it "the Southern Conference massacre."

And after PC's back-to-back hatchet job on the Citadel and Furman, pre-season favorites to win the title of that major conference, Blue Hose coaches and players facetiously laid claim to the league championship.

The convincing victories on the opponents' home fields also propelled Presbyterian to sixth place nationally in the NAIA rankings.

While enjoying the applause, Cally Gault now focuses his attention on the NAIA road ahead—where trouble lurks every weekend. For example, Lenoir Rhyne and Wofford round out September. It may not seem as formidable, but the SAC-8 is considered perhaps the fastest small-college conference in the country.

The record books shows the opening triumphs of 21-13 over the Citadel and 17-10 over Furman may represent the best start ever for a PC football season. They were fashioned by a team well-balanced offensively and defensively.

The PC offense accumulated almost 700 yards from scrimmage in the two games. Quarterback Jimmy Spence, with 66 percent accuracy, hit on 21 of 32 passes for 310 yards—mainly to ends Jesse Cason and Danny Thornton. Clayton Burk topped 100 yards each Saturday in rushing for a total 217 yards in 56 carries—much of it behind tackle R Walker. And Willie Mason added a yard kickoff return against Furman.

Defensively, the big honors went end Jim McCoun, middle guard Joe Grant and a defensive secondary (Heyward Hinton, Willie Cooper, Erskine Reed and Hal Brannen) that intercepted five passes by a Furman quarterback who lost only six all of year when he ranked as an NCAA leader.

South Carolina sport writers took special note of their work in these games by choosing for state honors Spence, offensive back-of-the-week Walker, offensive lineman-of-the-w and Hinton, defensive back-of-the-week. And as a final accolade, one writer reminded that PC provi only 25 football grants compared to for the Citadel and 50 for Furman.

Notable Quotes Regarding Furman University

"David only had to play Goliath once. If he had to play him twice, I don't think he would be able to win with the slingshot. And that's the position we find ourselves in this week. We used the slingshot against The Citadel, but we won't be able to do it against Furman."
    - Presbyterian College Head Football Coach Cally Gault, 1979

"After the Citadel win, our confidence was high for Furman."
    - David Neisler LB, 2023

"Willie Mason ignited that win!"
    - Randy Morris WR, 2023

"I hope I'm on the side where I'm losing a little bit of pleasure because of beating a friend rather than being in the situation where a friend loses some pleasure by beating me."
    - Presbyterian College Head Football Coach Cally Gault, 1979

"I had great respect for Coach Sheridan and Furman. Willie Mason made an incredible kickoff return."
    - Jay Byars WR, 2023

"We were bridesmaids before we finally got to the altar. But we know the honeymoon's over."
    - Presbyterian College Head Football Coach Cally Gault, 1979

"The week prior to our game, Furman had lost to Clemson 21-0. I remember how hot it was."
    - Bruce Ollis OG, 2023

"We've won the Southern Conference Championship. Now it's time to get back where it is tough."
    - Presbyterian College Head Football Coach Cally Gault, 1979

"I'll be frank. This game today was gravy. Next week we have to get back to the grits, fatback and turnip greens (referring to the SAC-8)."
  - Presbyterian College Head Football Coach Cally Gault, 1979

"During the Furman game I had an interception. I caught a tipped ball and ran with it and was tackled. Coach Gault wanted me next time to bat it away. He didn't want me to get hurt!"
  - Roy Walker OT, 2023

"I wrote David Henderson (Furman QB who threw 5 interceptions against PC) a letter after we got back. I told him he wouldn't have many games like that. I tried to tell him we had great respect for him as a class individual. Our players do. He was the first man on the field to congratulate our players Saturday, and feeling as he must have, that took class."
  - Presbyterian College Head Football Coach Cally Gault, 1979

Week 3

- September 15, 1979, The Presbyterian College Blue Hose Football team was ranked #6 in the NAIA Division I poll.
- September 23, 1979, St Louis Cardinals baseball Hall of Famer Lou Brock steals the 938th and final base of his career.
- September 22, 1979, The Presbyterian College Blue Hose football team defeated the Lenoir Rhyne Bears 28-14 at College Field in Hickory, North Carolina. Kickoff was at 7:30PM.

GO BLUE HOSE!

**Catch All The Action
Scores - Sports Stories**

**Listen To
Saturday Afternoon Scoreboard
With
Larry Gar**

**Over
WLBG - AM - Laurens
860**

The Presbyterian College Blue Hose go on the road for the third straight week to play their first SAC-8 opponent, the Lenoir Rhyne Bears in Hickory, North Carolina.

First conference game

Blue Hose face Bears

After conquering the Southern Conference, Presbyterian "gets back to where it's tough" this Saturday when they travel to play SAC-Eight rival Lenoir Rhyne.

Reports from Presbyterian say that the players have calmed down after convincing wins over The Citadel and Furman but that Coach Cally Gault "is still in the clouds." No so, says Cally.

"It didn't take us long to get calm," he said. "We went right back to work Saturday night by going to the Lenoir Rhyne-Wofford game. After seeing that, we realized we have no reason not to work right up to Thanksgiving Day."

What Gault saw was that both teams have more speed than the Blue Hose's previous two foes and are large on both offense and defense. "I've heard that people in Hickory are saying that this game will decide the conference championship," said Gault.

Presbyterian beat Lenoir Rhyne 14-7 last season. The Bears finished 6-5, winning their last five games of the season. Thus far this season they have defeated J.C. Smith 33-8 and Wofford 13-10.

Lenoir Rhyne operates out of the veer offense and has two quarterbacks, senior Jeff Flowe and junior Craig Corbett. Together the two could manage only 78 yards passing against Wofford. Both, however, are threats to run.

Joining Corbett and Flowe in the backfield is tailback Don Strayhorn, who rushed for 967 yards last season while averaging 5.1 yards per carry. Strayhorn rushed for 82 yards in 16 carries against the Terriers.

The Bears return 44 lettermen and 16 starters, including eight on offense and eight on defense. They average about 230 pounds on the defensive line and all four starters from last year's defensive secondary are back from last year. The Blue Hose will again face a good punter this week in Greg Marshburn, who averaged 47 yards per boot against Wofford.

Tailback Clayte Burke and flanker Jay Byars were named the Presbyterian offensive Players of the Week. Burke, a senior, carried 24 times for 100 yards and one touchdown against Furman. Byars was honored for his fine blocking, including one that sprung Willie Mason enroute to his 98-yard kickoff return.

Defensive end Jim McCoun and defensive back Heywood Hinton were Players of the Week on defense. McCoun, a tri-captain, had eight individual tackles including two for losses. Hinton picked off two of David Henderson's five errant passes and recovered a fumble. He was also in on seven tackles.

Willie Mason returned Furman kick 98 yards

SPORTS

Southern Massacre

Week 3

Presbyterian College   28   Lenoir Rhyne   14
Blue Hose   Bears

Hickory, North Carolina   September 22, 1979   7:30 PM
Presbyterian Overall Record   3-0   SAC-8 Record   1-0
NAIA Division 1 Ranking #2

Statistics	PC	Lenoir Rhyne
First Downs	15	13
Rushes / yards	50 / 102	32 / 110
Passing yards	213	142
Passes	15-21-0	13-27-0
Fumbles / lost	2-1	3-1
Penalties / yards	6-50	7-75
Punts / average	5-41	7-46

Scoring Summary

Q1 LR....PC 0 – LR 7....32 yard drive....Strayhorn 3 yard run.... PAT Good....6:09 remaining

Q2 PC....PC 7 – LR 7....45 yard pass from QB Spence to WR Porter.... Bishop PAT....14:53 remaining

Q2 PC....PC 14 – LR 7....13 yard drive....Hood 3 yard run.... Bishop PAT....13:10 remaining

Q2 PC....PC 21 – LR 7....72 yard drive....Hood 5 yard run.... Bishop PAT

Q3 LR....PC 21 – LR 14....93 yard drive....1 yard HB pass from Kirkpatrick to Nooe....PAT Good

Q4 PC....PC 28 – LR 14....93 yard drive....8 yard pass from QB Spence to RB Burke....Bishop PAT

Highlights
Presbyterian College Blue Hose vs Lenoir Rhyne Bears

- Lenoir Rhyne was ranked #18 in the NAIA Division 1 national ranking hosting #6 Presbyterian College.
- Presbyterian College Blue Hose QB Jimmy Spence threw for 213 yards and 2 touchdowns including a fourth quarter 57 yard completion to WR Jay Byars to set up the final touchdown of the game.
- In the 2nd quarter, as Lenoir Rhyne was driving, Blue Hose LB Steve Stalvy recovered a fumble resulting in a PC touchdown drive.
- Presbyterian College Blue Hose RB Ben Hood ran for two touchdowns.
- The Presbyterian College Blue Hose football team trailed for the first time in the 1979 football season 7-0. In the second quarter, the Blue Hose scored 21 unanswered points.

SHEALY'S FLORIST

"Flowers Especially For You"

Telephone: 833-1551

Jacobs Highway Clinton, S.C.

Spence leads Blue Hose win

Quarterback Jimmy Spence hit on 15 of 21 passes and threw for 213 yards as Presbyterian downed Lenoir Rhyne 28-14 in their first SAC-Eight contest of the season Saturday in Hickory.

The Bears were able to capitalize on a Blue Hose fumble in the first quarter when tailback Don Strayhorn went in from the three.

Presbyterian exploded for 21 points in the second quarter. Spence hit David Porter on a 45-yard pass play and fullback Ben Hood scored from the two-yard line and the five. Chuck Bishop hit all three conversions and the Blue Hose took a 21-7 lead. Lenoir Rhyne's only other score came on a one-yard pass from Don Kirkpatrick to Bruce Nooe in the third quarter.

Presbyterian tailback Clayto Burke closed out the scoring on an eight-yard reception from Spence.

"We're real pleased to get this one over with," said Presbyterian Coach Cally Gault. "Anytime you have a conference game you have a lot of emotion so you're ready to get that one out of the way."

The punting game, which had been a point of concern for Gault over the past three games, was solved for at least one Saturday as Lamar Roberts, who hadn't punted since high school, booted the ball five times for a 40.8

Week 4

- September 26, 1979, 1984 summer Los Angeles Olympic coverage was sold to ABC for $225 million.
- September 28, 1979, Boxer Ernie Holmes beats Ernie Shavers by TKO to win the WBC heavyweight boxing title.
- September 29, 1979, The Presbyterian College Blue Hose football team was defeated by the Wofford Terriers 23-21 at Johnson Field in Clinton, South Carolina. Kickoff was at 7:30 PM.

Randy Randall, Presbyterian College Women's Head Basketball Coach was the voice of Johnson Field on gameday. He and Bruce Wismer are pictured in the Bailey Stadium press box.

Mark Kay

Frank Kube

Erskine Reed

Walter Todd
Ex-Laurens quarterback

Blue Hose host Wofford

The Blue Hose of Presbyterian get to don their blue jerseys for the first time this year as they face Wofford in their first home game of the season this Saturday.

The Terriers are winless in two games but Presbyterian Coach Cally Gault still sees the game as a "toss up situation.

"The previous games don't make a bit of difference," he said. "It doesn't matter what their record is we're still going to have to get ready for them. I didn't even give the players a pep talk this week," Gault said. "They remember what happened last year."

In case anyone has forgotten, the Blue Hose were ntionally ranked last year when they traveled to Spartanburg where they were dumped by the Terriers 14-12. The previous year Presbyterian won 10-7 over a nationally ranked Wofford team.

However, the Terriers have been plagued with turnovers, suffering seven last week in a 21-12 loss to Carson-Newman at Jefferson City, Tenn. Six of those turnovers were passes. Wofford's other defeat came at the hands of Lenoir Rhyne 13-10. The Bears were victims of PC last week, 28-14.

"We did not play well against Carson-Newman," said Wofford Coach Buddy Sasser. "Our offensive line pretty much speaks for itself.

"We must correct mistakes made in our first two games and not let ourselves get down. We have to be ready when we go to Clinton Saturday."

Offensively, the Terriers will rely on the running of tailback Lenny Best, who entered the Carson-Newman as the top NAIA rusher in the nation. He suffered a minor leg injury Saturday, but should be at full speed for this week's game.

The quarterback position was up for grabs between sophomores Walter Todd, Barry Thompson and Tim Crumb at the start of the season. So far Todd, a former Laurens quarterback, has logged the most time, hitting on 13 of 28 passes for 46 percent and 165 yards. Thompson has played enough to have attempted two of six passes for 22 yards. The Carson-Newman game was Todd's first collegiate start.

The Blue Hose are currently ranked sixth in the NAIA and were sparked by Jimmy Spence, who hit on 15 of 21 passes for 213 yards against Lenoir Rhyne. The junior from Lexington is averaging 182 yards a game in total offense. Senior halfback Clayto Burke has been the Blue Hose' top rusher with 301 yards in three games.

Players of the week on defense were Mark Kay and

WOFFORD VS. PRESBYTERIAN

Johnson Field, Clinton, S.C.
Sept. 29, 1979, 7:30 p.m.

Price: $1.00

Next Home Game:
ELON
Oct. 13, 1979, 7:30 p.m.

The 1979 Presbyterian Blue Hose Football Team

P.C. CAPTAINS—Jim McCoun, left, Roy Walker, Bruce Ollis, right, with SAC-8 championship trophy.

Week 4

Presbyterian College   21   Wofford   23
Blue Hose   Terriers

Clinton, South Carolina   September 29, 1979   7:30 PM
Presbyterian Overall Record   3-1   SAC-8 Record   1-0
NAIA Division 1 Ranking #13

Scoring Summary

Q2 Wofford....PC 0 – Wofford 7....29 yard drive....Brady 4 yard run....Andrews PAT....12:56 remaining

Q2 PC....PC 7 – Wofford 7....91 yard drive....Burke 1 yard run....Bishop PAT....2:41 remaining

Q2 Wofford....PC 7 – Wofford 10....31 yard drive....Andrews 30 yard field goal....0:02 remaining

Q3 Wofford....PC 7 – Wofford 13....86 yard drive....Andrews 24 yard field goal....4:02 remaining

Q4 Wofford....PC 7 – Wofford 16....80 yard drive....Andrews 30 yard field goal....12:02 remaining

Q4 PC....PC 14 – Wofford 16....84 yard drive....QB Spence 8 yard pass to RB Ben Hood....Bishop PAT....7:48 remaining

Q4 Wofford....PC 14 – Wofford 23....80 yard drive....Brady 60 yard run....Andrews PAT....5:49 remaining

Q4 PC....PC 21 – Wofford 23....77 yard drive....QB Spence 1 yard run....Bishop PAT....2:40 remaining

Highlights
Presbyterian College Blue Hose vs Wofford Terriers

- Wofford came to Clinton, South Carolina with an 0-2 record.
- Wofford's offensive game plan included both the I formation and wishbone, confusing the PC coaching staff and defensive personnel.
- It was the first game and start for Wofford freshman quarterback Charlie Bradshaw.
- The Wofford offense generated over 250 yards rushing including a 60 yard rushing touchdown by Frank Brady in the fourth quarter.
- After being on the road this was the Presbyterian College Blue Hose first home game of the 1979 season.
- In 1979, the NAIA introduced a rule that had an impact on the game. Offensive pass interference in the end zone resulted in a loss of possession. In the third quarter, PC WR Donald Porter got tied up with a Wofford defender in the end zone. The call went against PC and resulted in a loss of possession at a critical moment in the game. The rule was discarded by the NAIA in the 1980 season.
- The Presbyterian College Blue Hose football team got the ball with 1:38 remaining in the fourth quarter down by 2 points. The Wofford team prevailed.
- Despite the steady rain, Johnson Field at Presbyterian College was packed, with an estimated 5,000 in attendance.
- Wofford freshman quarterback Charlie Bradshaw played like a veteran, calling audibles all evening and in complete control.

The Presbyterian College Blue Hose regroup after a loss at Wofford at home in Clinton, South Carolina. An independent NAIA school, many players on the Blue Hose never beat the Wofford Terriers.

Wofford dumps Hose again

It happened again.

When Presbyterian met Wofford last season the Blue Hose were nationally ranked but sustained a 14-12 loss at the hands of the Terriers. Saturday night the result was the same and the margin was the same, only the score was different as Wofford defeated number six-ranked PC 23-21 at Johnson Field.

The Terriers were able to hold on to the ball longer than PC and when they didn't have the ball the Blue Hose held possession deep in their territory as a result of a fine Wofford punting game.

A pleasant surprise for Wofford coach Buddy Sasser was freshman quarterback Charlie Bradshaw, who, as a freshman, was starting his first game and was calling audibles at the line and reading defenses like a senior. Also, runningback Lenny Best punished the Presbyterian defensive line, picking up 178 yards in 27 carries. Terrier kicker Ronnie Andrews booted field goals of 30, 30, and 23 yards. The Terrier defense held PC to only one first down in the first half.

Trailing 16-7, the Blue Hose pulled to within two points on a Jimmy Spence to Ben Hood pass play to culminate a 13-play, 84-yard drive followed by a Chuck Bishop extra point. But Wofford added another touchdown when Brady scampered 60 yards for a touchdown with 5:49 left to play in the game. PC again got within two when Spence went over from the one. They got possession one more time but that drive stalled at the Wofford 26 when Spence's pass to Jesse Cason was nullified due to an offensive interference penalty on Cason resulting in loss of possession.

Blue Hose are trying to get over loss

Cally Gault's Blue Hose are understandably a little down this week after absorbing a 23-21 loss at the hands of Wofford Saturday.

"We're getting over the withdrawal sypmtoms of losing," said Gault. "We were deadly disappointed. We acted as we normally do over any loss. A lot could be said, but we didn't play the kind of defense that we have thus far this season. But that's over. We get over our wins and our losses."

The Blue Hose will travel to Salisbury, N.C. this weekend where they will face Catawba which is winless so far. But Gault is not underestimating them.

"They've always been a dangerous team and we've sometimes had problems with them," he said. "We're wary of any team in our conference."

Notable Quotes Regarding Wofford

"Wofford? We never beat them!"
   - Frank Kube C, Robbie Way OG, Willie Cooper DB,
    Chris D'Andrea DT, Tom Steele TE, Randy Morris, WR 2023

"I transferred to PC. My first scrimmage was against Wofford. It turned into a brawl. Wofford is always a tough game. The loss helped us get even closer."
   - Jo Nell RB, 2023

"Wofford was well disciplined and had an outstanding game plan. Wofford was an independent NAIA Division 1 school. The loss did not affect the SAC 8 standings. If we had to lose one, that was the game to lose."
   - Jimmy Spence QB, 2023

"The Wofford loss was the most devastating loss in my football career."
   - John D'Andrea OG, 2023

"Offensive game plan by Wofford had our coaches scrambling."
   - Walt Atkins DB, 2023

"It was a packed house at PC as it was our first home game of the season. The offensive pass interference in the endzone which resulted in the loss of possession (a one year trial rule by the NAIA) was the difference."
   - Presbyterian College Assistant Football Coach John Perry, 2023

"The offensive interference in the endzone was most memorable. We refocused after the Wofford loss."
   - Bruce Ollis OG, 2023

"It was a rainy and misty evening. Wofford ran the wishbone and they had a great game plan."
   - Joe Grant MG, 2023

Andy Forrest OG holding his 4 year roommate and his best friend's jersey, the late OT Tommy Wade.

Week 5

- October 6, 1979, Pope John Paul II is the first Pope to visit the White House. He met with President Jimmy Carter.
- October 6, 1979, The Baltimore Orioles defeat the California Angels to advance and represent the American League in the World Series.
- October 6, 1979, The Presbyterian College Blue Hose football team defeated the Catawba Indians 21-0 at Shufford Stadium in Salisbury, North Carolina. Kickoff was at 2:00 PM.

Week 5

Presbyterian College   **21**   **Catawba**   **0**
Blue Hose   Indians

Salisbury, North Carolina   October 6, 1979   2:00 PM
Presbyterian Overall Record   4-1   SAC-8 Record   2-0
NAIA Division 1 Ranking #11

Statistics	PC	Catawba
First Downs	21	13
Rushes / yards	44 / 328	51 / 171
Passing yards	37	95
Passes	5-11-0	3-14-0
Fumbles / lost	4-3	4-2
Penalties yards	65	77
Punts / average	4-41	7-36

Scoring Summary

Q1 PC....PC 7 – Catawba 0....80 yard drive....Burke 5 yard run....Bishop PAT....6:15 remaining

Q2 PC....PC 14 – Catawba 0....69 yard drive....Spence 1 yard run....Bishop PAT....12:45 remaining

Q2 PC....PC 21 – Catawba 0....56 yard drive....QB Spence 1 yard pass to Burke....Bishop PAT....7:12 remaining

Highlights
Presbyterian College Blue Hose vs Catawba Indians

- Presbyterian College Blue Hose RB Clayo Burke broke the PC single game rushing record with 202 total yards. David Eskstein had held the record with 182 yards since 1972 also against Catawba.
- Presbyterian College Blue Hose Quarterback Jimmy Spence reportedly played with soreness in his right knee in the first half of the game.
- Reserve quarterbacks for the Presbyterian College Blue Hose football team Ward Gatlin and Paul Scott played the second half for the Blue Hose.
- Late in the second quarter and throughout the second half, the Presbyterian College Blue Hose offense and defense features reserves for valuable experience and playing time.

Get 21-0 win

Hose blank Catawba

Clayto Burke rushed 25 times for 202 yards and scored two touchdowns as Presbyterian blanked Catawba 21-0 Saturday at Shuford Stadium in Salisbury.

Burke's 202 yards broke the school record of 188 set by David Eskstein in 1972, also against Catawba. The Blue Hose jumped out to a 21-0 halftime lead and played mostly substitutes offensively throughout the second half.

PC was ranked number six nationally before falling to Wofford 23-21 last weekend in Clinton. They went into the Catawba game ranked 13th. Despite blanking the Indian offense, Gault admittedly was not pleased with the amount of penalties PC sustained plus some pushing incidents that took place following the first half.

Burke's first TD came with 6:15 left to go in the first period, when he broke in from the five-yard line. The touchdown capped a 12-play, 80-yard drive following a Catawba punt. Burke carried eight times for 61 yards to keep the drive going.

The Hose added another seven points early in the second quarter when quarterback Jimmy Spence, who played on a sore knee, scored from the one. The Lexington junior carried five times for 45 yards during the 69-yard drive. Chuck Bishop added the point after. Spence passed for 19 yards, hitting on four of five passes during the short time he played. Ward Gatlin and Paul Scott filled in for Spence.

PC scored again five minutes later as Spence tossed a three-yard pass to Burke on a fourth and two situation. Bishop's point after was good and the Hose went up by 21.

PC is now 2-0 in the SAC-Eight and 4-1 overall while Catawba is 0-5 and 0-3 in the SAC-Eight. The Blue Hose play host to Elon Saturday.

Week 6

- October 12, 1979, Boston Celtics guard Chris Ford scores the first 3 point basket in NBA history. Hall of Famer Larry Bird makes his NBA debut in the same game.
- October 12, 1979, Magic Johnson makes his NBA debut for the Los Angeles Lakers.
- October 13, 1979, The Presbyterian College Blue Hose football team defeated the Elon Fightin' Christians 30-14 at Johnson Field in Clinton, South Carolina. Kickoff was at 2:30 PM.

Presbyterian faces 'smarting' Elon team

Coach Jerry Tolley will bring what he believes to be his best team ever to Clinton Saturday as Presbyterian hosts Elon at 7:30.

The Fighting Christians finished second in the nation Angelo (Texas) State last season. In a preseason comment, Tolley said "on paper we look to be better than last season." But an upset loss to Mars Hill and a defeat at the hands of Western Carolina have left Elon with a 2-2 record and in PC Coach Cally Gault's words "left them smarting."

"They've got the best personnel of any team we've played so far," said Gault. "They've got 18 of 22 starters returning from last year and they should outweigh us by about 20 pounds on both lines, and we're bigger than normal."

Elon brings back eight starters from offense, among them All-American halfback Bobby Hedrick, who gained over 1,500 yards rushing and scored 20 touchdowns as a sophomore last year. He will be joined by the remainder of last year's starting backfield, quarterback Mike Currin and fullback James Dove.

It is a possibility that linebacker James Riddle, injured in the Western Carolina game, could miss this Saturday's game. Riddle, a team captain, led the Fighting Christians in solo tackles last season with 100.

"They had an open date last weekend, so they've had two weeks to get ready for us. We're expecting some new wrinkles, they might try to jazz it up," said Gault. "They're the kind of ballclub that'll try to stick it at you. They'll ram it at you for a while and if that doesn't work they'll go into the shotgun."

Gault's main concern for this game is trying to cut out penalties. The Blue Hose had more penalties in their 21-0 win over Catawba Saturday than in any of the four previous games (65 yards against the Indians).

The Hose picked tailback Clayto Burke as their offensive player of the week. The senior from Macon carried the ball 25 times for 202 yards and scored two touchdowns against Catawba. Tight end Danny Thornton, who Gault refers to as "an unsung hero," shared offensive honors with Burke. Larry Bridges, a senior linebacker from Greenville, was named defensive player of the week.

Presbyterian tailback Clayto Burke set school record
...Gained 202 yards against Catawba

The 1979 Presbyterian Blue Hose Football Team

ELON VS. PRESBYTERIAN
Johnson Field, Clinton, S.C.
Oct. 13, 1979, 7:30 p.m.

Price: $1.00

Next Home Game:
MARS HILL
(Homecoming)
Oct. 20, 1979, 3 p.m.

Week 6

Presbyterian College 30   Elon 14
Blue Hose   Fightin' Christians

Clinton, South Carolina   October 13, 1979   3:00 PM
Presbyterian Overall Record   5-1   SAC-8 Record   3-0
NAIA Division 1 Ranking #8

Statistics	PC	Elon
First Downs	24	21
Rushes / yards	55 -231	31 / 116
Passing yards	156	256
Passes	12-15-0	20-37-2
Fumbles / lost	0-0	1-0
Penalties / yards	2-10	8-60
Punts / average	4-29	5-41

Scoring Summary

Q1 PC….PC 6 – Elon 0….70 yard drive…. QB Spence 15 yard pass to RB Atkins ….Bishop missed PAT

Q1 PC….PC 13 – Elon 0….60 yard drive…. QB Spence 14 yard pass to WR Cason….Bishop PAT

Q2 PC….PC 16 – Elon 0….Bishop 30 yard field goal

Q3 PC….PC 23 – Elon 0….60 yard drive…. QB Spence 59 yard pass to WR Cason….Bishop PAT

Q3 Elon….PC 23 – Elon 7….31 yard drive…. RB Hendrick 3 yard run….PAT Good

Q4 PC….PC 30 – Elon 7….73 yard drive….RB Burke 5 yard run….Bishop PAT

Q4 Elon….PC 30 – Elon 14….QB Currin 18 yard pass to WR Smith….PAT Good

Highlights
Presbyterian College Blue Hose vs Elon Fightin' Christians

- Presbyterian College Blue Hose RB Clayo Burke rushed for 159 yards and 1 touchdown.
- The Presbyterian College Blue Hose offense had 231 yards rushing and 156 yards passing for 387 yards.
- Presbyterian College Blue Hose QB Jimmy Spence was 12-14 for 156 yards with 3 touchdown passes.
- Presbyterian College Blue Hose WR Jesse Cason caught 7 passes for 98 yards and 2 touchdowns including a 59 yard score.
- Elon, the 1978 NAIA Division 1 football runner-up and co-SAC-8 Champion with Presbyterian College, was held scoreless in the first half.
- A blocked punt by Elon led to one of their touchdowns in the second half.
- Down 16-0, Elon drove to the Presbyterian College 1 yard line late in the second quarter, and the Blue Hose defense held as time ran out in the quarter.

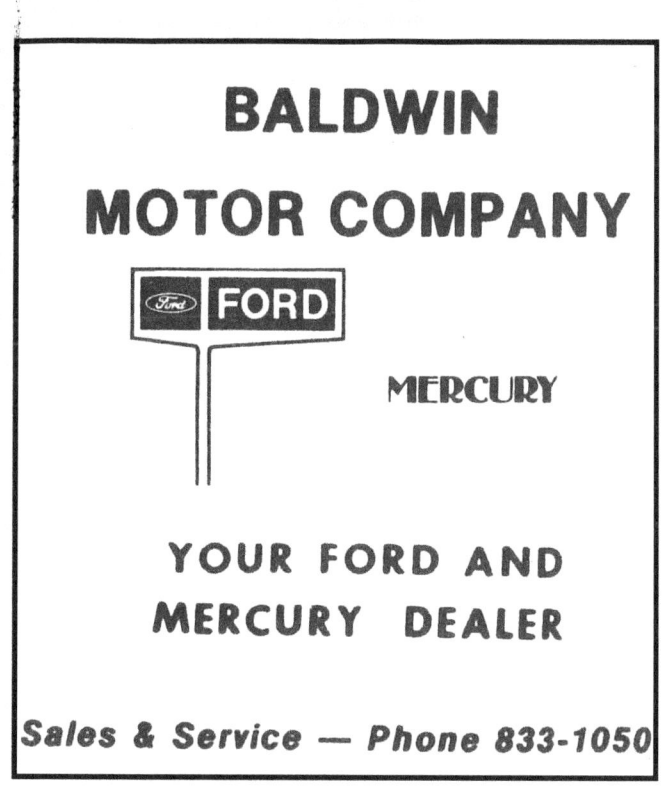

Blue Hose Top Elon, 30-14; Face Mars Hill

Saturday night the Blue Hose sought to heighten their chances at winning sole possession of the SAC-8 by defeating last year's co-conference champion Elon. PC stormed past Elon for a relatively easy 30-14 victory to up their record to 5-1. The excitement generated by the Hose's offense kept the fan's minds off of the cold biting wind that blew throughout the game. The Fighting Christians came into the game with the third best team defense in the nation; but PC paid little attention to that fact as they compiled 388 yards of total offense. Quarterback Jimmy Spence was equally unaffected by the fact that Elon's pass defense had only given up an average of 48 yards per game. Spence threw for over 150 yards.

Although they are usually overlooked, PC's offensive line played their best game of the year. They continually opened up gaping holes in the middle of Elon's defense to allow Clayto Burke to gain 171 yards. (Last week against Catawba, the offensive line helped Burke set a new school rushing record of 202 yards in one game, breaking the old record of 188 yards set in 1972 by David Eckstein against Catawba). Jimmy Spence was given ample time to throw by the offensive line as evidenced by his completion percentage of 92 percent. Spence was 11 for 12, including a new school record of 11 consecutive completions. (The old record, set by Jack Harper, was 9; the record stood for 28 years).

The hose seemed to be able to do everything right as they scored on two of their first three possessions. The only problem PC experienced was a blocked punt that led to Elon's first score. On the Hose's second possession they marched 70 yards in 7 plays to take the lead. Spence dropped back to pass with an Elon defender hanging on to him, and he hit Walter Atkins all alone in the end zone for the score. On the Hose's next possession, they profited from a poor punt by Elon to score their second touchdown. Spence, apparently trying to hit Atkins who was wide open in the end zone, fired crossfield to Jesse Cason for six points. Chuck Bishop missed his first PAT this year and the Hose led 13-0. After Spence's TD toss to Cason, Spence was nearly decapitated by an onrushing lineman and had to be helped off the field. However, Spence stayed in the game.

The only score of the second quarter came on a 30 yard field goal by Chuck Bishop. Elon had an excellent scoring opportunity near the end of the first half. The Hose defense and the inaccuracy of Elon's quarterback hindered any drives the Fighting Christians might have had but with seconds remaining in the half Elon had a first down on the two. The PC defense held the Christians who couldn't get off another play and the half ended with PC leading 16-0. The hardest hitting of the night occurred during halftime as Hose fans battled each other for the little footballs that are thrown into the stands.

The Hose opened the second half in grand style by putting another seven points on the board. The TD came on a 59-yard pass play to Jesse Cason. It was the longest pass play this year for the Hose. Elon finally got on the board following a blocked punt and entertained hopes of a comeback. QB Mike Cumin continued to go to the air and Elon went to the spread or shotgun formation. All hopes Elon had ended when a Willie Cooper interception was turned into a PC touchdown by Clayto Burke to give PC a commanding 30-7 advantage. Elon scored one more to make the score 30-14, but the game was never in doubt.

This week's homecoming game brings the well-balanced attack of the Mars Hill Lions (4-0-1) to PC. Mars Hill is the Cinderella team of the SAC-8 this year, but they are no fluke. Their offense is equally dangerous with the run as it with the pass. The Lions have speedy running back and a good corps of receivers. Mars Hill's defense is a tight one; it has given up very few points this season. The star of the Lions' defense is #72 linebacker Don Gulledge. Last year's Mars Hill defense was the best in the conference. The major factor in the Lions' success this season is their ability to not make mistakes.

Jimmy Spence drops back to throw one of PC's spectacular touchdown scoring passes.

The 1979 Presbyterian Blue Hose Football Team

Hose down Elon

	Presbyterian	Elon
First downs	24	21
Rushes-yards	55-231	31-116
Passing yards	156	256
Passes	12-15-0	20-37-2
Return yards	46	66
Punts	4-28.8	5-40.8
Fumbles-lost	0-0	1-0
Penalties-yards	2-10	8-60

By SAM REGISTER

The general consensus following the Presbyterian-Elon confrontation Saturday night at Bailey Stadium was that Elon's chances of winning ended after the first half.

The Blue Hose jumped out to a 16-0 first half lead and coasted to a 30-14 win over Elon, which went into the game rated as the number one defensive team in the South Atlantic Conference.

The final four minutes of the second quarter played a large part in the PC win. The fighting Christians drove down to the Blue Hose one yard line time ran out on second down and goal. "That goal line stand was the greatest thing that happened to us," said Presbyterian Coach Cally Gault.

The game was billed by Gault as one of the team's toughest games of the year. Elon, who shared a championship with PC in the SAC-Eight last year, was believed by Coach Jerry Tolley to be fielding a better team than last season's.

The hose scored two of the first three times they got the ball. Their initial TD came when they marched 71 yards on seven plays. Following a Phillip Melton punt, PC moved to the 43 yard line on a 14 yard run by Clayto Burke, who finished the game with 176 yards rushing on 32 carries, 14 of which came in the first quarter. Quarterback Jimmy Spence then dropped back, stepped into the pocket and fired a pass to Jesse Cason to move to Elon's 46.

On second and six, Spence was dropped for a six-yard loss but defensive end John Richards was called for a personal foul to give the Blue Hose a first down on the Elon 25. Burke then started toward the middle of the line but saw no opening and broke outside for a 10 yard gain. On the following play, Spence dropped back but was hit by Richards who had him around the ankles. However, he was able to maintain his balance for three to four seconds, enough time to spot fullback Walter Atkins all by his lonesome in the end zone, Chuck Bishop's extra point gave them a 7-0 lead.

After an Elon punt, PC gained possession again, this time on their 40. Following a six-yard pass to Cason, Burke got loose down the right sideline where he was finally dragged down by Richards on the Elon 20-yard line. On third down and five from the 15, Spence dropped back and took advantage of some fine pass blocking to find Cason coming across field at the goalline to give Presbyterian a 16-0 lead.

"Offensively we were ready," said Gault "We've been a good offensive team all year and tonight everybody was blocking well, the offensive line, the fullbacks, and the receivers. And that's an All-American if there ever was one," he said, pointing a finger at Roy Walker.

The Blue Hose were able to shut down Elon's feared ground game, led by junior Bobby Hedrick, who has rushed for over 3,000 career yards. Instead the Fighting Christians were forced to go to the air where they rolled up 256 yards, compared to 116 on the ground. Quarterback Michael Currin hit on 20 of 37 passes.

"They showed us more offense than any previous game," said Gault.

After adding a field goal to make a 16-0 lead, the Blue Hose defense dug in and took the punch out of the Fighting Christians. With four minutes remaining in the first half, Michael Edmondson returned Larry Bridges kickoff to the 27. With less than three minutes remaining Elon found itself on the 44. Currin dropped back and hit Hedrick who was streaking down the left side. He was finally tackled at the PC 44. On third and 10 at the 44, Currin again dropped back and fired and Wayne Smith jumped up in a crowd and came down with the ball on the 25.

Four plays later, Currin again found Hedrick over the middle. He caught the ball at his shoetops and barrelled down to the five. On fourth and inches Currin picked up the first down on a keeper with 41 seconds remaining. On first and goal from the two, Currin failed to get in when he rolled left. With 14 seconds remaining Currin tried a quarterback sneak and again the Blue Hose line held. Elon was out of timeouts and failed to get another play off before the gun sounded.

SELL, SELL, SELL
with Classifieds!
Dial 984-2888

Clayto Burke after scoring Presbyterian's final touchdown
...Burke rushed for 176 yards, 116 in the first half

Week 7

- October 14, 1979, Wayne Gretzky scores his first NHL goal as a member of the Edmonton Oilers.
- October 17, 1979, The Pittsburgh Pirates beat the Baltimore Orioles 4 games to 3 to win the Major League Baseball World Series.
- October 20, 1979, The John F. Kennedy Library was dedicated in Boston, Massachusetts.
- October 20, 1979, Boxer John Tate defeats Gerrie Coetzee in 15 rounds for the Heavyweight boxing title.
- October 20, 1979, The Presbyterian College Blue Hose football team defeated the Mars Hill Lions 34-6 at Johnson Field in Clinton, South Carolina. The Homecoming kickoff was at 3:00 PM. The 20th anniversary of the January 1, 1960 Blue Hose appearance in the Tangerine Bowl was celebrated.

Jesse Cason and Mars Hill's J.C. Burkett battle for the ball

...Cason came down with the ball during second quarter action

The 1979 Presbyterian Blue Hose Football Team

P.C. Vs. Mars Hill

Oct. 20, 1979
3:00 P.M.

Johnson Field,
Clinton, S.C.

HOMECOMING

Next Home Game:
Oct. 27,
7:30 P.M.
Central Florida
(Parents' Night)

Price: $1.00

20th ANNIVERSARY of the 14th Annual Elks TANGERINE BOWL

Orlando, Florida
January 1st
1960
Presbyterian College vs.
Middle Tennessee State

Week 7

Presbyterian College 34   Mars Hill 6
Blue Hose   Lions

Clinton, South Carolina   October 20, 1979   3:00 PM
Presbyterian Overall Record   6-1   SAC-8 Record   4-0
NAIA Division 1 Ranking #6

Statistics	PC	Mars Hill
First Downs	18	15
Rushes / yards	44 / 155	33 / 79
Passing yards	204	315
Passes	12-23-0	18-32-3
Fumbles / lost	3-3	1-0
Penalties / yards	10-107	3-57

Scoring Summary

Q1 PC....PC 7 – Mars Hill 0....80 yard drive.... QB Spence 12 yard pass to RB Burke....Bishop PAT

Q1 PC....PC 10 – Mars Hill 0....Bishop 28 yard field goal

Q2 PC....PC 17 – Mars Hill 0....QB Spence 65 yard pass to TE Thornton....Bishop PAT

Q2 PC....PC 24 – Mars Hill 0.... RB Hood 11 yard run....PAT Good

Q2 PC....PC 27 – Mars Hill 0.... Bishop 41 yard field goal

Q4 PC....PC 34– Mars Hill 0....RB Jo Nell 5 yard run....Bishop PAT

Q4 Mars Hill....PC 34 – Mars Hill 6....QB Clark 27 yard pass to WR Jones....PAT Good

Highlights
Presbyterian College Blue Hose vs Mars Hill Lions

- Mars Hill came to Clinton, SC ranked #10 in the NAIA Division 1 ranking. Mars Hill was undefeated with a record of 4-0-1.
- Mars Hill scored on the final play of the game.
- The Presbyterian College Blue Hose has only allowed 20 points in the last 3 games.
- Presbyterian College Blue Hose Quarterback Jimmy Spence completed 12 of 22 passes for 204 total yards and 2 touchdowns.
- Presbyterian College Blue Hose RB Clayto Burke rushed for 80 yards on 23 attempts.
- The Presbyterian College Blue Hose defense only allowed Mars Hill 79 total running yards.
- Presbyterian College Blue Hose TE Danny Thornton pulled in 80 receiving yards.
- The Presbyterian College Blue Hose control their own destiny in the SAC-8 Conference as they are the only team without a conference loss.
- In the fourth quarter, reserves entered the game giving the starters a rest and experience for the future Blue Hose.
- There was a moment of disappointment by the defense at the end of the game as Mars Hill had scored on the final play of the game. The players wanted a shutout.
- Coaches and media continue to praise The Presbyterian College Blue Hose defense.

Southern Massacre

Presbyterian downs Mars Hill in 34-6 rout

By SAM REGISTER

What started out looking like a slow Mars Hill death turned out to be a mercy killing as Presbyterian erupted for 17 second-quarter points to overpower the Lions 34-6 before a homecoming crowd of 4,500 in Clinton Saturday.

It looked as if Mars Hill, which went into the game undefeated, might go in or a score on their first possession as they reeled off eight plays before having to punt from midfield. On PC's first play from scrimmage Clayto Burke fumbled after a bone-jarring tackle. But once again, quarterback Jimmy Spence maintained his cool and marched the Hose 80 yards in 11 plays for their first touchdown. From then on, they scored on five of their first seven possessions.

"We didn't run the ball as much as we wanted to," said Coach Cally Gault. "But they were shooting all of their linebackers so they were obviously giving us the pass."

Mars Hill's effort to stymie the Blue Hose ground game forced Spence to go to the air more than Gault had planned to, but the gutsy junior picked apart the Lions' defensive secondary, hitting on 12 of 22 passes for 204 yards and two touchdowns. Despite the fact that Mars Hill was keying on the run, Burke still managed to have a fine day as he picked up 80 yards rushing. Once, with PC ahead 10-0 in the second quarter, Spence handed off to Burke and it appeared he would be thrown for about a five yard loss. He was hit around the knees and stopped momentarily, but broke away and shedded three more tackles before picking up nine yards. "He ran fifteen yards to get nine," said Gault.

Burke figured on six of the first 11 plays on the initial touchdown drive. On third and six from the 12, Spence faked a handoff to Burke who hurtled into the line and seemingly vanished until he reappeared in the right side of the end zone on the other end of a Spence pass.

Spence made good use of his receivers too, throwing to Danny Thornton four times for 90 yards, Jesse Cason twice, Jay Byars twice, and Donald Porter twice.

After a second quarter field goal by Ben Lewis fell short, Presbyterian took over on their own 19. After a trap play to Burke gained six, Spence dropped back and found the 205-pound Thornton cutting across midfield. A Cason block, a Thornton stiff-arm, and 50 yards later, Thornton crossed the goal line.

Mars Hill began sinking fast at that point. On their first play from scrimmage after the kickoff defensive back Hal Brannen picked off a Mark Clark pass and returned it to the Mars Hill 21. Three plays later Ben Hood belted his way into the end zone from the 11 to give the Blue Hose a 24-0 lead.

Later in the second quarter, a short punt by the Lions Lewis put PC on the Mars Hill 42. Spence then faded back and lofted a pass to Cason who went up with J. C. Burkett and came down with the ball at the 18. On the following play Spence was hit hard by Clayton Curry and lost the ball but he recovered at the 33. He got the ball within Chuck Bishop's range by hitting Thornton over the middle at the 24 and Bishop's boot gave PC a 27-0 halftime lead.

"Mars Hill is a young team and they made some mistakes," said Gault. "We just took what they gave us, that's what we've been trying to do all year."

With the score 34-0 later in the fourth quarter and 11 non-starters playing defense, the starters were on the sideline shouting "goose egg." But with no time showing on the clock, Clark threw a touchdown pass to Mark Jones from the 27-yard line. The attempted two point conversion was no good.

"They're a much tougher team than the score indicates," said Gault of Mars Hill. "Our folks wanted a shutout but they worked hard for that touchdown."

With Presbyterian upping its record to 6-1, the entire team drew praise from Gault. "They've done everything I've asked them to do all year," he said. "This is a fine group of folks. They've got a lot of character."

RUSHING: Mars Hill, Clark 8(-17), Miller 8-26, Phillips 12-60, Mitchell 1-1, King 1-8, Allen 3-1; Presbyterian, Burke 23-80, Atkins 6-27, Hood 7-48, Spence 2-(-12), Hinton 1-7, Chupp 3-12, Nell 1-5, Gatlin 1-(11).

PASSING: Mars Hill, Clark 18-32-3 215; Presbyterian, Spence 12-22-0 206, Gatlin 0-1-0 0.

RECEIVING: Mars Hill, Watts 3-74, Phillips 3-16, Miller 3-19, Jones 2-50, Garren 1-10, Allen 2-15, Maeaole 1-14; Presbyterian, Thornton 4-90, Cason 2-37, Byars 2-22, Porter 2-43, Burke 1-12.

Joe Mooneyham runs back his second interception of the day

...This one came in the fourth quarter

Week 8

- October 27, 1979, The New York Islanders of the National Hockey League scored 2 goals within 6 seconds and 3 goals within 44 seconds.
- October 27, 1979, The Presbyterian College Blue Hose football team defeated the University of Central Florida Knights 48-0 at Johnson Field in Clinton, South Carolina. This was the UCF Knights inaugural football season. The Knights were a perfect 4-0 on the season coming into Johnson Field. Parents Night kickoff was at 7:30 PM.

Itinerary: Central Florida 1979

Friday Oct. 26
- 2:00 - 3:00 Training and Equipment Room Open.
- 11:15 Meeting in the Classroom.

Saturday Oct. 27
- 3:30 Pre Game Meal
- 4:45 FCA
- 5:00 - 6:00 Taping
- 6:05 - 6:25 Meeting Classroom
- 6:25 Walk to Leroy Springs.
- 6:40 Spec. on field
- 6:50 Linemen on field
- 7:15 Return to Dressing Room
- 7:30 Game Time. Beat Central Florida.

Turn in game equipment and pick up box lunches following game.

Sunday Oct. 28
- 5:30 - 6:30 Treatment
- 6:30 Meeting in Classroom.

The Presbyterian College Blue Hose take on the University of Central Florida (UCF) Knights in their inaugural season. The Knights come to Clinton, South Carolina 4-0, including a win over the SAC-8 conference member Carson Newman.

PC faces new opponent

Despite the fact that they're in their first year of football, the University of Central Florida will bring an undefeated team to Clinton Saturday as they take on Presbyterian in a 7:30 p.m. matchup.

"We're concerned about Central Florida simply because we don't know too much about them," said Presbyterian Coach Cally Gault.

Among UCF's victims have been Carson-Newman, which the Blue Hose face Nov. 10. The remainder of the teams that Central Florida, 4-0, have beaten, are Florida schools.

Defensively they have had only 13 points scored against them and according to Gault they are armed with a fine passing attack. "They're a team that likes to throw rather than run" he said. So it should be a pretty exciting ballgame. The defense is anchored by two tackles, one at 260 pounds and one at 240."

The school, which is based in Orlando, has an enrollment of 12,000 and is likened to Francis Marion in size by Gault.

Players of the Week for PC were Danny Thornton, who caught four passes and scored on a 65-yard pass play and Jesse Cason, who caught three passes for 57 yards. Joe Grant was named Player of the Week on defense. Grant had eight individual tackles and caused two fumbles in a 34-6 win over Mars Hill.

SALLY HADDON of Greenville was named Homecoming Queen at halftime ceremonies of the Presbyterian-Mars Hill football game. Miss Haddon is the daughter of Mr. and Mrs. F.J. Haddon. She was escorted by Jeff Wilson of Atlanta.

Central Florida Vs. Presbyterian

[Parents' Night]
Johnson Field, Clinton, S.C.
Oct. 27, 1979, 7:30 p.m.

Next Home Game:
CARSON-NEWMAN
[Youth Day]
Nov. 10, 1979, 2:30 p.m.

Price: $1.00

The 1979 Presbyterian Blue Hose Football Team

Southern Massacre

Week 8

Presbyterian College 48   University of Central Florida 0
Blue Hose   Knights

Clinton, South Carolina   October 27, 1979   7:30 PM
Presbyterian Overall Record   7-1   SAC-8 Record   5-0
NAIA Division 1 Ranking #6

Statistics	PC	UCF
First Downs	20	14
Rushing yards	359	29
Passing yards	71	174
Passes	6-12-0	15-28-1
Fumbles / lost	2-1	5-4
Penalties / yards	5-42	3-34
Punts / average	2-43	3-25

Scoring Summary

Q1 PC....PC 7 – UCF 0....69 yard drive....RB Burke 12 yard run....Bishop PAT....12:04 remaining

Q2 PC....PC 14 – UCF 0....63 yard drive....RB Burke 5 yard run....Bishop PAT....14:24 remaining

Q2 PC....PC 21 – UCF 0....24 yard drive....QB Spence 24 yard run....Bishop PAT....10:43 remaining

Q2 PC....PC 23 – UCF 0....Bishop 33 yard field goal....8:35 remaining

Q2 PC....PC 27 – UCF 0....Bishop 28 yard field goal....0:32 remaining

Q3 PC....PC 34 – UCF 0....RB Burke 7 yard run....Bishop PAT....12:18 remaining

Q3 PC....PC 41 – UCF 0....DB Gason intercepts and returns 15 yards....Bishop PAT....7:00 remaining

Q4 PC....PC 48 – UCF 0....RB Jo Nell 1 yard....Bishop PAT....9:35 remaining

Highlights
Presbyterian College Blue Hose vs UCF Knights

- Presbyterian College Blue Hose DB Heyward Hinton had 2 fumble recoveries and one interception to lead the defense.
- Presbyterian College Blue Hose RB Clayto Burke ran for 123 yards and scored three rushing touchdowns.
- The Presbyterian College Blue Hose has allowed only 20 points in the last four games.
- The Presbyterian College Blue Hose defense only allowed UCF 4 yards rushing in the first half.
- Presbyterian College Blue Hose Quarterback Jimmy Spence threw for 71 yards and also rushed for 95 yards on 11 carries.
- The Presbyterian College Blue Hose capitalized on 5 turnovers by the young UCF Knights.
- A lopsided victory by The Presbyterian College Blue Hose enables valuable playing time for the PC reserves.
- Presbyterian College Blue Hose LB Alan Gaston intercepted a 3rd quarter UCF pass and returned it for a touchdown.
- Presbyterian College Blue Hose players had high expectations late in the 4th quarter as they wanted to hit the 50 mark on the Johnson Field scoreboard.

Southern Massacre

Knights Handed First Loss

The PC Blue Hose welcomed the University of Central Florida into the real world of college football Saturday night. The Hose handed the Knightss the first loss of their short football existence in a 48-0 thrashing.

PC capitalized on nine UCF turnovers, six interceptions and three fumbles, in the annihilation of the Knights. The Hose racked up 430 yards of total offense in the game. (They had 261 yards of total offense in the first half alone.). Clayto Burke, 129 yards on 25 carries and three touchdowns, led a ground attack that netted 359 yards. Playing only the first half, Jimmy Spence completed 6 of 7 tosses for 71 yards. Spence gained 95 yards rushing on 11 attempts. Leading the receiving team was Danny Thornton with two catches for 42 yards. A major factor in the Hose's success against UCF was that the Hose took the running game away from the Knights, who gained only 29 yards in the game. When the Knights went to the air, they were a little more effective; however, the defensive secondary came up with the big play when it was needed as evidenced by the secondary's four interceptions and two fumble recoveries.

The Hose wasted no time putting points on the board as they drove 69 yards following the opening kickoff to take a 7-0 lead, Clayto Burke scored the TD on a nine yard end around. Clayto also scored the Hose's next touchdown on a five yard run. Following an 8 yard punt by UCF, the Hose built a 21-0 lead when Spence cut through the Knight's defense for a 24 yard score. On UCF's first play following the kickoff, they fumbled. Heyward Hinton, who had one interception and a fumble recovery in the game, came up with the ball. PC converted it into a 33 yard Chuck Bishop field goal. A Joe Mooneyham interception stopped a steady drive by the Knights. On the punt, the Knights fumbled again, this time the ball was recovered by Thornton. The fumble recovery set up a record tying field goal for Chuck Bishop. Bishop's 26 yarder tied him with Sandy Cruickshacks for most field goals in a season for PC with six. The half end with the Hose out in front 27-0. There was some confusion at the half, as to whether the

cont. on p. 3

A PC defender stops an attempt by the University of Central Florida in a SAC-8 conference win Saturday.

Knights Crushed, 48-0

cont. from p. 1

Knights would go to the lockerroom or to their team bus.

The Knights did return for the second half...physically. Larry Bridges intercepted a UCF pass on the Knight's first possession to set up an eventual seven yard score by Burke. Steve Stalvey followed with PC's third interception of the night; but the Hose couldn't move and had to punt. UCF got the ball and ran 15 yards to give the Hose a huge 41-0 advantage. The Hose's defense kept heavy quarterbacks throughout the game. Hal Brannen's fumble recovery set up the last Hose score. Joe Nell took it in from the one and the Hose had the game 48-0. The Hose ran down the final minutes with a time consuming drive started by a Mark Leverette Interception.

The Hose tied a conference record with six interceptions and Chuck Bishop broke the school's season record of 26 PATs. Bishop is 28 out of 29 on PAT attempts. Clayto Burke has a shot at breaking the school records for most yards rushing in a season (1126 by Elliot Pauling) and highest rushing average per game (103.6 yards by David Eckstein). Clayto is averaging 119 yards a game and has rushed for 952 yards this season.

Bulldogs in Boiling Springs, N.C. The Bulldogs are 2-5 having lost four consecutive games. They tend to get behind in many of their games; therefore, they use their passing attack more often than their running game. Gardner-Webb's top running back is No. 40 Robbie Barnes. The QB No, 14 Chip Stuart is just behind Spence statistically.

SAC-8 STANDINGS

	Conf.			All Games		
	W	L	T	W	L	T
P.C.	4	0	0	7	1	0
Newberry	3	1	0	5	2	0
Mars Hill	4	1	1	5	1	1
Carson-Newman	2	2	0	4	3	0
Elon	2	2	0	4	3	0
Lenoir Rhyne	1	2	0	4	3	0
Gardner-Webb	1	5	0	2	5	0
Catawba	1	5	0	1	7	0

SATURDAY'S SCHEDULE
*P.C. at Gardner-Webb, 2 p.m.
*Lenoir Rhyne at Carson-Newman, 7:30 p.m.
Catawba at Wofford, 7:30 p.m.
*Elon at Newberry, 7:30 p.m.
Mars Hill at Georgetown, 1:30 p.m.
*-Conference Game

STATS
CONFERENCE STATS
Hose #1 in team offense
Spence #1 in individual team offense
Cason leading receiver
Burke leading scorer and rusher

Passing	Att.	Compl.	PCT.	TD	Int.	Yds.
Spence	131	85	65%	10	1	1197
Receiving	Recpt.	Yds.	Avg.	TD		
Cason	38	420	11.1	2		
Thornton	21	396	18.9	2		
Rushing	Att.	Yds.	Avg.	TD		
Burke	211	952	4.5	8		

RETRACTION: In last week's preview of Central Florida, I erroneously stated that UCF was averaging 23 points a game when in fact they were only averaging 15 pts. a game. (Following the 48-0 trouncing by the Hose, they are now only averaging 11.6 a game).

The 1979 Presbyterian Blue Hose Football Team

Presbyterian rolls over Knights, 48-0

By SAM REGISTER

For most spectators at the Presbyterian-University of Central Florida game Saturday night in Clinton, it was the longest four quarters of football they could remember, or would want to. But for the second and third stringers on the Blue Hose team, it was a whale of a football game.

"Have we got 50 yet," asked All-SAC-Eight defensive end Jim McCoun as he sat in a chair on the sidelines while the Blue Hose held a 40-0 lead in the third quarter. Most of McGoun's starting teammates joined him there during the second quarter as the subs scored two more touchdowns and PC routed Central Florida 48-0.

"We're glad we got to look at a lot of players," said Presbyterian Coach Cally Gault. "It's the first time we've had a chance to relax for a whole half of football this season."

It appeared that the previously undefeated Knights might be in for a long night when Clayto Burke waltzed into the end zone from 11 yards out to cap a seven-play drive of 69-yards with 12:04 left in the first quarter. Burke rushed for 123 yards in 22 carries and scored three touchdowns on runs of 11, five, and seven, despite the fact that he played very little in the second half.

Just as the eyelids of the 5,000 in attendance for Parents' Night began to droop from the predictability of PC romp, Charlie Ziegler fielded Larry Bridges kickoff at the 15, cut to his left and handed the ball to a sweeping Jonas Haggins who churned up the right side line to the Blue Hose 45 yard line. The Knights moved to the 30 on four plays before Mike Williams caught a Mike Cullison pass and fumbled where Heyward Hinton recovered on the 34. Hinton later recovered another fumble and intercepted a pass to set up a Chuck Bishop field goal.

Jimmy Spence, who led that first TD drive by rushing three times for 24 yards, rushed for 95 yards in 11 carries. On Presbyterian's second possession the Hose moved to midfield before Burke was hit hard going into the line and coughed up the ball. Central Florida took over but on third and 10 from the 41 middle Guard Leonard Howard appeared in the CF back field seemingly before the ball did and he chased Cullison down for an 11 yard loss.

With 14:24 remaining in the second quarter, Burke capped a 12-play drive when he burst in the end zone from five yards out to make it 13-0. Bishop's point after was good. Spence tacked on another touchdown when he went in on a keeper two minutes later. Bishop added another field goal after Hinton's fumble recovery to give the Hose a 24-0 lead.

UCF rode the passing combination of Cullison to Williams down to the PC 35 before he rolled right and fired into the hands of Joe Mooneyham at the 10 where he returned it to the 24. The Hose sustained two busted plays and were forced to punt from their 30. But Williams fumbled Lamar Roberts' 45 yard punt and tight end Danny Thornton recovered at the 26 for Presbyterian. The offense moved the ball to the 18 where Bishop kicked his second field goal of the evening for a 27-0 half time score.

Substitutes played much of the second half for PC with the exception of Burke, who scored his third touchdown with 12:18 gone in the third quarter. Later in that quarter the first-string defense was called in after UCF moved within the PC 25.

Presbyterian's final scores came when Allan Gaston returned an intercepted pass 15 yards for a touchdown and Joe Nell went over from the one with 9:35 remaining in the game.

"As you could see we didn't cover the reverse well on the kickoff and we had too many penalties," said Gault. "You've got to correct your mistakes, no matter what the score is. We made some mistakes tonight that if they had come against a better team they could have hurt us."

Statistics

	C. Fla.	PC
First down	14	20
Yards rushing	29	359
Passing	174	71
Passes	28-25-1	12-6-0
Total yards	203	430
Fumbles-lost	5-4	2-1
Penalties	3-31	5-42
Punts avg.	3-24.7	2-43

Central Florida—0 0 0 0—0.
Presbyterian—7 20 14 7—48.
A—5,006.

Week 9

- November 1, 1979, The United States federal government proposes making a $1.5 billion loan to Chrysler Corporation.
- November 2, 1979, Studio 54's owners were arrested for tax evasion.
- November 3, 1979, The Presbyterian College Blue Hose football team defeated the Gardner Webb Bulldogs 21-3 at Spangler Stadium in Boiling Springs, North Carolina. Kickoff was at 2:00 PM.

The 1979 Presbyterian Blue Hose Football Team

The Presbyterian College Blue Hose go on the road to Boiling Springs, North Carolina to face SAC-8 member Garner Webb. The Hose are 7-1.

The Laurens County Advertiser — October 31, 1979

Face Gardner-Webb

Blue Hose hit the road

After playing its three opening games away, Presbyterian will hit the road again this weekend for the first time in four weeks as they travel to Boiling Springs, N.C. to play Gardner-Webb Saturday at 2 p.m.

The Bulldogs have an unimpressive 2-5 record, but according to Presbyterian Coach Cally Gault, this record is not indicative of the Bulldogs' talent.

"They've had some fine offensive efforts, but their defense has given up a lot of points," said Gault. "They've just had the misfortune of running into some very hot teams lately. They're capable of making mistakes at the worst possible moment."

But Gault is quick to point out that one of the Bulldogs' two wins has come against Newberry, currently in second place in the SAC-Eight. It has been the Indians' only loss thus far.

Gardner-Webb, which has beat the Blue Hose twice in the past three years, claims the top passer in the conference in Chip Stuart, a 6-2, 177 pound sophomore from Georgia. He is joined in the backfield by runningback Robbie Barnes, a senior at 5-11, 190 pounds. Barnes was named to the All-Conference, All-District and honorable mention All-American teams last season. He has been hampered with injuries this fall however and may not see much playing time Saturday.

The Hose will be coming off a 48-0 shellacking over the University of Central Florida, a game in which they rolled up 430 yards in total offense, 359 on the ground. PC jumped out to a 27-0 halftime lead, scoring 20 points in the second quarter and sending the reserves in for the second half to finish off the Knights.

Players of the Week for the Hose were Leonard Howard and Allan Gaston. Howard, a 6-2, 227-pound senior from Doraville, Ga., started his first game at defensive tackle Saturday in the place of the injured Mark Kay and came through with some key tackles. Gaston, a 5-10, 158-pound senior from Carrollton, Ga., intercepted a pass and scored to give the Blue Hose defense its first touchdown of the year.

On offense Jimmy Spence and Clayto Burke received Player of the Week honors, Burke for rushing for 123 yards and scoring three touchdowns, and Spence for completing six of 12 passes for 71 yards and two touchdowns passing. Spence also rushed for 95 yards in 11 carries and added another TD on the ground.

Advertiser Sports

Southern Massacre

Gardner-Webb College

**BULLDOGS VS PRESBYTERIAN
NOVEMBER 3, 1979
Spangler Stadium**

Week 9

Presbyterian College 21   Gardner Webb 3
Blue Hose   Bulldogs

Boiling Springs, North Carolina   November 3, 1979   2:00 PM
Presbyterian Overall Record   8-1   SAC-8 Record   5-0
NAIA Division 1 Ranking #2

Statistics	PC	Gardner Webb
First Downs	20	10
Rushes / yards	61 / 305	39 / 68
Passing yards	142	131
Passes	6-12-2	9-30-4
Fumbles / lost	4-4	1-0
Penalties / yards	8-73	2-30
Punts / average	4-30	7-39

Scoring Summary

Q1 PC....PC 7 – GW 0....83 yard drive....QB Spence 53 yard pass to WR Porter....Bishop PAT....13:16 remaining

Q1 GW ....PC 7 – GW 3....Koonts 38 yard field goal....9:07 remaining

Q2 PC....PC 14 – GW 3....72 yard drive....QB Spence 17 yard run....Bishop PAT....14:11 remaining

Q2 PC....PC 21 – GW 3....57 yard drive....RB Burke 1 yard run....Bishop PAT....9:29 remaining

Highlights
Presbyterian College Blue Hose vs Gardner Webb Bulldogs

- Presbyterian College Blue Hose RB Clayto Burke rushed for 168 yards.
- Gardner Webb only managed 68 rushing yards on 39 attempts.
- The Presbyterian College Blue Hose defense has only allowed 23 points in the last 5 games.
- Presbyterian College Blue Hose running backs ran for 305 yards.
- The Presbyterian College Blue Hose offense turned the ball over 6 times which included 4 fumbles and 2 interceptions.
- In the second half, the Blue Hose had 3 fumbles, 1 interception and a blocked punt.
- The deepest penetration by the Presbyterian College Blue Hose offense in the second half was to the Gardner Webb 22 yard line.
- Neither team scored in the second half of the game.
- Presbyterian College Blue Hose WR Donald Porter was on the receiving end of a 54 yard strike for a touchdown from QB Jimmy Spence.
- Presbyterian College Blue Hose QB Jimmy Spence was 6-12 for 142 yards with 3 interceptions.
- The media is beginning to look ahead to the annual Thanksgiving game with Newberry, a SAC-8 Conference Championship and a berth in the NAIA Division 1 playoffs.
- Presbyterian College Head Coach Calley Gault is ready to get on the practice field in preparation for Carson Newman.

The 1979 Presbyterian Blue Hose Football Team

November 9, 1979 The Blue Stocking, Clinton, S.C. 29325 Page 3

Turnovers Highlight Contest at Boiling Springs

Saturday afternoon the Blue Hose's offense defined the word "opposite". In the first half of the game against the Gardner-Webb Bulldogs, PC's offense played to the tune of 21 points. In the second half the offense couldn't drum up a melody because of four turnovers (one interception and three fumbles.)

PC's defense was the key to the victory. Gardner-Webb could only muster 68 yards on the ground against the Hose. The defense, which has given up only nine points in the last three games, limited the Bulldogs to 199 yards of total offense in the game (55 yards coming in the first half compared to PC's 255 yards of total offense in the opening half). The deepest Gardner-Webb could get into the PC territory was the 21-yard line. Despite numerous turnovers by the PC offense, they chalked up nearly 450 yards of total offense. Jimmy Spense hurled for 142 yards and one TD by completing 6 of 12 passes. He rushed for 55 yards and another touchdown on 9 carries. Clayto Burke led all rushers with 168 yards on 31 carries.

The entire Gardner-Webb team only gained 68 yards in the game- 100 less than Clayto. The SAC-8's leading rusher now has 1,120 yards: six yards shy of Elliot Pauling's school record. Clayto is also well ahead of David Eckstein's school record of 103.6 yards averaged per game. Clayto is averaging 124.4 yards per game.

The Hose began the game in typical fashion by scoring on their initial possession. PC followed the opening kickoff with a four play, 83-yard scoring drive. The touchdown came on a 53-yard pass play to Donald Porter. Gardner-Webb then capitalized on the first of six PC turnovers by converting a fumbled punt into a 38-yard field goal. Those three points would be the last points PC's defense would allow the rest of the afternoon. Jimmy Spence upped the Hose's lead to 14-3 by darting 18 yards for a score. PC put seven more points on the board on their next possession. Spence hit Jesse Cason with a big gainer to set up the score. After a series of runs, the Hose faced a fourth and goal at the one; Clayto dove over the line to widen PC's lead. Chuck Bishop's third PAT of the day ended the scoring at 21-3. Following the last score, both teams' offenses played sloppily as displayed by a combined total of nine turnovers. Hal Brannon intercepted a Gardner-Webb pass to get the turnovers going. Jimmy Spence later threw an interception to give the Bulldogs the ball back. Gardner-Webb tried to score before the half ended by going for a fourth and long; but Mark Wheless sacked the quarterback to give the Hose control of the ball, the half ended the way the game would end 21-3. 21-3.

The second half continued to be a battle of mistakes. Spence underthrew Cason for another interception; but the Hose's defense held the Bulldogs. The Hose fumbled the ball away only to get the ball back on Hal Brannon's fourth interception of the year. This time Lamar Roberts' punt was blocked, but once again the stubborn PC defense stopped Gardner-Webb. The turnovers became so commonplace in the second half that even Coach Gault intercepted a pass on the sideline. He was stopped for no gain. The Bulldogs recovered another PC fumble; but they immediately threw another interception. A fierce rush by Jim McCoun forced the miscue: a Joe Grant interception. However, the Hose fumbled again. Heyward Hinton's interception late in the game closed out the battle of turnovers. Coach Gault attributed the increased amount of turnovers to a lack of concentration by the offense.

This Saturday at 2:00 the 5th ranked Blue Hose (8-1) take on the hottest team in the SAC-8, the Carson-Newman Eagles, before a youth day crowd. The Eagles (5-3) have won their last three games scoring around 110 points and giving up only 34 points.

Last year the Hose drubbed Carson-Newman 42-22. Pending the outcome of PC's last two games, the Hose have an excellent chance of getting a playoff bid. The matter of deciding where the game is to be played rests solely on the financial attractiveness of the location, in other words, whoever can draw the largest crowd would get the home field advantage. Get out and support the Hose. Note: In this week's polls the Hose moved up to second in the NAIA.

SAC-8 STANDINGS

	Conf.			All Games		
	W	L	T	W	L	T
P.C.	5	0	0	8	1	0
Mars Hill	4	1	1	6	1	1
Carson-Newman	3	2	0	5	3	0
Newberry	3	2	0	5	3	0
Elon	3	2	0	5	3	0
Lenoir Rhyne	1	3	0	4	4	0
Gardner-Webb	1	6	0	2	6	0
Catawba	1	5	0	1	8	0

SATURDAY'S RESULTS
*P.C. 21, Gardner-Webb 3
*Carson-Newman 31, Lenoir Rhyne 0
*Elon 14, Newberry 6
Wofford 28, Catawba 10
Mars Hill 39, Georgetown, Ky. 20

SATURDAY'S SCHEDULE
*Carson-Newman at P.C., 2:30 p.m.
*Lenoir Rhyne at Elon, 2:00 p.m.
*Newberry at Mars Hill, 7:30 p.m.
Guilford at Catawba, 2:00 p.m.
Emory & Henry at Gardner-Webb, 2:00 p.m.

STATISTICS

	PC	GW
First Downs	24	10
Yards Rushing	305	68
Yards Passing	142	131
Total Yards	447	199
Passes Attempted	17	30
Passes Completed	6	9
Passes Intercepted By	4	2
Penalties	8	3
Yards Penalized	83	15
Fumbles Lost	4	0

Scoring:
P.C.—Porter, 53-yd. pass from Spence, 13:16 first quarter. Chuck Bishop kick EP.
GW—Koontz, 38 yd. field goal, 9:07 first quarter.
P.C.—Spence, 37 yd. run, 14:11 second quarter, Bishop kicked EP.
P.C.—Burke, 1 yd. run, 9:29 second quarter. Bishop kicked EP.

Rates: $10 & $13 Singles;
$13 & $15 Double

Telephone: 833-1630 Clinton, S.C.

PC hangs on for 21-3 win

Presbyterian jumped out to a 21-3 first-half lead and managed to hang on from there as they defeated Gardner-Webb 21-3 at Boiling Springs, N.C. Saturday.

However, the Hose were unusually sloppy, especially in the second half, when they suffered three fumbles, one interception, and a blocked punt. But in the first half they were unstoppable.

They traveled 83 yards in four plays for their first touchdown, a 53-yard touchdown pass from Jimmy Spence to Donald Porter. Chuck Bishop's extra point made it 7-0. Carlisle Koonts kicked a 38-yard field goal after a PC fumble to narrow the Hose lead to four.

With 14:11 remaining in the second quarter, Spence scored on a 17-yard run and Bishop's kick made it 1-3. The Blue Hose also scored on their next possession when Clayto Burke went over from the one to cap a seven play drive that covered 57 yards. Burke finished the day with 168 yards in 23 carries, 68 more yards rushing than the entire Gardner-Webb offense. Presbyterian got no farther than the Bulldog 22 in the second half, however.

PC, now 5-0 in the conference and 8-1 overall, will host Carson-Newman next week.

Statistics

	PC—G. Webb
First down	10
Rushing yards	39-65
Passing yards	131
Passes attempted	9-30
Interceptions	4
Total offense	199
Penalties	2-30
Fumbles-lost	1-0
Punts	7-39.4

Presbyterian	7 14 0 0 — 21
Gardner-Webb	2 0 0 0 — 3
A—4,000	

Crouch Hardware

FORMERLY COPELAND HDW.

True Value - Not Just A Name
It's Our Way Of Doing Business!

110 N. Broad St.   Ph. 833-1020

Week 10

- November 4, 1979, In Iran, fifty-two US diplomats and US citizens were detained and held hostage for 444 days by a group of militarized college students.
- November 5, 1979, The Ayatollah Khomeini describes the United States as "The Great Satan."
- November 6, 1979, The Ayatollah Khomeini takes over in Iran.
- November 7, 1979, MLB Chicago Cubs reliever Bruce Sutter wins the National League Cy Young award.
- November 10, 1979, The Presbyterian College Blue Hose football team defeated the Carson Newman Eagles 34-28 at Johnson Field in Clinton, South Carolina. Youth Day kickoff was at 2:30 PM.

Itinerary: Carson-Newman 1979

Friday Nov. 9
    2:00 - 3:00   Equipment & Training Room Open.
    11:15   Meeting

Saturday Nov. 10
    10:15   Pre Game Meal
    11:45   FCA
    11:55 - 12:55   Taping
    12:55   Meetings
    1:25   Walk to Leroy Springs
    1:40   Spec. on Field
    1:50   Linemen on Field
    2:15   Return to Dressing Room
    2:30   Game Time Beat Carson Newman

Sunday Nov. 11
    No Meeting, Training Room Open For Treatment

Monday Nov. 12
    Check Bulletin Board for Announcements
    JV Game Monday Night

The 1979 Presbyterian Blue Hose Football Team

Carson Newman Vs. Presbyterian
[Youth Day]
Johnson Field, Clinton, S.C.
Nov. 10, 1979, 2:30 p.m.

Price: $1.00

Southern Massacre

Week 10

Presbyterian College 34   Carson Newman 28
Blue Hose   Eagles

Clinton, South Carolina   November 10, 1979   2:30 PM
Presbyterian Overall Record   9-1   SAC-8 Record   6-0
NAIA Division 1 Ranking #1

Statistics	PC	Carson Newman
First Downs	19	14
Rushes / yards	67 / 415	58 / 354
Passing yards	88	26
Passes	5-14-2	2-12-5
Fumbles / lost	3-3	5-2
Penalties / yards	6-47	5-60
Punts / average	2-32	4-40

Scoring Summary

Q1 PC....PC 7 – CN 0....50 yard drive....RB Burke 24 yard run....Bishop PAT....4:55 remaining

Q1 PC....PC 14 – CN 0....35 yard drive....RB Burke 6 yard run....Bishop PAT....2:10 remaining

Q2 PC....PC 21 – CN 0....68 yard drive....RB Burke 68 yard run....Bishop PAT....5:37 remaining

Q2 CN....PC 21 – CN 7....63 yard drive....Andrews 3 yard run....Grisby PAT....2:16 remaining

Q2 PC....PC 28 – CN 7....56 yard drive....QB Spence 1 yard run....Bishop PAT....1:14 remaining

Q3 CN....PC 28 – CN 14....53 yard drive....Rutledge 1 yard run....Grisby PAT....5:30 remaining

Q4 CN....PC 28 – CN 21....94 yard drive....Rutledge 4 yard run....Grisby PAT....14:23 remaining

Q4 PC....PC 34 – CN 21....90 yard drive....QB Spence 1 yard run....Bishop PAT no good....3:27 remaining

Q4 CN....PC 34 – CN 28....15 yard drive....Andrews 1 yard run....Grisby PAT....2:00 remaining

Highlights
Presbyterian College Blue Hose vs Carson Newman Eagles

- The Presbyterian College Blue Hose survived the 1979 season "trap" game. Carson Newman was a formidable opponent. Carson Newman gave PC all they could handle. PC took care of business with plenty of outside distractions such as national ranking and the annual turkey day classic on the horizon against Newberry College in 11 days.
- Presbyterian College Blue Hose RB Clayto Burke rushed for 187 yards on 25 attempts. Burke scored 3 touchdowns. PC RB Ben Hood had his best performance of the year rushing for 121 total yards. PC QB Jimmy Spence also rushed for 92 yards.
- In 1977, Blue Hose RB Elliott Paulding set the PC rushing record with 1126 total rushing yards. With the 187 yard performance against Carson Newman, Burke became the PC all time single season rushing leader with one regular season game remaining.
- The Presbyterian College Blue Hose defense once again stepped up forcing 7 Carson Newman turnovers. The Blue Hose recovered 2 fumbles and recorded 5 interceptions.
- Presbyterian College Blue Hose DB Hal Brannen had an outstanding performance with 3 interceptions against Carson Newman.
- In the last 2 games, The Presbyterian College Blue Hose offense has had 7 fumbles, and have lost each of those 7 fumbles. In addition, PC QB Jimmy Spence has thrown 4 interceptions in 2 games. PC Head Coach Calley Gault certainly knows what to work on with 10 practice days in preparation for Newberry College on Thanksgiving Day.
- With the victory over Carson Newman, coupled with a loss by #1 Central State Oklahoma, The Presbyterian College Blue Hose found themselves at #1 in NAIA Division 1 Football.

The Laurens County Advertiser November 12, 1979

Brannen's three thefts pace Presbyterian

	C-N	PC
Rushing (attempts-yards)	58-358	67-400
Passing yards	26	58
Passing (attempts-yards)	2-12-5	5-14-2
Fumbles-lost	5-2	3-3
Penalties	5-60	6-47
Punting	4-40	2-32
First downs	11	19

Defensive back Hal Brannen had three interceptions and Clayto Burke scored three touchdowns as Presbyterian defeated high powered Carson-Newman 34-28 in Clinton Saturday.

The Blue Hose jumped out to a 28-7 halftime lead but the Eagles erupted for three touchdowns in the second half to narrow the margin. Carson-Newman started a drive with two minutes remaining in the game but Brannen's third interception killed a possible comeback by the Eagles.

Brannen's previous interceptions were also key ones, the first of which set up a touchdown and the second halted an earlier Eagle drive. The junior from Unadilla, Ga., has seven thefts for the season.

The Hose set a game rushing mark for this season, racking up 400 yards in 67 carries. Quarterback Jimmy Spence, Burke, and Ben Hood, a fullback from Greensboro, Ga., were the Hose's only ballcarriers. Spence rolled for 92 yards on 23 carries and two touchdowns and Hood had his finest day of the season with 121-hard-earned yards on 16 carries.

Burke broke two PC records Saturday, carrying 28 times for 187 yards. His 1,307 yards this season breaks the mark set by Elliott Pauling and his career mark of 2,426 breaks that held by David Eckstein. Burke's three touchdowns makes him the leading scorer in the SAC-Eight Conference with 90 points. He is also among the top three rushers in the nation.

Burke scored the first three touchdowns of the game on runs of 24, six, and 48 yards. His final TD was his longest run from scrimmage this season. Spence's one-yard plunge rounded out the Hose's first-half scoring.

Carson-Newman picked up 376 total yards, 350 rushing. Their first touchdown, which came in the first half, was on a three-yard carry by quarterback Jay Andrews. Andrews also scored the Eagles' final TD on a one-yard keeper. Jeff Rutledge scored Carson-Newman's other two touchdowns on runs of 10 and four yards.

Linebacker Steve Stalvey paced the defense along with Brannen, with eight solo tackles and 14 assists. Defensive end Jim McCoun had six tackles, 10 assists and one fumble recovery.

Quarterback Jimmy Spence added two TDs
...And rushed for 92 yards on 23 carries

Tailback Clayto Burke set two PC rushing records Saturday
...The senior tailback rushed for 187 yards and three touchdowns against Carson-Newman

| Carson-Newman | 9 7 7 14-28 |
| Presbyterian | 14 14 0 6-34 |

Week 11

- November 10, 1979, A 106 car train derails in Mississauga, Ontario, Canada forcing an evacuation of 200,000 people in the area.
- November 13, 1979, Ronald Reagan announces his candidacy for President of the United States.
- November 17, 1979, The Ayatollah Khomeini frees most black and female US hostages detained in Iran.
- November 17, 1979, Daniel Okrent sketches out the first draft rules for Rotisserie Baseball on a flight to Austin, Texas.
- November 19, 1979, Chuck Berry is released from prison for tax evasion conviction.
- November 19, 1979, MLB Houston Astros sign Nolan Ryan to a record 4 year $4.5 million contract.
- November 22,1979, The Presbyterian College Blue Hose football team defeated the Newberry Indians 16-14 at Setzler Field in Newberry, South Carolina. The annual Thanksgiving day kickoff for the Bronze Derby was at 2:00 PM.

12 The Laurens County Advertiser, November 21, 1979

In Bronze Derby

Gault eyes Newberry

By SAM REGISTER

"Our immediate attention is on Newberry. They're the thing that counts right now more than anything," said Presbyterian Coach Cally Gault Tuesday. "This game is the season itself."

Gault and the Blue Hose are gearing up for this Thursday's annual Bronze Derby Thanksgiving contest against the Indians, to be played at Newberry at 2 p.m.

Although Newberry has not had the success the Hose have enjoyed this season, Gault is not underestimating the opponent.

"This game needs nothing else to make it big, like rankings or playoff berths," he said. "There is no outside incentive."

How about the Hose's number one national ranking?

"Well, there could be an extra incentive to knock us off," he said, "but we should have the extra incentive of wanting to remain where we are."

The Indians come into this Turkey Day battle, which began in 1912, with a 5-4 record, having lost its last three games to Jacksonville St., Elon, and Mars Hill. But Gault is quick to point out that Newberry was a "bruised football team" over those three games, with a total of six starters out for the Mars Hill game. All except linebacker Dennis Yarborough, are expected to start Thursday's game.

The Hose have a 42-21-4 edge in the series and toppled the Indians 26-0 last year in Clinton.

Should Presbyterian beat Newberry, they will host Saginaw Valley State (Mich.) in the first round of the NAIA national playoffs. If the Hose lose to Newberry, Gault said there is a very big "if" involved whether PC gets invited or not. If they lose and still receive an invitation, there's a chance Presbyterian would have to travel to Saginaw or elsewhere to play.

Eight teams will be invited to participate in the playoffs, with the final two teams meeting Dec. 15 in McAllen, Texas for the national championship.

But for right now, Gault's thoughts are about 20 miles southeast of Clinton.

"A 5-4 record in our league is good," he said. "Newberry has proved to be a fine football team defensively and offensively. They're probably the only people that were pleased more than we were when the rankings came out."

Presbyterian will go into Thursday's game ranked second in passing offense, first in rushing offense, and first in total offense in the SAC-Eight Conference.

Junior quarterback Jimmy Spence is first in total offense in the conference, averaging 177.9 yards per contest. He is also first in passing, having hit on 96 of 157 passes for 1,427 yards and 11 touchdowns.

Burke is first in the SAC-Eight among the top three in rushing with 1,307 yards in 10 games and a 130.7 yard per game average. He is first in the conference in scoring with 90 points. Kicker Chuck Bishop is third with 57.

Jesse Cason has 44 receptions in 10 games which ranks first among conference receivers as does his 54.0 yards per game average. Tight end Danny Thornton is fourth in the conference with 22 receptions. Willie Mason is number one in the SAC-Eight in kick returns with a 29.0 average and 203 total yards. His 98-yard kick return for a touchdown highlighted the Furman game. Also tops in the conference is Hal Brannen, who has picked off seven enemy aerials.

The Bronze Derby game has been played every Thanksgiving Day since 1966. The concept of playing for the derby came about in the late 1940s when a Presbyterian student named James Kellet, whose uncle owned a clothing store in Fountain Inn, purchased a Stetson Derby from there and started wearing it for fun.

Kellet happened to be wearing it one night in 1947 when he and a group of friends went to see the Presbyterian basketball team play at Newberry. Some Newberry students put a ladder up outside the gym, climbed through the window at the top of the visitors' section, and made their way down through the crowd and one of them snatched the derby off Kellet's head and made off with it. He and his friends chased the Newberry group but Kellet went back to Clinton minus his derby.

Charles MacDonald, PC sports information director, suggested to Frank Kinard, the SID at Newberry that it the hat could be recovered it might become a symbol for athletic supremacy between the two schools.

It was decided that it would go to the winner of any athletic event between the two schools, so the derby changed hands through football, baseball, and basketball seasons from 1947 to 1965. To keep the importance of the derby from diminishing, the schools agreed in 1966 that it would be claimed only by the winner of the annual Thanksgiving Day football game.

It is noteworthy to mention that a member of the PC entourage which made the trip to Newberry that night in 1947 was a student named Calhoun Gault.

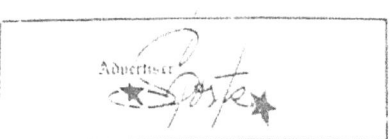
Advertiser Sports

This display in the lobby of Ross Templeton gymnasium is a reminder of the Blue Hose' ranking.

NAIA National Rankings

TEAM	1st PLACE VOTES	RECORD
PRESBYTERIAN	9	9-1-0
TEXAS A & I	7	8-1-0
KEARNEY ST. NEB.		8-1-0
WISCONSIN-RIVER FALLS		9-1-0
CENTRAL STATE OKLA.		8-1-0
WESTERN ST. COLO.		7-1-0
ANGELO ST. TEX.		7-2-0
SAGINAW VALLEY ST. MICH.		8-1-1
MARS HILL N.C.		7-1-1
FAIRMONT ST.		8-1-1
ARKANSAS-MONTICELLO		8-2-0
NORTHEASTERN OKLA.		8-2-0
OREGON COLLEGE		7-1-1
SOUTHERN COLORADO		7-2-0
OREGON TECH.		7-2-0
W. LIBERTY ST.		7-2-1
STEPHEN F. AUSTIN		7-3-0
SOUTHWEST TEXAS ST.		7-3-0

The 1979 Presbyterian Blue Hose Football Team

Every Thanksgiving Newberry and Presbyterian Fight It Out For

The Bronze Derby

by Billy Deal

When James Kellett was a student at Presbyterian College in the late 1940s, he acquired a sartorial habit which was to affect the destiny of one of the state's oldest athletic rivalries.

"My uncle operated a clothing store in Fountain Inn," Kellett recalls today, "and men's hats were pretty popular in those days. So, I started wearing a Stetson derby, just for fun, and I happened to be wearing it one night in 1947 when a bunch of us went to see the Presbyterian basketball team play at Newberry.

"It was a pretty exciting game, and some Newberry students put a ladder up against the outside of the gym and climbed through a window at the top of the visitors' section. They worked their way down through the crowd and one of them snatched the derby from my head and ran outside. We chased them and a few skirmishes occurred, but I ended up without my derby. We looked for it all over the Newberry campus but I finally went home hatless." (The identity of the Newberry student who swiped the hat has long since faded into obscurity.)

What might have ended as another in a series of increasingly hostile student pranks between rivals was turned into a legend by the quick thinking of cooler heads.

Charles MacDonald, Presbyterian College sports information director, suggested to counterpart Frank Kinard at Newberry College that if the derby could be recovered it might become a symbol for athletic supremacy between the schools. The idea won quick approval from the student bodies, and the hat was recovered and bronzed for posterity.

It was decied that it would go to the winner of any athletic contest between the schools, so it changed hands repeatedly through baseball, basketball and football seasons from 1947 through 1955.

Realizing that such frequent contests diminished the importance of the trophy, the schools agreed in 1956 that it would be claimed only by the winner of the annual Thanksgiving Day football game.

So, the Bronze Derby Classic became official and the turkey day battle now stands as one of the country's few remaining college rivalries which is (1) still played on Thanksgiving Day and (2) symbolized by a permanent trophy.

Unlike the rivalry between the University of South Carolina and Clemson, which dominates the state in football frenzy, the Bronze Derby series is wine of a different vintage.

The proximity of the towns (Clinton is only 20 miles from Newberry) and the genuine friendships among the opposing players and coaches add a touch of sanity to the proceedings. Talk to players or coaches from any era and that quickly becomes evident.

Adding to the "small home town" flavor of the series are the small student populations (900 at Presbyterian, 800 at Newberry) and limited stadium capacities (5,000 at Presbyterian, 4,000 at Newberry).

Perhaps the ultimate rapport occurs before the game each year. The host school serves Thanksgiving lunch in its cafeteria, and fans from both schools share a meal before going out to stare at each other across 100 yards of grass with white stripes.

It is refreshing and somehow reassuring to find an athletic rivalry which combines intensity and common sense.

Harvey Kirkland, now a member of the athletic department at The Citadel, was head coach at Newberry from 1952 through 1967. He believes the Thanksgiving date helps keep the rivalry in perspective.

"Before I came the game was played on Saturday, but we got it moved to Thanksgiving my first year at Newberry," Kirkland explained. "It used to be played on Thanksgiving at some point in the past but had been shifted back to a Saturday date.

"There is a natural rivalry between the two schools and playing the game on Thanksgiving Day just adds to the meaning. But I don't recall a single incident of real animosity between the communities. Oh, we always wanted to beat their socks off and we pulled no punches on the field, but I always had dear friends in Clinton and at Presbyterian. It was just a fine, friendly rivalry and I treasure the days I was associated with it."

Kirkland also remembers some tender moments on the field. "I won't ever forget one year Bobby Waters [Presbyterian quarterback who later played professionally with the San Francisco 49ers] killed us with his throwing, and there were other moments, good and bad, that stay with me. But to look back and pick out the great players and the great games now is difficult to do. Any time we beat them, it was very satisfying [an occurrence that happened only five times during Kirkland's tenure.]"

There is a postcript to that January night in 1947 when James Kellett's pilfered derby set destiny in motion. One member of the Presbyterian entourage was a young football player who also was to have an important part in the future of the Bronze Derby.

That young man's name was Calhoun (Cally) Gault, and he has probably had more impact on Presbyterian football and the Bronze Derby series than any other individual. After graduating in 1948, he became head coach at North Augusta High School, where he compiled an outstanding record of 88 wins, 13 losses and seven ties. In 1963 he was named head coach of Presbyterian and his record with the Blue Hose reads 89-73-6.

With his unruly salt and pepper hair sprouting in different directions and a full-face, leprechaun's smile, Gault resides in the limbo of his profession.

As a small college coach he will never attain the recognition reserved for those who direct the athletic destinies of the major universities, but he is content to live in the world he knows best. And within that realm, he has no peers.

He is renowned for his emotional, straight-up approach to football, and his record reflects the intensity of his efforts. He is the type of coach for whom every man would like his son to play. He is fatherly, yet tough; demanding, yet understanding. And he speaks of the Bronze Derby with a genuine reverence.

"The Newberry game is a different season for us," Gault said. "Our philosophy up here is that we play ten ball games, then we beat Newberry. There's no question that we have a very special series. If both teams have poor records, it's still a good rivalry, but if both teams have good records, it's a great rivalry."

Like Kirkland, Gault thinks playing the game on Thanksgiving adds to the importance. "I think that's the only time to play it. It's the only time when we have the whole state to ourselves, and that's part of the tradition."

Another part of the tradition is the friendship of the coaches. Gault's chief adversary at Newberry was Fred Herren, who guided the Indians' football fortunes from 1968 through 1977.

"Having such respect for Fred as a gentleman and a coach added greatly to the rivalry for me," Gault noted, "but it didn't add to the satisfaction when we won. One of the things I don't like about the coaching business is seeing a friend lose. I consider Fred a very close friend, and it hurt to see him lose."

Then, with the leprechaun's smile turning up the corners of his mouth, he added, "But I'd rather hurt for him than have him hurt for me."

Although Presbyterian holds a decided edge in victories since the rivalry began in 1913 (42-21-4), the series has produced some thrilling contests—but none better than the four games from 1969 through 1972.

While Gault mentions his first win

The 1979 Presbyterian Blue Hose Football Team

over Newberry (14-7 in 1963) and his last (26-0 in 1978) as among the most satisfying, he also points to the 1969-70 victories with pride. These two games were perhaps the most exciting in the series, thanks to the heroic efforts of Presbyterian quarterback Allen McNeill.

Now head football coach at Loris High School, McNeill remembers how the 1970 game nearly ended in disaster for the Blue Hose. "That game really stands out," he said, "because we had a real good club and Newberry was just so-so. We jumped out in front, twenty and oh, and then just let down. Well, they came back and went ahead, twenty-three—twenty, and time was running out. We finally scored in the closing minutes to win, twenty-seven to twenty-three."

McNeill's modesty disguises the truth of that exciting finish, but Gault remembers it well.

"It was third down and he was back to pass. He couldn't find a receiver open so he went around right end, turned the corner and ran fifty-five yards for a touchdown." McNeill's game-winner overshadowed outstanding performances by two Newberry players that day. Redskin quarterback Tommy Williamson completed 11 out of 25 passes for 214 yards and tailback Donald Garrick picked up 146 yards on 32 carries.

McNeill's leadership was also responsible for the 23-21 victory in 1969. He guided the Blue Hose on a 75-yard, fourth-quarter touchdown drive to clinch the victory, sealing Newberry's fate with an 11-yard touchdown pass to Bill Caldwell.

The 1971 game is remembered vividly in both camps. Newberry entered the game with a 7-2-1 record and Presbyterian was sporting an 8-2 worksheet. A good, close game was expected.

It could be termed "good" only from a Newberry point of view and "close" by nobody's. In what might have been Herren's finest moment as a coach, the Indians smacked the Hose, 34-0, in one of the most one-sided games in the series.

"That was definitely my finest game against PC," noted Herren, now director of alumni affairs at Newberry.

Newberry used the offensive talents of Garrick and Williamson to pile up the points and relied on a record-setting defensive unit to keep the explosive

Southern Massacre

Hose bottled up. The Indian secondary intercepted five passes for a season total of 41, an NAIA team record.

Realizing that Presbyterian would be anxious to retaliate for such a humiliating loss the following year, Herren came up with a gimmick to divert their attention.

When the teams took the field at Presbyterian on Thanksgiving in 1972, the Indians presented a special guest— a huge, white turkey, wearing a red halter with a block N.

"We named him Killer and he was to become the property of the winning team, along with the Derby," Herren recalls. "As it turns out, it wasn't too funny to us because we got beat, seventeen-oh, but old Killer got a lot of attention."

Most of the attention came from the late Billy Tiller, a member of the PC coaching staff and a mountainous man with a sense of humor to match.

"Billy had a big white apron, a chef's hat and a big knife and fork," Gault recalls, "and when they brought Killer out, Billy looked at me, and I just pointed to the field. I didn't know what he was going to do but I knew it would be funny. When he walked out onto the field, the crowd roared. It was one of the lighter moments in the series."

Newberry was to find out that Presbyterian had a "killer" of its own that day in David Eckstein, the school's all-time rushing leader. He ripped through the Newberry defense for 152 yards and two touchdowns (on runs of 58 and two yards). Eckstein closed his brilliant career at Presbyterian with 1,022 yards for the season and a career total of 2,361.

But the turkey episode typifies the community spirit which accompanies the Bronze Derby. "It's got to be one of the friendliest football games you'll ever see," Gault notes.

Again, a sentiment echoed by Herren.

"Our fans aren't like Carolina fans or Clemson fans. They don't get rabid and completely caught up in the game. They get excited but they maintain control. Maybe it's the smallness of the communities and the schools, but I think it's good, whatever the reason.

"I also think the holiday mood affects them. It's almost like old-home week when these teams play. Some folks have asked us to change the game from Thanksgiving, but we won't do it. That's our day without competition from the big schools. We feel the advantages of playing on Thanksgiving far outweigh the disadvantages."

Ken Pettus, an outstanding linebacker on Herren-coached teams of 1969-72, agrees that the game has special meaning.

"We played against most of their guys in high school, so we usually knew each other pretty well," said Pettus, now a member of the Furman University coaching staff. "Besides, we usually scrimmaged them twice in the spring and that helped maintain a friendly atmosphere."

Pettus is described by Herren as "the most intense player" he coached. "I never saw a player get up for a game like he did."

In his senior year, Pettus got everybody's attention when he painted his helmet with an Easy Rider design. "One of their linemen had done it the year before so I thought I'd try it."

The PC-Newberry series, with the Bronze Derby and Thanksgiving heritage, would seem to be safe from the modern trend away from traditional thinking, but times change and thus opinions.

Reed Charpia, a former Newberry

player (1962-65), replaced Herren as head coach last year and finished the season with a 7-3 record and national ranking (12th).

But Charpia is a new breed, and one suspects the old traditions might be less important to his generation.

"When I was in school, the PC game seemed to be a very important game for everybody," he says. "That has changed since I came back to coach. Our players get enthusiastic about playing and I think our fans like the Thanksgiving rivalry, but I don't think it means that much to our student body. I think that's true partly because the students really don't know what the rivalry is about and partly because school is out and they simply aren't here.

"You don't see the student pranks anymore, and I think that's bad because you need that student involvement to keep the interest up. Personally, I like to play on Thanksgiving, but I don't think our players are crazy about it. Everybody goes home for Thanksgiving and they want to go home, too. I just don't think the Bronze Derby means that much to the players and students anymore.

"Tradition used to be a big factor in football," Charpia continued, "but I don't think it is anymore. I think tradition still helps in recruiting, but what happened last year won't affect this year what you get on the field."

But what does the fan think of all this? Does tradition matter to the guy who pays the tab?

Harold Folk of Newberry has been attending PC-Newberry games since 1954. What makes that game different from the others?

"The atmosphere is different. You can feel it. The Bronze Derby is on the line and everybody gets caught up in it. You go to a Carolina or Clemson game and you look through binoculars to see the players. When you go to a game here or at Presbyterian, you can hear them hit and grunt on the field from your top row seat. It's more personal. I think the size of the schools and the fact that the towns are so close accounts for most of the interest."

The cornerstone of collegiate sports is tradition and nowhere is that truer than among small colleges. With no major bowl berths available and relatively little publicity outside their own regions, small colleges take the players the big schools overlook and play a different game.

That's the kind of game you can see at Newberry's Setzler Field on Thanksgiving Day. Jim Kellett will be there. And Harold Folk. And down on the field, an aging leprechaun will be matching wits with a smooth newcomer.

When the dust settles, someone will hoist a strange looking trophy high into the air as a symbol of victory. And somewhere at the edge of the crowd, Fred Herren will wend his way to Cally Gault and they will speak quietly for a moment. Friendly rivals, one hurting for the other. The true meaning of college athletics.

And that's what some folks had in mind when they covered an old derby hat in bronze in 1947.

Billy Deal, public relations director for Standard Savings and Loan, is a graduate of Georgia Southern. For eight years he was a sportswriter, then sports editor, of the Savannah Morning News, *and during that time covered the PGA golf circuit, Atlanta Braves Baseball and college football. Deal lives in Columbia.*

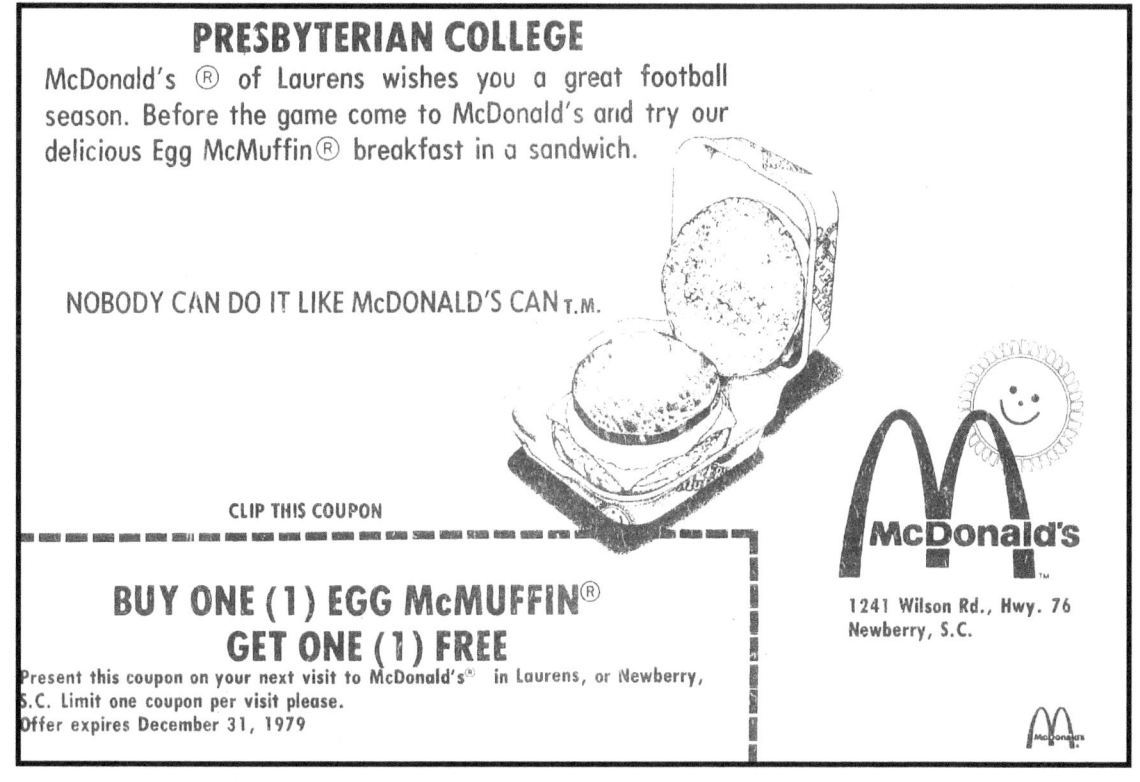

Southern Massacre

Week 11

Presbyterian College   16   Newberry College   14
Blue Hose   Indians

Newberry, South Carolina   November 22, 1979   2:00 PM
Presbyterian Overall Record   10-1   SAC-8 Record   7-0
NAIA Division 1 Ranking #1

Statistics	PC	Newberry
First Downs	11	14
Rushes / yards	55 / 180	37 / 127
Passing yards	75	134
Passes	10-17-1	12-27-3
Fumbles / lost	2-0	6-3
Penalties / yards	3-31	10-78
Punts / average	8-30	5-39

Scoring Summary

Q1 PC....PC 3 – Newberry 0....75 yard drive....Bishop 35 yard FG....3:50 remaining

Q2 PC....PC 6 - Newberry 0....38 yard drive....Bishop 22 yard FG....14:09 remaining

Q2 PC....PC 13 - Newberry 0....35 yard drive....QB Spence 2 yard run....Bishop PAT....9:12 remaining

Q2 Newberry....PC 13 - Newberry 7....73 yard drive....QB Tate 14 yard pass to Wilson....Spencer PAT....6:07 remaining

Q3 Newberry....PC 13 - Newberry 14....White 22 yard interception return....Spencer PAT....7:03 remaining

Q4 PC....PC 16 - Newberry 14....80 yard drive....Bishop 21 yard field goal....0:47 remaining

Highlights
Presbyterian College Blue Hose vs Newberry College Indians

- The Presbyterian College Blue Hose football team survived an outstanding game with the Newberry College Indians. The Blue Hose, after the 16-14 victory, were SAC-8 Champions and would be hosting an NAIA Division 1 quarterfinal game in Clinton, SC versus the Saginaw Valley State College Fighting Cardinals, from Saginaw, Michigan.

- The Presbyterian College Blue Hose went all year without any major injuries. However, QB Jimmy Spence reinjured a right knee that he had injured and rehabilitated this past year. Spence indicated that his knee was a little sore after the game and he was OK. He could move front and back in the game, but was having difficulty with his lateral movement. DB Hal Brannen suffered a broken collar bone and was unfortunately out for the playoffs.

- Newberry shut down the Blue Hose running attack, allowing RB Clayto Burke only 90 yards on 34 carries. Newberry kept Blue Hose RB's Burke, Hood and Atkins out of the endzone.

- Blue Hose WR Jesse Cason made the biggest six yard catch of the year. After the late 4th quarter catch, a Newberry defender hit him out of bounds. The 15 yard penalty extended the game winning drive.

- Presbyterian College Blue Hose K Chuck Bishop had the day he will never forget. Bishop accounted for 10 of the 16 points scored by the Blue Hose, including a 21 yard last minute field goal to win the game and retain the Bronze Derby.

- The Blue Hose did a much better job holding on to the ball. QB Jimmy Spence did throw a pick six to Newberry defender Jimmy White in the third quarter after returning to the game from his knee injury.

The 1979 Presbyterian Blue Hose Football Team

November 30, 1979 The Blue Stocking, Clinton, S.C. 29325 Page

PC Completes 10-1 Season

Before the post-season play begins, it is only fitting to review the Hose's most successful regular season and the records that fell in the past eleven games. As the season began Coach Gault felt PC was to face its "toughest schedule ever;" the Hose seemed to disprove that fact by beating over half of their eleven opponents by more than two touchdowns. PC opened the 1979 campaign with three consecutive road games. Undaunted by the fact that they were 15 point underdogs to The Citadel opening night, the Hose outlasted the Bulldogs 21-13. Spence threw for nearly 200 yards and Burke ran for 109 yards to set the pace they would match numerous times during the season.

The Furman Paladins were the next challenge the Hose faced, but Willie Mason's 98-yard kickoff return spelled defeat for PC's second consecutive foe. The Hose defeated Lenior Rhyne, 2-0 at the time, by the score of 28-14 and moved up to sixth in the national rankings. PC fans were beginning to prepare for the SAC-8 championship; but on a rainy day the Wofford Terriers brought the Hose back to earth with a 23-21 upset of the highly favored PC team. The Wofford loss seemed to ignite the Hose as they annihilated their next five challengers. Catawba was shellacked 21-0; Elon fell 30-14; Mars Hill was creamed 34-6; Central Florida was devasted 48-0; and Gardner-Webb was dropped 21-3. The Hose then met a little stiffer competition in the "never-say-die" Carson-Newman Eagles. The Eagles got within five points of defeating the now 2nd ranked Blue Hose but the Hose defense held off Carson-Newman to give PC another victory 34-28. Following the victory over the Eagles, the Hose became the number one ranked team in the nation.

The final test PC faced was the Bronze Derby Classic versus Newberry. The comeback victory against Newberry typified the year PC had (The offense scoring the points needed and the defense coming up with the big play when needed.).

The '79 campaign saw the fall of 11 school records. 1) Jesse Cason broke his record of 46 receptions in a season by netting 48 tosses this year. 2) Chuck Bishop set new school records by kicking nine FGs in a season (ties SAC-8 record) and 36 PATs. He also set a new career record for PC fieldgoals eclipsing the old record of 19. 3) Clayto Burke set three new school records: most yards rushing in a game with over 200 yards; most yards rushing season with 1397; most yards rushing per game average with 127 yards per game (The old record was 103 yards per game.). Clayto also set two SAC-8 records, breaking the old record of 123.6 yards per game rushing average, and the record for the most net yards rusing in a season of 1380. 4) Spence broke his own record for best completion percentage by completing 62 percent of his passes (the old record was 58 percent.). The PC team set three school records: most interceptions season-29, most wins season-10, and most yards of total offense per game average-371.4. (The old records were 27.9 and 368.2 respectively.)

Bishop Kick Lifts Hose, 16-14

The PC Blue Hose took their number one ranking and 9-1 record to Newberry on Thanksgiving Day to challenge the Newberry Indians (5-4) in the annual Derby Classic. After four quarters of football the Hose chalked up another victory as they sneaked past the Indians 16-14. PC made the most of three of six Newberry turnovers by cashing in 13 valuable points.

As usual, the Hose opened the scoring by marching 75 yards to set up a 23-yard Chuck Bishop field goal. Bishop's three pointer was his seventh of the year, breaking Sandy Cruickshank's school record of six field goals in one season. Bishop later increased his record and the score with a 22-yard field goal to give PC a 6-0 lead over the Indians. The Hose extended their lead to 13-0 when Spence scored on a two-yard run. All of PC's first three scores were set up by Newberry's turnovers.

However, Newberry, still seeking revenge for last year's 26-0 thumping from the Hose, came right back with a pair of touchdowns to take the lead. Backup quarterback Jeff Tate threw a 14-yard scoring strike to pull the Indians to within six points of PC. A battered Jimmy Spence then made his only mistake of the day as Newberry's Jimmy White intercepted Spence's pass and waltzed untouched for a 22-yard score. Newberry had the lead 14-13. All through the entire second half, the Indians had excellent field position. Their worst field position during the final half, with the exception of their last possession, was on their own 46-yard line. However, the Hose's stubborn defense held Newberry to give PC's offense the chance it needed. Jimmy Spence, knocked out of the game twice, came back to engineer the Hose's dramatic last minute victory. Spence moved the offense 80 yards in 13 plays; but the clock was the final obstacle. Forty-seven seconds remained in the contest which now rested on the toe of kicker Chuck Bishop. The tension mounted; but Bishop's 21-yard attempt was good and the Hose were on their way to the playoffs. Bishop's three field goals gave him nine for the season, tying Tom Sexton's SAC-8 record for the most field goals in a season.

FINAL STATS
Burke 2nd in NAIA for rushing
Bishop 8th in NAIA for kick scoring

Rushing	Att	Yds	Avg	TD
Burke	304	1597	4.6	12
Spence	130	421	3.2	7
Hood	62	308	5.0	3

Passing	Att	Compl	Yds	Int	Pct	TD
Spence	171	106	1302	6	62%	11

Season Avg	PC	Opp
Rush	233.3	153.2
Pass	138.2	132.1
Total Off	371.4	285.3

Receiving	Recpt	Yds	Avg	TD
Cason	48	556	11.6	2
Thornton	25	441	17.6	2

Score By Quarters	1	2	3	4	Total
PC	75	134	21	61	291
Opp	10	38	37	40	125

Playoff-bound Hose dispose of Newberry

	Newberry	PC
First downs	14	11
Rushes-yards	37-127	55-180
Passing yards	134	75
Return yards	35	45
Passes	12-27-3	10-17-1
Punts-avg.	5-37.8	8-30.5
Fumbles-lost	6-3	2-0
Penalties-yards	10-75	5-31

By SAM REGISTER

If by chance there was someone who saw the Thanksgiving Day matchup between Presbyterian and Newberry, knowing that one of the two teams was playoff-bound but not exactly which one, it wouldn't have been an easy guess.

In fact, they would have probably chosen Newberry.

PC dominated the first quarter, but the second, third and most of the fourth quarter belonged to Newberry until Chuck Bishop's 21-yard field goal with 47 seconds remaining in the game gave the Blue Hose a 16-14 win over the Indians in the 68th Bronte Derby Classic.

Presbyterian jumped out to 13-0 lead in the second quarter but it looked as if the team that went in the Newberry locker room at the half was not the same team that came out at the second half. It also did not help that Jimmy Spence, the SAC-8 Player of the Year, went down late in the second quarter, reinjuring the knee that he underwent an operation on last spring for torn ligaments.

Backup quarterback Ward Gatlin filled in for Spence on the first three offensive plays of the second half, but something was definitely lacking. That something was Spence. He hobbled back in to start PC's next possession on a knee that Coach Cally Gault revealed was so heavily taped that the junior from Lexington could hardly move it.

He was unable to scramble out of the grasps of the charging defensive lineman Thursday, a Spence trademark throughout the season. He also threw an interception that went for a touchdown, something he'd never done before at PC. But with the exception of those first three plays, he was on the field throughout the second half.

"Jimmy's the kind of boy who doesn't know pain," said Gault. "He never has.

"We weren't going to play him unless the doctor gave the OK," Gault said. He told us he could play but he'd be in pain."

It was bad enough that Spence was not his usual agile self, but Clayto Burke, who went into the game having rushed for 1,307 yards this season, was having a hard time getting out of the backfield. And when he made it out of the backfield, he seldom got to the line of scrimmage. He rushed for 90 yards but it took him 34 carries. However, most of his yardage came on the Hose's final scoring drive which covered 60 yards in 13 plays and culminated with Bishop's field goal.

"Newberry was tremendous today," said Gault. "They did a tremendous job of stopping our offense. They closed Burke down and let Spence run.

"But when the chips are down—I've never seen anybody come back as well as we did. Chuck Bishop came through as he has all year."

The Indians had a little trouble on offense during the first half, sustaining three crucial penalties on their opening drive which ended at the PC 25 with a field goal that was wide to the right.

Presbyterian took over from there. A screen to Jesse Cason netted a loss of two yards and a draw play to Burke picked up one. On third and 11 Spence dropped back to pass, but finding everybody covered he scampered out of the pocket and straight up the field for a first down at the 48.

Ben Hood fumbled on the following play but Frank Kube fell on it for a three yard gain. On second and seven Spence faked a handoff to Burke and again cut up-field, rambling all the way down to the Newberry nine. But the Indian defense held and the Hose had to settle for a field goal.

The Indians used both Jeff Tate and Eddie Pettus at quarterback throughout the first half, but it was Tate who connected with C.W. Wilson in the end zone with 6:07 remaining in the first half to cut the PC lead to 13-7.

Presbyterian 3 10 0 3-16
Newberry 0 7 7 0-14
A-5,500

PC's Clayto Burke carries his weight and that of about three others ...C.W. Wilson (bottom) scored the Indians opening touchdown

The 1979 Presbyterian Blue Hose Football Team

How 'bout them Hose! . . .

The PC defense has smothered opponents, yielding 11.13 points per game

Jimmy Spence has hit on 106 of 171 passes for 1,502 yards and 11 touchdowns

Jimmy Spence unloads against Elon
...Ready to lower the boom, John Robinson (81) and John Richards (89)

Chuck Bishop's 21-yard field goal helped the Hose edge Newberry 16-14

Three happy Presbyterian College Assistant Coaches .... Wayne Renwick, Elliot Poss and Bob Strock are all smiles on Thanksgiving Day November 22, 1979 after the Blue Hose defeated Newberry 16-14 to win the annual Bronze Derby game. The win guaranteed Presbyterian College a berth and first round home game in the Division 1 NAIA playoffs.

The Southern Massacre completed. 7-0 SAC 8 Champions, NAIA # 1 Ranking.

Notable Quotes Regarding Newberry

"That was some kind of good feeling."
    - Chuck Bishop K, 1979

"That game is like a turkey day game should be!"
    - Jo Nell RB, 2023

"I thought we had it won. Maybe that is why we got beat. Jimmy Spence was the difference in the game."
    - Newberry Head Football Coach Reed Charpria, 1979

"That was the most emotional football game I've ever been part of, and while I'm very disappointed we didn't win, we all wish them (PC) well in the NAIA Playoffs."
    - Newberry DE Jimmy White, 1979

"The Newberry game is always close."
    - John D'Andrea OG, 2023

"At Newberry, we had it fourth and short in the closing minutes. We hit Jesse Cason outside and he came up short but was hit out of bounds resulting in a penalty to extend the drive."
    - Presbyterian College Assistant Coach Bob Strock, 2023

"After the Newberry game and win, there were cigars and celebration!"
    - Bob Peterson, 2023

"The Newberry game we all took personally. It was a hard hitting defensive battle. Chuck Bishop!"
    - Joe Grant MG, 2023

"I told Chuck Bishop before he went on the field to kick the winning field goal, to keep his head down and follow through. The crowd will let you know if you made it!"
    - Ronnie Hollier WR, 2023

"Newberry was a dogfight. We were glad to get out with a win!"
    - Frank Kube C, 2023

"Newberry was tremendous today. They did a tremendous job of stopping our offense. They closed Burke down and let Spence run. But when the chips are down, I've never seen anybody come back as well as we did. Chuck Bishop came through as he has all year."
    - Presbyterian College Head Football Coach Cally Gault, 1979

"I may have had the best tackle of the day. Coach Gault got extremely upset and was heading after an official. I gave him a bear hug and redirected him to the sidelines. He thanked me later! After the incident, if he were introducing me to other people, he would tell them that I was responsible for saving his career!"
    - Ronnie Hollier WR, 2023

Len Howard and Joe Grant converge on a Newberry defender.

The 1979 Presbyterian Blue Hose Football Team

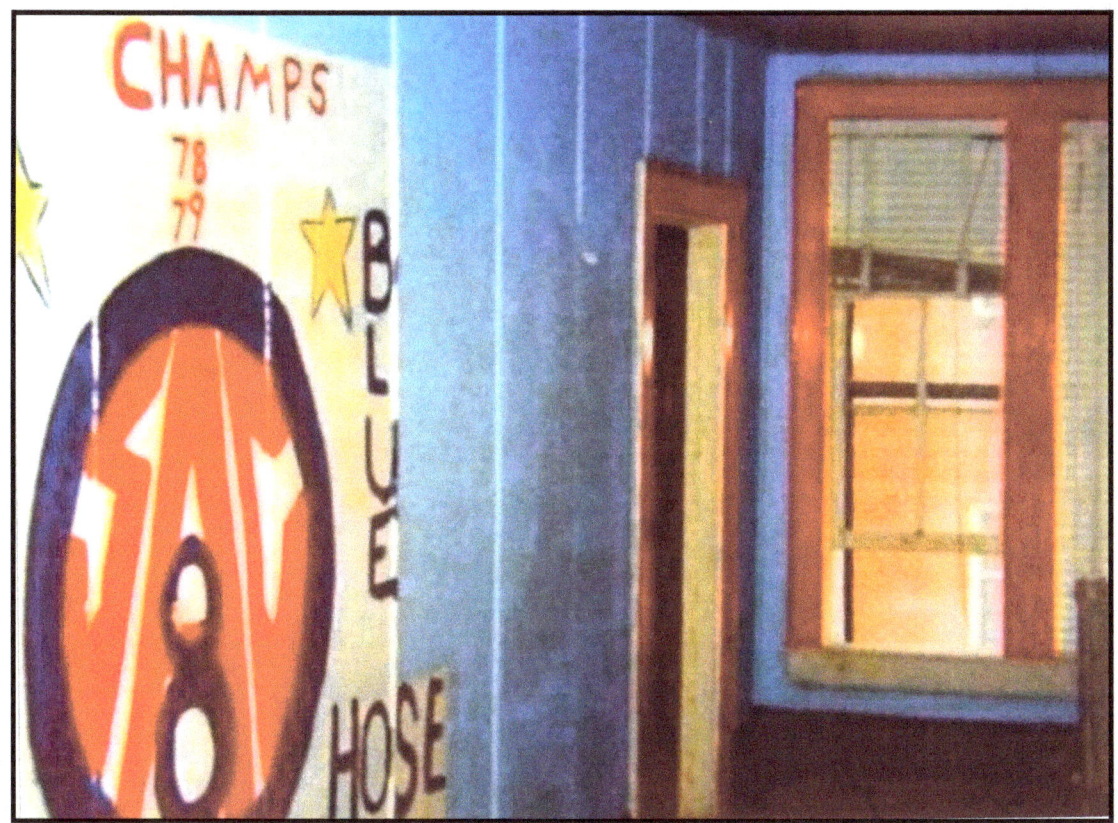

Above: Wall art painted in Doyle Hall on PC campus. Artist unknown.

Below: MG Joe Grant enjoying a moment with the Bronze Derby.

Southern Massacre

Burke keeps on churning

By SAM REGISTER

After rushing for 1,397 yards in 11 games this year Sunday mornings are a little tougher to deal with than they were at the beginning of the season. But according to Clayto Burke, that's one of the prices you pay for being number one.

"I'm getting kinda worn down," said Burke, the nation's third leading NAIA rusher, "Especially the way people are after us now, hitting ~~~ per ~~~. The Newberry game was the hardest hitting game all year."

Although he would just as soon forget it, Burke remembers the Newberry game too well. It was the only game this season in which the 5-11, 194-pound senior was not able to run with his usual authority—until the final minutes of the game when the Blue Hose marched 74 yards in 12 plays. Burke carried the ball on eight of those plays, picking up 45 yards to set up Chuck Bishop's 21-yard field goal with less than a minute remaining in the game. Burke said his main concern was "getting downfield into field goal position."

Before coming to Presbyterian, Burke attended Southwest High School in Macon, which at that time was the largest secondary school in the nation. He played tailback and was being courted heavily by South Carolina, Clemson, Vanderbilt, and Florida during his senior year.

But an injury to the team's starting quarterback forced Burke to step in at that position. After that many of the bigger schools lost interest in him.

During his first couple of years at PC, he played a little at receiver, but he soon found himself back at the tailback position. And although its hard to fathom, Burke was not a polished runner two years ago.

"It took me the whole spring to learn everything," he said. "I was hitting the hole full speed and Coach (Wayne) Renwick told me to feel my way through.

"I haven't really patterned myself after anyone. After the Gardner-Webb game (168 yards rushing, one TD) someone compared me to Wilbert Montgomery of the Philadelphia Eagles. I like to watch other runningbacks but I haven't patterned myself after anyone. I just take what the defense gives me. I'm a picky runner."

Burke was named to the All-Conference and All-District teams last year and, as was expected, he's had an outstanding season this year. In the Hose' 34-28 win over Carson-Newman Burke carried for 187 yards and scored three touchdowns. He also set single season and career rushing marks at PC.

A Pre-Law major, Burke is soft-spoken and lucid. Despite being on the number one team in the nation he is not a braggart, although that could very well be justified.

"I haven't given it that much thought," he said. "I always thought if we stayed at the top and kept winning and others kept losing we'd get there. But I didn't anticipate it at the first of the

Face Saginaw Valley State Saturday

Clayto Burke set single-season and career rushing marks at PC this season

Week 12

- November 24, 1979, A United States Senate report proves US troops in Vietnam were exposed to the toxic chemical Agent Orange.
- November 25, 1979, Pat Summerall and John Madden broadcast their first game together. Their partnership lasted 22 years and became one of the most well known in TV sportscasting history.
- November 30, 1979, Ted Koppel becomes late night ABC anchor of "American Held Hostage."
- December 1,1979, The Presbyterian College Blue Hose football team defeated the Saginaw Valley State Cardinals 36-6 at Johnson Field in Clinton, South Carolina. This was the final game for Saginaw Valley State Head Coach "Muddy" Waters with Saginaw Valley State. The following year he became Head Football Coach at Michigan State. In 2000, he was inducted into the College Football Hall of Fame. The NAIA Division I Quarter Final Championship game kickoff was at 1:30 PM.

Hose To Face Saginaw Valley

The dream has become a reality. After twelve weeks of regular season preparation the Blue Hose are ready to engage in the struggle that could lead them to the NAIA championship. Following an impressive 10-1 season and two weeks as number one in the nation, the PC Blue Hose will put their intimidating statistics on the line Saturday, December 1 at 1:30 against the Saginaw Valley State Cardinals.

The Cardinals bring an 8-1-1 record and a Great Lakes Intercollegiate Athletic Conference Championship to Clinton as they attempt to move closer to the NAIA finals. The Saginaw Valley State defense had a banner year. Allowing only two teams to score more than 14 points, the Cardinal defense gave up an average of 9.4 points a game with three shutouts. In comparison, P.C.'s defense gave up an average of 11.3 points a game, registered two shutouts, and also permitted only two teams to score more than 14 points. The Cardinal defense is an excellent one equally adept to stopping the pass (the pass defense finished 8th in the nation) as they are against the run.

Saginaw Valley State's offense, like its defense, has no real weakness. They have a very explosive offensive unit as evidenced by scores of 51-0 and 77-0. The Cardinals use their aerial attack effectively because of the capabilities of their quarterback Steve Zott, and the speed and hands of receiver Melvin Mathews. On the ground Saginaw Valley State fake to apply their running attack. The Cardinals have averaged 28.9 points a game while P.C has averaged 26.5.

Although the Cardinals are ranked 8th in the nation, they should not be taken for granted. They are a well coached and very impressive football squad. Coach Gault has the utmost respect for Saginaw Valley State. P.C. fans should realize that just because the Hose are number one, it doesn't mean this game will be easy by any measure. Saturday's battle relies on the misdirection or the NAIA quarterfinal championship, is only the beginning of a tough struggle to a NAIA Championship. (If, P.C. wins Saturday they would like play the winner of the Kearney State-Central State (Okla. game).

Possible the toughest decision the P.C. coaching staff had to make this past week was cutting the team roster down for Saturday's game. NAIA rules only allow 40 players to dress for the contest.

THE BLUE STOCKING

VOL. LXII NO. 20   PRESBYTERIAN COLLEGE CLINTON, S.C. 29325   NOVEMBER 30, 1979

And Then There Were 50!

On December 1, 1979, The Presbyterian College Blue Hose hosted a NAIA Division 1 quarterfinal football game on Johnson Field in Clinton, South Carolina. Seventy two players were on the regular season roster, but only 50 were dressed and were on the field.

The NAIA has a rule for post season football mandating that the participating teams may only dress 50 players. The Presbyterian College Blue Hose coaching staff had some tremendous decisions to make. In particular, the quarterback position. Jimmy Spence was having problems moving laterally, and would be limited to practice. Does PC carry one or two backup quarterbacks? The young men on special teams and backup roles that busted their tails throughout the year had to be evaluated. There were a dozen players that knew they would not dress, but the last ten were difficult decisions.

When I talked to Presbyterian College Blue Hose assistant coaches Strock, Perry and Renwick, each told me the exact same thing. It may have been the most difficult meeting they had in their college coaching careers. A dozen players were being reevaluated. Who could do what? Who could contribute in case of the unexpected?

I asked the coaches how they told the players. Each player was talked to individually. Each player knew when they hit the practice field on Monday who was on the roster. For a dozen players, the news was bittersweet. At the time, it was tough. But when they look back years later, they recognize that the coaches had to make a tough decision and respected their choices.

The players found out hours later that there were multiple players that heard "You were the 51st player and we had a tough decision to make."

The coaches wanted to take them all, and it was their way of telling them how valuable they were to the team. Practice the week prior to the quarterfinal game was upbeat and spirited.

Four freshmen, RB Jo Nell, LB's Marty Martin and David Wise, and OG Robbie Way were selected to dress for the quarterfinal game. The final decision was made to dress three quarterbacks, Jimmy Spence, Ward Gatlin and Paul Scott.

> **LEADERSHIP AND MANAGEMENT**
>
> Getting ahead in any carreer means proving you've got the leadership and management abilities it takes to be succesful. That's why Military Science Cadets at Presbyterian College get a head start. The new Army ROTC puts the emphasis on evaluating and developing your leadership and management potential to the fullest. It's one reason ROTC is frowing so fast. Grow with it.

Presbyterian College Vs. Saginaw Valley State College

First Round NAIA Playoffs
Johnson Field
Clinton, S.C.

December 1, 1979

Price: $1.00

The 1979 Presbyterian Blue Hose Football Team

WELCOME TO
Presbyterian College

DR. KENNETH ORR
...President, Presbyterian College

We are pleased to have you on campus to attend this football game. May your visit to the home of the Blue Hose be a pleasant one.

As the new President of Presbyterian College, I look forward to each game. Football is such an exciting and colorful sport. Regardless of our age, we can appreciate the high degree of teamwork, discipline and stamina that good teams always exhibit. It is the result of many, many hours of rugged practice, mental concentration, and careful coaching.

Presbyterian College is proud of its long tradition of fine football teams guided by skillful coaches. Over the years these players and coaches have demonstrated the highest qualities of character and sportsmanship, qualities that represent well the spirit of Presbyterian College.

This year's team, under the leadership of Cally Gault, Director of Athletics and Head Football Coach for sixteen years, continues this fine tradition. Coach Gault, his coaching staff, and his players have worked hard to prepare for this contest. Regardless of the score, I am sure we will see a highly competitive squad giving its best effort.

Thank you for attending this game, and for supporting athletics at PC. We cordially invite you to return to the campus often.

WELCOME, SCOTLAND HIGH SCHOOL BAND AND THANKS FOR YOUR PRE-GAME AND HALFTIME SHOW

Scotland High School Band - Laurinburg, North Carolina
"THE FIGHTING SCOT BAND"

Director: Mr. Bert Owen
Marching Director: Mike Robinson
Drum Major: Ronnie Ollis
Drum Majorette: Jenny Thomas

Sponsored by the Band Booster Club: Co-President Mr. & Mrs. J.B. Ollis

175 piece band outfitted in authentic imported Scottish Kilts, including a Bagpipe Corps

Has received numerous citations including: 1st place in the Land of the Sky Festival held in Asheville, North Carolina, 1978 and most recently a Superior rating in the 4A Division competition held in Mullins, S.C. this fall.

Southern Massacre

National Association of Intercollegiate Athletics

THE NAIA CHAMPIONSHIP FOOTBALL PLAYOFF SYSTEM

DIVISIONS AND AREAS

Unlike basketball, where NAIA institutions compete in Districts, NAIA football institutions are classified according to Divisions I or II. When the NAIA divided into divisions in 1970 member institutions were given an opportunity to declare in which division they wished to compete. The NAIA Football Coaches Association Review Board has had the authority to rule on changes within divisions and an institution is required to spend at least two seasons in a given division once it is placed there.

Within each division member institutions are arranged according to geographic areas:

DIVISION I

Area 1—Alaska, Colorado, Hawaii, Idaho, Kansas, Minnesota Missouri, Montana, Nebraska, North Dakota, Oregon, South Dakota, Utah, Washington, Wyoming.

Area 2—Arizona, Arkansas, California, Nevada, New Mexico, Oklahoma, Texas.

Area 3—Connecticut, Illinois, Indiana, Iowa, Maine, Massachusetts, Michigan, New Hampshire, New Jersey, New York, Ohio, Pennsylvania, Rhode Island, Vermont, West Virginia, Wisconsin.

Area 4—Alabama, Delaware, District of Columbia, Florida, Georgia, Kentucky, Louisiana, Maryland, Mississippi, North Carolina, South Carolina, Tennessee, Virginia.

DIVISION II

Area 1—Alaska, Hawaii, Idaho, Montana, Nebraska, North Dakota, Oregon, South Dakota, Washington, Wyoming.

Area 2—Arizona, California, Colorado, Kansas, Nevada, New Mexico, Oklahoma, Texas, Utah.

Area 3—Connecticut, Iowa, Maine, Massachusetts, Michigan, Minnesota, Missouri, New Hampshire, New Jersey, New York, Rhode Island, Vermont, Wisconsin.

Area 4—Alabama, Arkansas, Delaware, District of Columbia, Florida, Georgia, Illinois, Indiana, Kentucky, Louisiana, Maryland, Mississippi, North Carolina, Ohio, Pennsylvania, South Carolina, Tennessee, Virginia, West Virginia.

THE RATERS

Teams selected for participation in the NAIA playoffs are determined by weekly ratings throughout the season. Selected members of the NAIA Football Coaches Association submit a weekly rating during a specified rating period to determine which teams will participate in the post-season playoffs.

Each of the four geographical areas (see above) within the Division are allocated four raters, thus making 16 raters per division.

In 1979 the Division II rating period runs from Wednesday, September 19 to Wednesday, November 7 and the Division I rating period goes from Wednesday, September 19 to Wednesday, November 14.

SELECTION OF TEAMS

• Teams must declare their intent to participate in the NAIA championship football program by October 1.

• Teams must be ranked in the top 12 in the last regular-season weekly rating (Nov. 7 for Division II, Nov. 14 for Division I) to be considered for the playoffs.

• The top-ranked team from each of the four geographical areas (in each division) within the top 12 is automatically selected for the playoffs.

• The next four highest-ranked teams, **regardless of geographic area,** and not already selected, complete the eight-team field.

• No more than two teams from the same conference (within the same division) are selected for the playoffs.

• Teams may be paired according to geographic proximity to each other for the first round (quarterfinals) and members of the same conference would play each other in quarterfinal or semifinal rounds.

• Teams with four or more non-winning games will not be selected for participation in the playoffs.

1979 PLAYOFF DATES

DIVISION II

Quarterfinals — Saturday, November 17
Semifinals — Saturday, December 1
Championship — Saturday, December 8,
site of participant

DIVISION I

Quarterfinals — Saturday, December 1
Semifinals — Saturday, December 8
Championship — Saturday, December 15,
Palm Bowl, McAllen, TEX

The 1979 Presbyterian Blue Hose Football Team

Eight-Team Playoff Begins Second Year

This is the second year of the NAIA's eight-team playoff format with the two teams participating here today having earned a playoff spot by their ranking in the final regular-season ratings conducted by the NAIA Football Coaches Association.

The winner of today's game advances to the Division I semifinals to be played December 8 with those winners advancing to the second annual Palm Bowl on December 15 in McAllen, Texas.

On behalf of the Association's more than 500 member institutions we thank those present today for your loyal support and for providing a vehicle for alumni and community involvement on campus while providing a robust and desirable activity for the students.

It is the strong feeling of the NAIA that football, one of 15 national championship events conducted by the Association, is an integral aspect of the total educational program.

Harry Fritz
NAIA Executive Director

HARRY FRITZ

Welcome & Thanks From NAIA President

On behalf of the NAIA we wish to extend our greetings to all of the football fans, the two outstanding teams and their coaches assembled here today for the first round of Division I football competition.

Sponsorship of this event involves cooperation between college officials and community leaders and is a tribute to the importance of the young people being educated in our great colleges and universities.

The NAIA strives for a well-balanced and comprehensive program of activities - one that meets the needs of its total student population of 950,000 students. Currently, the NAIA conducts 15 national championships in 14 different sports.

We thank those present today for your loyal support in making this post-season game an outstanding athletic competition in the best tradition of American higher education.

W.C. (Red) Myers
NAIA President
Erskine College, SC

W.C. "RED" MYERS

Southern Massacre

Facts About Today's Playoff Opponents

Presbyterian College

President: Dr. Kenneth Orr
Enrollment: 900: 500 men; 400 women
Athletic Director: Calhoun F. "Cally" Gault
Head Football Coach: Cally Gault
Presbyterian College 1948-AB University of South Carolina 1956 M-Ed.
Coaching Record: 89-73-6 (16 seasons)
Assistant Coaches: Bob Strock - Erskine College 1955 Def. Backs, John Perry - Presbyterian 1972 Off. Line, Elliot Poss - Presbyterian 1971 Def. Line, Wayne Renwick - Presbyterian 1973 Receivers
Sports Information Director: Hunter Reid

Saginaw Valley State College

2250 Pierce Road
University Center, MI 48710

President: Dr. Jack M. Ryder
Enrollment: 3,800
Athletic Director: Frank "Muddy" Waters Jr.
Football Coach: Frank "Muddy" Waters - Michigan State University, 1949 - Collegiate Record, 163-73-7 (24 seasons)
Assistant Coaches: James A. Larkin, Offensive Coordinator - Steve Reese, Defensive Coordinator - Frank "Murky" Waters III, Passing Game Coordinator - Al Doty, Defensive Backs - Joe Flynn, Special Teams, Scouting - Bob Spencer, Linebackers - Charles Goss, Offensive Backfield
Sports Information Director: Greg Branch

Game Officials

Referee - Ray Beasley
Umpire - R.N. Ognovich
Linesman - William Michael
Line Judge - Monte Williams
Back Judge - Malcolm Erwin
Clock Operator - Frank Gibson

Game Officials provided by the Southern Conference, Dallas Shirley, assistant to Commissioner

Presbyterian College

Presbyterian College, owned by the Synods of South Carolina and Georgia, enjoys an established reputation for its educational product.

Here is a 99-year tradition spotlighted by the accomplishments of distinguished alumni in every field of endeavor. The rolls include college presidents, leaders of business and industry, churchmen by the scores, men of medicine and of law, scientists probing into outer space, the creative, and those who guard our creations as ranking officers of the armed forces.

They are the products of a distinctive program of Christian higher education which trains the mind and develops the physical and moral fiber necessary for future leadership.

The program features: Academic excellence in the liberal arts and sciences; pre-professional study for the ministry, medicine, dentistry, law, engineering, teaching; ROTC training toward reserve commissions; a self-governed student body, athletics and other varied extra-curricular activities.

Upon this solid tradition, Presbyterian College stands and points with enthusiasm toward the future. An expanded campus, selected student body, new facilities, enriched curriculum are the order of the day.

The President

DR. KENNETH B. ORR
President of Presbyterian College

Dr. Kenneth B. Orr assumed office in July as Presbyterian College's 15th president, successor to

the retiring Dr. Marc C. Weersing.

He brought with him an unusual background that includes having been president of a religious graduate school, a pulpit minister, an All-City high school football player, an Air Force pilot, a salesman for Proctor & Gamble and the author of an award-winning doctoral dissertation.

Before stepping into the PC executive office, Dr. Orr earned distinction as president of Presbyterian School of Christian Education in Richmond, Va., where he served from 1974 to 1979. For ten years prior to that, he was assistant-to-the-president and then vice-president of Union Theological Seminary in Virginia. His career also includes a three-year tenure as minister of the 400-member West End Presbyterian Church of Roanoke, Va.

Ken Orr is a 46-year-old Charlotte native who comes from a family of ministers, educators and lay leaders.

PC's new president is married to the former Janice Ann Jarrett of Tallahassee, Fla., and they have three sons - Kevin (14), Jeffrey (10) and Jonathan (6).

PAGE 4

Saginaw Valley President

PRESIDENT RYDER

Guiding Saginaw Valley is Dr. Jack M. Ryder. Under his leadership since the fall of 1974, the college has taken gallant strides in asserting its leadership among Michigan's educational institutions.

Since the beginning of Dr. Ryder's tenure, SVSC has gained a perspective on its future - by setting solid goals and objectives. Some have already been met; the college has undertaken an energetic growth program to help meet others.

A Michigan State University graduate, Dr. Ryder served as vice-chancellor and dean for Administrative Affairs at the University of Indiana-Purdue in Indianapolis.

In many ways, he has been the Cardinals' number one fan for years. Not only does he, his wife Lila and daughter Suzanne attend nearly every home athletic event, but his enthusiasm and support of athletics have been one of the keys behind the success of SVSC's athletic program.

Dr. Ryder and his family reside in the presidential residence just north of the campus. Besides their spectator participation in SVSC sports, Dr. and Mrs. Ryder play racquetball and square dance.

Saginaw Valley State College

When Delta college, a two-year community college serving the Midland, Bay and Saginaw County area was founded in 1961, many area residents felt that higher education in the area should go a step further.

For, while Delta offered associate degrees and two-year certificates in many program areas, students still had to travel at least as far as Mount Pleasant, Lansing or Flint to attend a four-year college.

To help meet the higher education needs of the Tri-County area — which became in the Sixties one of the most rapidly-growing metropolitan areas in the Midwest — a private college, Saginaw Valley College, was founded in 1963. At first it offered only junior- and senior-level courses and held its classes on the Delta campus.

In the mid-Sixties, however, it became apparent that it was time for a vigorous building program to begin. The Project 66 and 68 Buildings were the first two construction endeavors on SVSC's present site; Wickes Hall was next. Since then, and since Saginaw Valley became a state-supported institution in 1967, it has added dormitories, the Athletic Center, Doan Center, a theatre and Pioneer Hall of Engineering and Technology.

The SVSC campus is bounded by Bay Road on the west, Pierce Road on the south and Davis Road on the east. It is nestled in the rich farmlands of Saginaw and Bay Counties, and lies a stone's throw from the county line.

Wickes Hall, Doan Center and the dorm complex are near a lush growth of pines, just off a tree dotted courtyard and fountain. Cardinal Gymnasium, home of the Cardinal cagers and athletic offices, rests on the edge of a wood filled with some of Michigan's most beautiful and majestic native flora.

The football stadium, built in 1975, lies just east of that wood. Beyond it is the newly constructed, 400-meter outdoor track.

Nearly 600 students live on campus in SVSC's apartment-style residence hall suites, and the 3,700 enrollment makes the college one of the fastest-growing in the nation.

The undergraduate college supports six schools: Arts and Behavioral Sciences; Business and Management; Education; Public Services; Science, Engineering and Technology and Nursing and Allied Health Sciences. The graduate college offers master's degree programs in Education and Business Administration.

SVSC's enrollment has more than doubled since 1974, and continues to grow. To meet this increase in enrollment the college plans another instructional facility, a new library facility, a heating and cooling plant and a new physical education facility and fieldhouse.

PAGE 5

The 1979 Presbyterian Blue Hose Football Team

Presbyterian College's Blue Hose

REESE AMMONS
DT

WALTER ATKINS
Back

HAL BRANNEN
DB

LARRY BRIDGES
Linebacker

CLAYTO BURKE
Back

JAY BYARS
Flanker

JESSE CASON
Split End

JIMMY CHUPP
Back

WILLIE COOPER
DB

JOHN D'ANDREA
OG

ALLAN GASTON
DB

WARD GATLIN
QB

JOE GRANT
MG

GENE HARPER
OT

HEYWARD HINTON
DB

BEN HOOD
Back

LEONARD HOWARD
MG

MARK KAY
DT

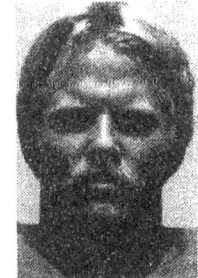
FRANK KUBE
Center

JOE LANE
DE

JIM McCOUN
DE

JOE MOONEYHAM
DB

JOE NELL
Back

BRUCE OLLIS
OG

115

Southern Massacre

| LARRY OWENS Linebacker | MIKE OWENS DB | DONALD PORTER QB-SE | DEAN PRICE TE-FB | ERSKINE REED DB | JARROLD REEVES Center |

  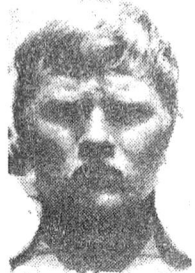   

| PAUL SCOTT QB | JIMMY SPENCE QB | STEVE STALVEY Linebacker | BARRY TAYLOR OG | DANNY THORNTON TE | ROY WALKER OT |

ROBBIE WAY OG

CHRIS WILLIAMS DT

PC Football

Football kicked off at Presbyterian in 1913; but it was not until two years later - with the arrival of Walter A. Johnson - that the college started playing a representative schedule.

Everett Boe coached the first pick-up squad in 1913. Student William P. Jacobs II, grandson of the founder and later president of PC, organized the team, played on it and served as assistant coach. His love of the game here motivated, years later, the establishment of the Jacobs Blocking Trophies, now perpetuated by his two sons.

Walter Johnson came to PC at 22 as a one-man coaching staff in 1915. He put football and other athletic activities on a solid intercollegiate basis, remained as head coach for 25 years and died in 1958 after 43 years as athletic director - dean of Southern sportsmen.

One of the stars of Johnson's first PC team was End Lonnie McMillan. He joined the coaching staff shortly after graduation and remained until his retirement in 1959. McMillian, succeeding Johnson as head coach in 1941, introduced the South to T-formation football by installing it here.

Frank Jones, succeeding Bill Crutchfield in 1957, headed the program for five years and carried the Blue Hose into the 1960 Tangerine Bowl. Upon the death of Clyde Ehrhardt in 1963, Cally Gault - who had played his football here under McMillian - assumed the reins.

The years since 1913 have seen colorful football played by outstanding athletes wearing the Garnet and Blue - a program continued without interruption despite two world wars.

The 1979 Presbyterian Blue Hose Football Team

1979 PRESBYTERIAN COLLEGE ROSTER

NO.	NAME	POS	HT	WT	CLASS	HOMETOWN
1	Chuck Bishop	K	5-11	148	Jr.	Lodge, S.C.
10	Ward Gatlin	QB	6-3	180	Sr.	Conway, S.C.
11	Donald Porter	QB	6-1	186	Jr.	Washington, D.C.
12	Jay Byars	FLK	6-1	172	Sr.	Cayce, S.C.
14	Paul Scott	QB	5-10	180	So.	Chamblee, Ga.
15	James Spence	QB	6-2	185	Jr.	Lexington, S.C.
23	Randy Morris	SE	5-9	143	So.	Marietta, Ga.
24	Jimmy Chupp	QB	6-½	172	Jr.	Doraville, Ga.
25	Lamar Roberts	P	5-11	160	Jr.	Greenwood, S.C.
26	Allan Gaston	DB	5-10	158	Sr.	Carrollton, Ga.
28	Erskine Reed	CB	5-10	185	Sr.	Orangeburg, S.C.
29	Mark Leverette	DB	5-11	170	So.	Simpsonville, S.C
30	Dean Price	TE-FB	6-2	234	Jr.	Anderson, S.C.
31	Jo Nell	OB	5-9	180	Fr.	Charleston, S.C.
32	Ben Hood	OB	6-½	209	Jr.	Greensboro, Ga.
33	Joe Mooneyham	DB	5-10	177	So.	Pauline, S.C.
34	Heyward Hinton	DB	5-11	199	Jr.	Columbia, S.C.
36	Willie Cooper	DB	5-8	168	Jr.	Gable, S.C.
37	Ricky Kirkpatrick	FS	5-9	160	So.	Milledgeville, Ga.
40	Clayto Burke	OB	5-11	194	Sr.	Macon, Ga.
43	Marty Martin	LB	5-10	185	Fr.	Hopkins, S.C.
44	Mike Owens	DB	5-11	170	So.	Spartanburg, S.C.
46	Walter Atkins	OB	5-11	200	So.	Greenville, S.C.
47	Hal Brannen	DB	6-1	188	Jr.	Unadilla, Ga.
50	Leonard Howard	MG	6-2	219	Sr.	Doraville, Ga.
52	Larry Owens	LB	6-1	205	Jr.	Greenville, S.C.
53	Steve Stalvey	LB	5-10	197	So.	Waycross, Ga.
54	David Wise	LB	6-0	191	Fr.	Columbia, S.C.
55	Robert Hannah	LB	5-11	210	Sr.	Fairburn, Ga.
56	Jarrold Reeves	OG	6-1	204	Jr.	Avondale, Ga.
57	Frank Kube	C	6-0	205	So.	Orlando, Fla.
61	Larry Bridges	LB	6-0	200	Sr.	Greenville, S.C.
63	John D'Andrea	OG	6-0	225	Jr.	Fairburn, Ga.
64	Bruce Ollis	OG	5-11	206	Sr.	Laurinburg, S.C.
66	Barry Taylor	OG	5-11	212	Sr.	Durham, N.C.
67	Mark Wheless	DE	6-1½	205	So.	Clearwater, Fla.
70	Charles Yarborough	OT	6-½	202	So.	Clinton, S.C.
71	Robert Peterson	DT	6-1	218	Jr.	Duluth, Ga.
73	George Martin	DT	6-1	224	So.	Pickens, S.C.
74	Robbie Way	OG	6-3	225	Fr.	Lugoff, S.C.
75	Joe Grant	MG	5-11½	251	Jr.	Charleston, S.C.
76	Gene Harper	OT	6-4½	258	Jr.	Eatonton, Ga.
77	Roy Walker	OT	6-3½	232	Sr.	Clinton, S.C.
78	Chris William	DT	6-2	210	Jr.	Lawrenceville, Ga
79	Reese Ammons	DT	6-2	230	So.	Darlington, S.C.
80	Jesse Cason	SE	5-9½	155	Jr.	Orlando, Fla.
81	Danny Thornton	TE	6-½	205	Jr.	Washington, Ga.
86	Hugh Bailey	DE	5-11	204	Jr.	Liberty, S.C.
88	Willie Mason	SE	5-0	158	Jr.	Laurens, S.C.
90	Mark Kay	DT	6-3	255	Sr.	Anderson, S.C.
95	Joe Lane	DE	6-0	187	Jr.	Tallahassee, Fla.
99	Jim McCoun	DE	6-2	209	Sr.	Decatur, Ga.

Southern Massacre

1979 Saginaw Valley Roster

No.	Name	Pos	Ht	Wt	Class	Hometown
1	Melvin Mathews	WR	6-1	170	Junior	Detroit, MI
2	Ken Tolfree	CB	5-11	180	Senior	Merrill, MI
3	Kevin Zott	DB	5-10	160	Freshman	Utica, MI
8	Kenny Johnson	CB	5-11	170	Senior	Pleasantville, NJ
9	Rick Kolb	QB	6-1	185	Freshman	Plantation, FL
10	Steve Zott	QB	5-10	180	Senior	Utica, MI
11	Bob Stacey	DB	6-0	170	Soph.	Burton, MI
12	B.J. Lathwell	TE	6-2	215	Senior	Frankfort, MI
14	Dave Larkin	QB	5-11	170	Senior	Mt. Morris, MI
15	Howard Harrison	DB	5-11	165	Freshman	Platation, FL
18	Tom Merkle	WR	6-4	205	Junior	Bay City, MI
21	Karl Darling	WR	5-8	170	Senior	Detroit, MI
22	Duane duChemin	WR	5-9	155	Soph.	Newaygo, MI
24	Terry Peabody	RB	6-2	200	Soph.	St. Clair Shores, MI
25	Fred Holubik	WR-P	6-2	190	Junior	Freeland, MI
29	Dennis Provins	DB	6-1	195	Freshman	Traverse City, MI
32	Sylvester Bush	RB	6-0	200	Soph.	Rockville Center, NY
33	Ben Laser	RB	5-10	190	Junior	Waldron, MI
34	Jim Martinez	RB	5-11	220	Senior	Drayton Plains, MI
35	Kirk McCarty	K	5-9	195	Soph.	Rapid River, MI
37	Dan DiTomaso	S	5-11	180	Junior	Warren, MI
38	Robert Forrest	S	5-11	170	Soph.	Pleasantville, NJ
39	Larry Leighton	RB	6-0	180	Freshman	Grosse Ile, MI
40	Mark Macken	MG	5-11	240	Freshman	Rockville Center, NY
46	Brad Elbers	LB	6-0	200	Soph.	Reese, MI
51	Steve Zuchnik	LB	6-2	215	Freshman	Kawkawlin, MI
52	Andy Wilson	C	6-2	195	Soph.	Portage, MI
54	Steve Bundy	T	6-2	205	Freshman	Battle Creek, MI
56	Tom Curl	DT	6-1	230	Soph.	Chicago, IL
57	Ross Gleason	LB	6-0	215	Junior	Negaunee, MI
59	John Pelkki	LB	6-0	215	Junior	Saginaw, MI
60	Brent Fackler	T	6-0	220	Soph.	Lima, OH
61	Scott Gostovich	C	6-1	245	Soph.	New Baltimore, MI
62	Steve Braun	DE	6-1	210	Freshman	Battle Creek, MI
63	Steve Aschbaucher	G	5-11	190	Freshman	Temperance, MI
64	Robert Beesley	G	6-2	200	Freshman	Ronkonkoma, NY
65	Mark Johncock	T	6-3	210	Freshman	Battle Creek, MI
66	Bob Paul	LB	6-0	210	Soph.	Marine City, MI
67	Dave Wendt	G	6-2	210	Senior	Oxford, MI
68	Bob Loftus	T	6-2	245	Junior	Northfield, NJ
69	Mark Zimmerman	G	6-0	210	Junior	Saginaw, MI
70	Al Stewart	DT	6-7	250	Senior	Detroit, MI
72	Jeff Major	DE	6-4	235	Senior	Burton, MI
73	Gary Provins	T	6-2	250	Junior	Traverse City, MI
74	Vince Williams	DT	6-2	195	Senior	Memphis, TN
77	Pete Bede	DT	6-1	240	Soph.	Frankenmuth, MI
82	Mike Rehm	TE	6-4	200	Soph.	Detroit, MI
84	Brian Drewniak	DE	6-2	200	Senior	Taylor, MI
85	Kurt Ebert	TE	6-3	210	Junior	Holly, MI
86	Eugene Marve	DE	6-3	220	Soph.	Flint, MI
89	Larry Bee	MG	6-2	220	Junior	Detroit, MI

"The Official NAIA football for 1979 is the Rawlings R-5, Rawlings Sporting Goods, Co., St. Louis, Missouri"

The 1979 Presbyterian Blue Hose Football Team

Saginaw's Fighting Cardinals

PETE BEDE
Defensive Tackle

DAN DITOMASO
Safety

BRIAN DREWNIAK
Defensive End

DUANE DUCHEMIN
Running Back, WR

KURT EBERT
Tight End

BRAD ELBERS
Linebacker

ROBERT FORREST
Safety

ROSS GLEASON
Linebacker

FRED HOLUBICK
Punter

KEN JOHNSON
Cornerback

DAVE LARKIN
Quarterback

BEN LASER
Running Back

B.J. LATHWELL
Tight End

BOB LOFTUS
Guard

KIRT MCCARTY
Kicker

JIM MARTINEZ
Running Back

TOM MERKLE
Quarterback

BOB PAUL
Middle Guard

MIKE REHM
Tight End

AL STEWART
Defensive Tackle

Southern Massacre

KEN TOLFREE
Cornerback

DAVE WENDT
Guard

ANDY WILSON
Center

STEVE ZOTT
Quarterback

Muddy's Record

Year	School	Record	Honors
1950	Walled Lake HS	4-4-0	
1951	Walled Lake HSS	8-0-0	State Champs
1952	Albion HS	5-3-0	
1953	Hillsdale College	*	
1954	Hillsdale College	7-1-1	MIAA Champs
1955	Hillsdale College	9-0-0	MIAA Champs
1956	Hillsdale College	9-0-0	MIAA Champs
1957	Hillsdale College	9-1-0	MIAA Champs
1958	Hillsdale College	7-2-0	MIAA Champs
1959	Hillsdale College	8-2-0	MIAA Champs NAIA Playoffs
1960	Hillsdale College	9-1-0	MIAA Champs
1961	Hillsdale College	6-3-0	
1962	Hillsdale College	5-3-1	
1963	Hillsdale College	6-3-1	
1964	Hillsdale College	7-2-1	
1965	Hillsdale College	6-3-0	
1966	Hillsdale College	3-5-1	
1967	Hillsdale College	3-5-0	
1968	Hillsdale College	6-3-0	
1969	Hillsdale College	9-1-0	NAIA Playoffs
1970	Hillsdale College	9-2-0	
1971	Hillsdale College	6-5-0	
1972	Hillsdale College	7-2-0	
1973	Hillsdale College	7-2-0	
1974	SVSC	No varsity schedule	
1975	SVSC	3-7-0	
1976	SVSC	4-7-0	
1977	SVSC	6-5-0	
1978	SVSC	4-5-1	

Career Record   172-79-6
*Assistant under Charlie Bachman

Saginaw Valley State College
Depth Chart

Offense

SE	1	Melvin Mathews, 25 Fred Holubik
LT	73	Gary Provins, 60 Brent Fackler, 54 Steve Bundy
LG	69	Mark Zimmerman, 63 Steve Aschbaucher
C	61	Scott Gostovich, 52 Andy Wilson
RG	67	Dave Wendt, 64 Robert Beesley
RT	68	Bob Loftus, 65 Mark Johncock
TE	12	B.J. Lathwell, 85 Kurt Ebert, 82 Mike Rehm
RB	39	Larry Leighton, 24 Terry Peabody, 32 Sylvester Bush
RB	34	Jim Martinez, 33 Ben Laser
FL	21	Karl Darling, 18 Tom Merkle, 22 Duane duChemin
QB	10	Steve Zott, 14 Dave Larkin, 9 Rick Kolb
K	35	Kirk McCarty
P	25	Fred Holubik, 3 Kevin Zott

Defense

LE	86	Eugene Marve, 72 Jeff Major
LT	70	Al Stewart, 56 Tom Curl
MG	89	Larry Bee, 40 Mark Macken
RT	77	Pete Bede, 74 Vince Williams
RE	84	Brian Drewniak, 62 Steve Braun
LLB	46	Brad Elbers, 66 Bob Paul
RLB	51	Steve Zuchnik, 57 Ross Gleason, 59 John Pelkki
LC	2	Ken Tolfree, 15 Howard Harrison
SS	37	Dan DiTomaso, 3 Kevin Zott
FS	38	Robert Forrest, 29 Dennis Provins
RC	8	Ken Johnson, 11 Bob Stacey

The 1979 Presbyterian Blue Hose Football Team

Cally Gault Is Dean Of Active S.C. Coaches

Presbyterian College Head Coach Cally Gault is the dean of active South Carolina college coaches. He's now in his 17th season as head coach of the Presbyterian College Blue Hose and this year guided the team to the school's best regular season record, 10-1, and the No. 1 NAIA national ranking.

Over the past two years, Coach Gault's Blue Hose have posted a record of 18-3-1, raising his college coaching career mark to 99-74-6. A 1948 graduate of Presbyterian College, Coach Gault had an outstanding high school coaching career prior to returning to P.C. as head coach. At North Augusta High School, his teams won 88, lost 13 and tied seven. That included three state championships and a four-year undefeated streak of 43 straight games (1954-58).

The 51-year-old coach has been "South Carolina College Coach of the Year" four times and has won the conference honor three times.

Gault is married to the former Joy Godfrey of Clinton and they have two daughters, Mrs. Stanley (Joy) Gruber and Mrs. Bob (Emmie An) McLean, and a son, Cal, who is a student at the University of South Carolina.

COACH CALLY GAULT

PC Coaching Records

Everett Boe	1913	4-3-0
B. Theller	1914	4-1-4
Walter Johnson	1915-17 1919-40	103-96-19
Gifford Shaw (acting)	1918	2-0-0
Lonnie McMillian	1941-53	61-58-2
Bill Crutchfield	1954-56	13-14-1
Frank Jones	1957-61	24-22-3
Clyde Ehrhardt	1962	1-9-0
Cally Gault	1963	99-74-6

COACH BOB STROCK

COACH JOHN PERRY

COACH ELLIOTT POSS

COACH WAYNE RENWICK

Saginaw Valley Coach
Frank 'Muddy' Waters

FRANK WATERS
Athletic Director
Head Football Coach

Keeping track of football coaches at SVSC has been pretty easy..."Muddy" has been at the wheel since the program started. This is his fifth year of football at SVSC, and the 29th year he's been on he sidelines as a coach.

In four years of varsity play, Waters' Cardinals have had one winning season - going 6-5 in 1977.

Waters' overall record is 172-79-6, and he holds honors that date all the way back to his playing days at Michigan State Univesity - where he set a rushing mark that still stands.

He has been installed in the National Association of Intercollegiate Athletics' (NAIA) Hall of Fame and has been named the NAIA District 23, AP and UPI Michigan Coach of the Year seven times. He was the National Coach of the Year in 1957, and the Sigma Chi Coach of the Year in 1969. Presently third vice-president of the NAIA, Waters has been president of the NAIA's Coaches Association and Football Coaches Association four times each.

Waters spent 20 years at Hillsdale College before coming to SVSC, and in that time established Hillsdale's as one of the most powerful small-college programs in the nation. His Chargers were seven-time Michigan Intercollegiate Athletic Association champs, and were nationally ranked 12 times.

Now 56, Waters played for Clarence "Biggie" Munn at Michigan State from 1947 through 1950. In 1945 he married Mary Lou Ginther, and they now live in Saginaw. Two of his sons - John, 23, and Bill, 22, were SVSC football and track standouts, and John still holds nearly all of the Cardinal rushing records. Waters' other son, Frank D. (Murky) III, is an assistant football coach.

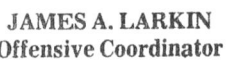

JAMES A. LARKIN
Offensive Coordinator

FRANK WATERS III
Passing Game Coordinator

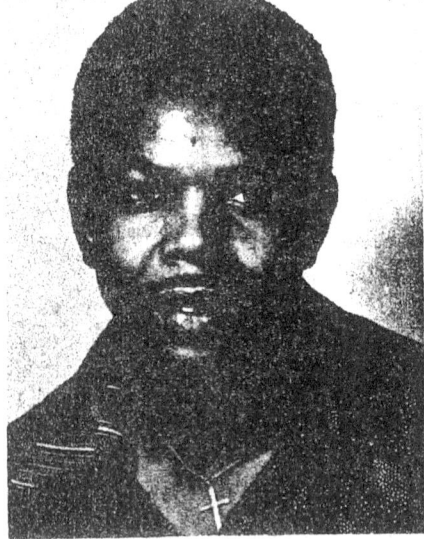

CHARLES GOSS
Offensive Backfield

STEVE REESE
Defensive Coordinator

NOT PICTURED: Joe Flynn, Special Teams and Offensive Ends; Bob Spencer, Linebackers.

Official Tie-Breaking Procedures
NAIA Football Playoff Games

If, at the end of the fourth quarter, the teams have identical scores, the tie will be resolved in the following manner:

1. The NAIA Game Committeeman will designate the end of the field on which the overtime period(s) will be played.

2. The Game Committeeman, the Game Officials, and the respective team captains shall assemble at the 50 yard line following a three minute intermission at the conclusion of the fourth quarter. The referee shall conduct a coin toss and the visiting team captain shall be given the privilege of calling the coin while it is in the air. The winner of the toss shall be given his choice of ball possession or defense for the first overtime period.

3. Each team shall put the ball in play from its opponent's 20 yard line, first down and 10 yards to go.

4. Teams shall alternate possessions until the tie is broken following an equal number of possessions.

All Other Official NCAA Football Rules Apply Except:

1. Each team is allowed one (1) timeout for each overtime period. Any unused regulation game timeouts may not be used during overtime period.

2. The same end of the field will be used for both possessions in order to insure equal game conditions for both teams.

3. Each overtime period will include one possession by each team.

4. The loser of the coin toss for the first overtime period shall have the option of ball possession or defense to begin the second overtime period. Should there be addition overtime periods, the choice will be alternated between the teams.

5. There will be a one minute intermission between each overtime period.

The team scoring the greater number of points in the overtime period(s) shall be declared the winner. The final score shall be determined by totaling all points scored by each team during the regulation and overtime period(s).

Starting Line-Ups

P.C. OFFENSE
- SE-80, Cason
- LT-77, Walker
- LG-64, Ollis
- C-57, Kube
- RG-66, Taylor
- RT-76, Harper
- TE-82, Thornton
- QB-15, Spence
- Flk-12, Byars
- FB-32, Hood
- TB-40, Burke

CARDINAL DEFENSE
- LE-86, Marve
- LT-70, Stewart
- MG-89, Bee
- RT-77, Bede
- RE-84, Drewniak
- LLB-46, Elbers
- RLB-51, Zuchnik
- LC-2, Tolfree
- SS-37, DiTomaso
- FS-38, Forrest
- RC-8, Johnson

P.C. DEFENSE
- LE-99, McCoun
- LT-78, Williams
- MG-75, Grant
- RT-90, Kaye
- RE-86, Bailey
- LB-53, Stalvey
- LB-61, Bridges
- LCB-47, Brannen
- RCB-34, Hinton
- FS-36, Cooper
- SS-28, Reed

CARDINAL OFFENSE
- SE-1, Mathews
- LT-73, Provins
- LG-69, Zimmerman
- C-61, Gostovich
- RG-67, Wendt
- RT-68, Loftus
- TE-12, Lathwell
- RB-39, Leighton
- RB-34, Martinez
- FL-21, Darling
- QB-10, Zott
- K-35, McCarty
- P-25, Holubik

Southern Massacre

AL MEYER

NAIA Coaches' Association Largest Coaches Group In The World

The NAIA Coaches' Association congratulates the two teams here today in this first round of the Division I football championship series.

Members of the NAIA Football Coaches Association play an integral role in selection of the teams for the playoffs. Teams are selected on the basis of weekly ratings from the Division I and Division II football rating committees.

The NAIA Coaches' Association is the largest organization of college coaches in the world. This organization has made it possible for coaches to conduct their business on a professional basis and affords the opportunity for leadership within the profession.

Al Meyer
NAIAC President
Mayville State College ND

NAIA Football Coaches Association

President: Don Larson, Illinois Wesleyan University, Bloomington

1st Vice President: Joseph Fusco, Westminster College, New Wilmington, PA

2nd Vice President: Thomas Parry, Central Washington University, Ellensburg

3rd Vice President: Forrest Perkins, U. of Wisconsin-Whitewater, Whitewater

4th Vice President: Pat O'Neal, East Central University, Ada, OKLA

Past President: Ron Randleman, Pittsburg State University, Pittsburg, KAN

Coordinator: Division I: Clark Swisher, Northern State College, Aberdeen, SD 57401

Division II: Frank Waters, Saginaw Valley State College, University Center, MI 48710

National Staff Liaison: Dr. Charles Morris, NAIA National Office, Kansas City, MO

NAIA Area Representatives

Area

1 Bob Shoup, California Lutheran College, Thousand Oaks

2 Ernest Hawkins, East Texas State University, Commerce

3 Ted Kessinger, Bethany College, Lindsborg, KS

4 Ken Gibler, Missouri Valley College, Marshall

5 Ralph Carpenter, Henderson State University, Arkadelphia, AR

6 Bill Ramseyer, Wilmington College, Wilmington OH

7 Jack Huss, Lenoir-Rhyne College, Hickory, NC

8 Denny Creehan, Edinboro State College, Edinboro, PA

The 1979 Presbyterian Blue Hose Football Team

HOW THEY GOT HERE

PRESBYTERIAN COLLEGE
(10-1 Overall, 7-0 SAC-8)
P.C. 21, The Citadel 13
P.C. 17, Furman 10
P.C. 28, Lenoir Rhyne 14
Wofford 23, P.C. 21
P.C. 21, Catawba 0
P.C. 30, Elon 14
P.C. 34, Mars Hill 6
P.C. 48, Central Florida 0
P.C. 21, Gardner-Webb 3
P.C. 34, Carson-Newman 28
P.C. 16, Newberry 14

SAGINAW VALLEY ST.
(8-1-1 Overall)
Great Lakes Conference Champs
Saginaw 51, NE Illinois 0
Saginaw 29, Indiana Central 12
W. Illinois 27, Saginaw 7
Saginaw 23, Evansville 0
Saginaw 21, Hillsdale 3
Saginaw 32, Grand Valley 24
Saginaw 20, Northwood 7
Saginaw 22, Ferris State 14
Saginaw 77, Mexico Ed. 0
Saginaw 7, Wayne State 7 (tie)

National Association of Intercollegiate Athletics

NAIA FOOTBALL

Established in 1940 as the National Association of Intercollegiate Basketball, the NAIA emanated from a "National Small College Basketball Tournament" inaugurated in 1937.

Football, one of 15 national championship events conducted by the NAIA, became part of the NAIA championship program in 1956. The first two years, only two teams were selected for the championship, but in 1958, the NAIA inaugurated a playoff system to determine which teams would advance to the championship game.

NAIA football teams were lumped together in one division for 13 years — from 1956 to 1969. Division II became a reality in 1970 following a year-long study of the membership and an endorsement by the NAIA Football Coaches Association.

Four teams made up the playoff field in each division until 1978 when the championship series was expanded to include eight teams and went from two weekends and seven playoff games to three weekends and 14 playoff games.

The first championship game was played in 1956 with St. Joseph, Ind. and Montana State battling to an 0-0 tie in the mud in the Aluminum Bowl in Little Rock, Ark. Moving to St. Petersburg, Fla., in 1957 until 1961, the championship game was called the Holiday Bowl. In 1961 the title game moved to Sacramento, Calif., became known as the Camellia Bowl and remained on the West Coast until 1964.

The Champion Bowl became the official name in 1964 and held that title through the 1976 championship game. The last two championship games have been played at neutral sites — Seattle (Apple Bowl, 1977) and McAllen, Tex. (City of Palms Bowl, 1978).

All nine of the Division II championship games have been played at either on-campus sites or nearby locations.

Texas A&I University, holders of the NAIA record for consecutive victories (42) and the longest unbeaten streak (46 games) has captured six of the previous 23 national championship title games.

Westminster PA has won three national titles and Texas Lutheran has taken two crowns since Division II was formed in 1970.

NAIA DIVISION I QUARTERFINAL GAME PAIRINGS
Saturday, December 1, all games 1:30 p.m., local times

Western State COLO (8-1-0) at Texas A&I (9-1-0)
Wisconsin-River Falls (9-1-0) at Angelo State TEX (8-2-0)
Central State OKLA (9-1-0) at Kearney State NEB (8-1-0)
Saginaw Valley State MICH (8-1-1) at Presbyterian, SC (10-1)

NAIA DIVISION II QUARTERFINAL GAME RESULTS
Saturday, November 17

Pacific Lutheran WASH 34, California Lutheran 14, at Thousand Oaks, CA
Bethany KAN 35, Austin TEX 24, at Lindsborg, KS
Northwestern IOWA 40, Midland Lutheran NEB 27, at Vermillion, SD
Findlay OHIO 41, Jamestown ND 15, at Findlay OHIO

NAIA DIVISION II SEMIFINAL GAME PAIRINGS
Saturday, December 1, all games, 1:00 p.m., local times

Pacific Lutheran WASH (9-0-0) at Findlay OHIO (8-1-1)
Bethany KAN (11-0-0) at Northwestern IOWA (9-1-0)

The 1979 Presbyterian Blue Hose Football Team

Program Sponsors

Gambrell and Hanvey
Goodman Insurance
Gray Funeral Home
Gulf Oil Co.
W.S. Hatton Ins.
Jacobs List
Leonard-Marler Ins.
Robert's Drive-In
Tiller's Interstate
D.E. Tribble
Mike Turner Co.
Shealy's Florist
Whiteford's Drive-In
Community Cash
Crouch Hardware
Copley's Clothing and Gifts
First State Savings
Lawson Furniture
Heritage Savings
Laurens Glass
United Agency
Sunshine Cleaners
McGee's
Carolina Service Station
Citizens Federal Savings

C-W-S Guano
Mac Duncan
Earl's EZ Mart
Joe's Gulf Station
Revco
Pitts Service Station
Laurens Mills
Greenwood Mills
Clinton Mills
M.S. Bailey & Son, Bankers
Industrial Supply
Torrington
Bailey Agency
Baldwin Motor Co.
Clinton Chronicle
Clinton-Newberry Nat'l Gas Authority
H.D. Payne
First National Bank
Bishop's Tire
Chancey's
Collins and Aikman
Ascoe Felts
3M Company
Lynn Cooper, Inc.

NAIA DIVISION I QUARTERFINAL GAME

INFORMATION SHEET

Compiled by Randy Randall-Presbyterian Student Activities Director

TIME: 1:30 P.M.
DATE: December 1, 1979
LOCATION: Johnson Field-Presbyterian College
AT STAKE: NAIA Quarterfinal Championship

PRESBYTERIAN COLLEGE BLUE HOSE VS. SAGINAW VALLEY STATE CARDINALS

BLUE HOSE FACTS

South Atlantic Conference Champs
'79 Regular Season Ranking - 1st
Head Coach: Cally Gault

1979 Schedule (10-1)

The Citadel (A)	21-13	W
Furman (A)	17-10	W
Lenoir-Rhyne (A)	28-14	W
Wofford (H)	21-23	L
Catawba (A)	21-0	W
Elon (H)	30-14	W
Mars Hills (H)	34-6	W
Central Florida (H)	48-0	W
Gardner-Webb (A)	21-3	W
Carson-Newman (H)	34-28	W
Newberry (A)	16-14	W

CARDINAL FACTS

Great Lakes Intercollegiate
Athletic Conference Champs
'79 Regular Season Rank - 8th
Head Coach: Frank "Muddy" Waters

1979 Schedule (8-1-1)

Northeastern Illinois (H)	51-0	W
Indiana Central (A)	29-12	W
Western Illinois (A)	7-27	L
Evansville IND (H)	23-0	W
Hillsdale MICH (A)	21-3	W
Grand Valley MICH (H)	32-24	W
Northwood Inst. MICH (A)	20-7	W
Ferris State MICH (A)	22-14	W
Mexico Education (A)	77-0	W
Wayne State MICH (H)	7-7	T

Game Outlook

The game pits two explosive offensive teams against one another. The Cardinals have averaged 28.9 points a game while allowing 9.4 points. The Blue Hose have averaged 26.4 points a game while allowing 11.13 points.

The Cardinals have a potent passing attack led by quarterback Steve Zott and wide receiver Melvin Mathews. Zott hit 55 percent of his passes for 1,650 yds and 12 touchdowns last year. Mathews caught 34 passes for 533 yds last year.

The Blue Hose counter with last years SAC-8 player of the year Jimmy Spence at quarterback and the nations 3rd leading rusher Clayto Burke. On the receiving end of Spence's passes will be P.C. record holder Jesse Cason and tight end Danny Thornton. The Blue Hose offensive line is led by All-American Roy Walker. The P.C. defense is a scrappy bend-but-not-break defense.

* * * * TICKET INFORMATION * * * *

		Available At	
Reserved Tickets	$6.00	The Mens Shop-Laurens	Mon-Thur 9am-6pm
Student Tickets	3.00		Friday 9am-4pm
All Tickets on Game Day	6.00	The Adairs Men Shop-Clinton	Mon-Thur 9-6
			Friday 9-4
		PC Athletic Office Mon-Fri	9am-5pm

The Box Offices on the east and west sides of the stadium will open Saturday at 9:30 A.M. The gates will open at 12:00 noon. Tickets will be sold five minutes into the third quarter.

Week 12

#1 Presbyterian College
Blue Hose

36

#8 Saginaw Valley State College
Fighting Cardinals

6

Clinton, South Carolina
PC Overall Record 11-1

December 1, 1979   1:30 PM

NAIA Division 1 Quarter Final Championship

Statistics	PC	Saginaw Valley
First Downs	26	10
Rushes / yards	73 / 299	35 / 74
Passing yards	188	61
Passes	16-17-0	5-15-2
Fumbles / lost	2-2	6-4
Penalties / yards	3-28	7-28
Punts / average	8-30	5-39

Scoring Summary

Q1 SV .... PC 0 - SV 6 .... 24 yard drive .... QB Zott 12 yard pass to Matthews .... Kick failed .... 12:14 remaining

Q1 PC .... PC 7 - SV 6 .... 53 yard drive .... RB Burke 2 yard run .... Bishop PAT .... 3:34 remaining

Q1 PC .... PC 14 - SV 6 .... 17 yard drive .... QB Scott 17 yard pass to WR Byars .... Bishop PAT ... 2:12 remaining

Q2 PC .... PC 17 - SV 6 .... 57 yard drive .... Bishop 23 yard FG .... 11:19 remaining

Q2 PC .... PC 24 - SV 6 .... 60 yard drive .... QB Scott 30 yard pass to WR Cason .... 7:33 remaining

Q2 PC .... PC 27 - SV 6 .... 46 yard drive .... Bishop 20 yard FG .... 0:00 remaining

Q4 PC .... PC 34 - SV 6 .... 68 yard drive .... Mason 1 yard run .... 4:47 remaining

Q4 PC .... PC 36 - SV 6 .... Safety after blocked punt by Wheless .... 2:59 remaining

Highlights
Presbyterian College Blue Hose vs Saginaw Valley State College

- Presbyterian College Blue Hose RB's Clayto Burke scored 1 touchdown and had 121 yards on 21 attempts. Ben Hood ran for 73 yards on 12 attempts. Walter Atkins ran for 38 yards on 9 attempts.
- WR Jesse Cason led the Presbyterian College Blue Hose receivers with 1 touchdown and 65 yards on 6 catches.
- QB Jimmy Spence was a perfect 2-2-0 for 20 yards before leaving the game in the middle of the first quarter as he had reaggravated his knee injury suffered Thanksgiving Day at Newberry. All week prior to the NAIA Division 1 Quarterfinal matchup, he was resting and being evaluated daily.
- Presbyterian College Blue Hose Head Football Coach Calley Gault told the media all week that he and the team had tremendous confidence in backup QB Ward Gatlin. When QB Jimmy Spence went down, it was Paul Scott who got the call. Coach Gault gave credit to his assistant coaches for preparing QB Scott. The decision to call Scott's number was the combination by PC to run the veer offense against Saginaw Valley and Scott's quickness.
- Blue Hose QB Paul Scott went 15-16 for 168 yards. Scott recorded 2 touchdown passes. The first was a 17 yard strike to WR Jay Byars in the first quarter. In the second quarter, Scott connected with WR Jesse Cason for a 30 yard touchdown.
- After Presbyterian College Blue Hose QB Paul Scott entered the game, he calmly drove the Blue Hose 57 yards down the field in 7 plays resulting in a 2 yard RB Clayto Burke rushing touchdown. The next four drives by QB Paul Scott resulted in his two touchdown passes and also two field goals by K Chuck Bishop.
- At halftime, The Presbyterian College Blue Hose were leading 27-6. The third quarter was scoreless. In the fourth quarter, Presbyterian College Blue Hose Willie Mason scored on a 1 yard run, and the defense

forced a safety to end the scoring as a result of a blocked punt.

- On the day, The Presbyterian College Blue Hose offense generated 487 yards of total offense against Saginaw Valley State College, 299 on the ground and 188 passing yards.
- The Presbyterian College Blue Hose defense sacked Saginaw Valley QB Zott 5 times for a net loss of 33 yards.
- Saginaw Valley State College was held to only 1 yard of rushing in the first quarter. They had a total of only 135 yards total offense for the game. The Presbyterian College Blue Hose defense was certainly the second half of the story.
- Presbyterian College Blue Hose QB Paul Scott was named the games most valuable player.
- In the 1979 NAIA Division 1 quarterfinal game, Presbyterian College Blue Hose Head Football Coach Calley Gault celebrated his 100th collegiate career win with the victory over Saginaw Valley State College coached by 2000 College Football Hall of Fame inductee Frank "Muddy" Waters.
- Central State Oklahoma beat (at) Kearney State Nebraska 42-22 to set up the semifinal matchup on December 8, 1979 in Edmond, Oklahoma.
- The Presbyterian College Blue Hose are one win away from playing in the NAIA Division 1 Championship game, The Palm Bowl, in McAllen, Texas.

Southern Massacre

Hose bump off Saginaw, enter semis

By SAM REGISTER

With the first quarter about half over, a hush fell over Johnson Field Saturday afternoon as Presbyterian quarterback Jimmy Spence was helped to the sidelines after reinjuring his knee.

The Blue Hose already trailed Saginaw Valley State 6-0 and without last year's SAC-Eight player of the year at the controls it looked as if PC might be playing its final game of the 1979 season. As Coach Cally Gault said following the Newberry game, "Just having a player like Jimmy Spence on the field means a lot."

But seven plays later that hush was transformed into a roar when Paul Scott, a 5-10, 160-pound sophomore from Chamblee, Ga., directed the Blue Hose offense into the end zone with 3:44 left in the first quarter. Chuck Bishop's field goal gave Presbyterian a lead which it never relinquished.

When Scott had awakened from his Walter Mitty-like afternoon, he had completed 14 of 15 passes for 168 yards and thrown two touchdown strikes while leading the Hose to a 36-6 win over Saginaw Valley. He also carried four times for 30 yards and was named the offensive player of the game.

Presbyterian will now travel to Edmund, Okla., Saturday where it will face Central State at 2 p.m. Central State defeated Kearney State, 48-22 Saturday.

On first and 10 from the Saginaw Valley 10, it became obvious that Scott would not be satisfied just to hand the ball off for the remainder of the afternoon. The gutsy quarterback faked to Clayto Burke and rolled to right, directing his blockers and carried down to the six. Two plays later, Burke, who rushed for 121 yards on 19 carries went in from the two.

"What can you say?" Burke replied when asked about Scott's performance. "He completed 14 of 15 passes. You can't do much better than that. We knew he was a good passer. He did a fine job of finding the open man. He didn't sit on it. He started throwing immediately and took advantage of things. He was well prepared."

"Scott is an intelligent young man and we knew he'd be cool," said Gault. "I'm surprised that he threw the ball as well and as accurate as he did, but I'm not surprised that he played a fine game. He's very obviously a young man who reacts to the pressures of the game."

Gault was also admittedly pleased with the way the Blue Hose shut down the Fighting Cardinals' offensive attack.

"Although we moved the ball well, I have to say, defense, defense, defense," said Gault.

The Presbyterian defense held Saginaw Valley to 74 yards on 35 carries and limited the Cards' aerial attack to only 61 yards. They came into the game averaging 150 yards through the air. Quarterback Steve Zott, who came into Saturday's contest with a completion average of 55 percent, managed to complete five of 15 passes. He threw two interceptions.

After the Hose went ahead 7-6, Karl Darling fumbled on the first play of the Cards' third possession and Mark Wheless recovered on the Saginaw Valley 19-yard line. On second and 11 from the 19, a draw play to Walt Atkins netted nine yards and on third and three from the 10 Scott found Jay Byars, who was hit but fell into the endzone for the Hose's second TD of the first quarter.

Byars, a senior flanker from Cayce who is oft praised by Gault for his blocking, took a couple of steps off the line of scrimmage and seemed to get lost in front of the goal line.

"Paul did a good job of finding me," said the 6-1, 171-pound Byars. "That pattern is keyed against man-to-man defenses. My job was to pick off the linebacker but he was playing back."

The Hose's third scoring march began with about nine minutes left in the first half. On first and 10 from the 40, Scott pitched to Burke, who juked his way down the left sideline to the Cardinal 38 yard line. Burke carried the next two plays and on third and seven, Jesse Cason picked up three yards on a reverse.

Faced with a fourth and four situation, Presbyterian opted to go for the first down with the ball on the 31. Scott took the snap, rolled to his right and lofted a pass over Cason's right shoulder on the one-yard line and inches from the right sideline. Cason tucked the ball in, shedded a tackle and succeeded in getting one foot in the end zone. Bishop added the extra point for a 24-6 lead.

Scott was named offensive player of the game in a postgame ceremony. Defensive tackle Chris Williams' three unassisted tackles, nine assists, and two quarterback sacks earned him the defensive MVP award.

	Saginaw	PC
First downs	10	26
Rushes-yards	35-74	73-299
Passing yards	61	168
Passes	5-15-2	16-17-0
Punts-avg.	7-28.0	3-28.0
Fumbles-lost	2-2	6-4
Penalties-yards	3-15	4-39
Saginaw	6 0 0 6-6	
Presbyterian	14-12 0 9-36	

Rushing, Saginaw Valley: Leighton 19-27, Martinez 3-7, Zott 13-41, Darling 2-9, Peabody 2-(-5); Presbyterian: Burke 20-121, Spence 1-4, Hood 12-72, Atkins 9-38, Scott 4-30, Cason 1-4, Mason 7-29.

Passing, Saginaw Valley: Zott 5-15-2 61; Presbyterian: Spence 2-2-0 20, Scott 14-15-0 168.

Receiving, Saginaw Valley: Martinez 2-21, Mathews 2-26, Leighton 1-14; Presbyterian: Cason 6-65, Byars 2-19, Porter 2-21, Atkins 2-40, Burke 1-16, Hood 2-12.

Willie Mason vaults over a Roy Walker block
...Mason scored on a one-yard plunge in the fourth quarter

The Blue Hose defense celebrates after a second half fumble recovery
...The Presbyterian defense held the Fighting Cardinals to 135 total yards

Sophomore quarterback Paul Scott looks downfield
...Scott was named the offensive player of the game

1979 NAIA Quarter Final Championship game ball.

A Jay Byars reception contributed to a Blue Hose Quarter Final win.

Southern Massacre

The Presbyterian College Blue Hose NAIA Division 1 quarter final victory over Saginaw Valley appeared in newspapers throughout the nation.

NAIA Playoffs

Soph QB Leads Blue Hose, 36-6

The Associated Press

CLINTON, S.C. — Sophomore quarterback Paul Scott came off the bench and threw two touchdown passes in the first half to start Presbyterian on its way to a 36-6 NAIA quarter-finals victory over Saginaw Valley State Saturday.

Scott, who replaced senior standout Jimmy Spence after he re-injured an ankle halfway through the first quarter, got his first touchdown on a fourth-and-three situation at the Saginaw 31 by passing to Jessie Cason in the end zone.

Power runner Cato Burke began the Blue Hose scoring with a 2-yard run that capped a 46-yard drive in the first period.

Willie Mason added a 1-yard touchdown run late in the game, Chuck Bishop kicked 23- and 22-yard field goals and Mark Wheless completed Presbyterian's scoring by falling on a blocked punt in the end zone for a safety shortly before the game ended.

Presbyterian Claims NAIA Playoff Win

From Wire Reports

CLINTON — Sophomore quarterback Paul Scott came off the bench and fired two touchdown passes in the first half to start Presbyterian on its way to a resounding 36-6 NAIA quarterfinals football victory over Saginaw Valley State Saturday.

Presbyterian, now 11-1 and ranked No. 1 among National Association of Intercollegiate Athletics Division I teams, plays Central Oklahoma State at Edmond, Okla., in a semifinal game next Saturday at 1 p.m. Angelo State plays Texas A&I in the other semifinal contest at Kingsville, Texas, 7:30 p.m.

Scott replaced senior standout Jimmy Spence after Spence re-injured an ankle halfway through the first quarter. He threw 10 yards to Jay Byars and on a fourth and three at the Saginaw 31 passed to Jessie Cason in the end zone.

Power runner Clayto Burke began the Blue Hose scoring with a two-yard run that capped a 46-yard drive in the first period.

Willie Mason added a one-yard touchdown run late in the game, Chuck Bishop kicked 23- and 22-yard field goals and Mark Wheless blocked a Saginaw Valley punt that led to the final points, a safety, when Ken Tolfree fell on the ball in the end zone.

Presbyterian, now 11-1 and ranked No. 1 among National Association of Intercollegiate Athletics Division I teams, goes to semifinal play next week against an opponent to be selected.

Saginaw Valley, No. 8 in NAIA rankings, finished 8-2-1.

Scott, a transfer from The Citadel who had seen just brief action in three games this year, hit on 14 of 15 passes for 168 yards and was named the outstanding player of the game.

He said winning over the Great Lakes Conference champs in Presbyterian's first playoff game ever was "like a dream. I hope I don't wake up until after Dec. 15." That's when the championship game is played at the Palm Bowl in McCallen, Texas.

Notable Quotes Regarding Saginaw Valley

"Presbyterian did what all great team seem to do. They lost somebody that everyone thought they couldn't afford to lose, but somebody nobody had ever heard about stepped in and filled up the gap in a hurry."
   - Saginaw Valley Head Coach "Muddy" Waters, 1979

"The toughest meeting I had in my football coaching career was when the PC coaching staff had to sit down and decide who the 50 were to dress for the playoff game. We had players who knew that they would not dress. When we came up with our agreed choices, we talked to every player that was not going to dress. Those players busted their tails all year. It was a tough day."
   - Presbyterian College Assistant Coach Wayne Renwick, 2023

"Freshman and players that did not dress for the quarter final game collectively made it happen (during practice) to prepare for Saturday."
   - Chris D'Andrea DE, 2023

"We had a beautiful week of practice. The media presence at the game stood out."
   - Ronnie Hollier WR, 2023

"Practice was a highly spirited week."
   - Jeff South OG, 2023

"I was a little hurt when I did not make the 50 to play in the game. We had a good week of practice. I do remember there was a lot of media at the game."
   - John Cann OG, 2023

"The playoff atmosphere was different. Hosting a dinner with the other team was a cool experience."
    - John D'Andrea OG, 2023

"I looked across the field and they had their winter jerseys on. The sun was beating on them."
    - Leonard Howard, 2023

"I don't remember much about the atmosphere. When I walked on the field I was focused and zoned in."
    - Erskine Reed CB, 2023

"Even though there were those of us that would not dress, no one slacked off. During practice we wanted to make the team better. Yes, I was one of the handful of 51st players. It was tough on all of us at the time."
    - Bob Peterson DT, 2023

"The playoff game was packed. It was the largest crowd ever to see a football game at Johnson Field. Bleachers were brought in to accommodate the crowd."
    - Randy Randall, Presbyterian College Head Basketball Coach, 2023

"We played a Catholic school from Green Bay, WI, and had to go up against the Holy rosary. Then we get in the playoffs and have to go up against a bunch of Presbyterians. This time we came up against the rolling hosiery!"
    - Saginaw Valley State Head Coach "Muddy" Waters, 1979

Week 13

- December 3, 1979, University of Southern California running back Charles White wins the 45th Heisman trophy award for the most outstanding college football player in 1979.
- December 3, 1979, 11 spectators were trampled to death at a Who concert at Riverfront Stadium in Cincinnati, Ohio trying to claim unreserved seats.
- December 7, 1979, "Star Trek: The Motion Picture" debuts starring William Shatner and Leonard Nimoy.
- December 8,1979, The Presbyterian College Blue Hose football team was defeated by the Central State University Bronchos in the NAIA Division I Semi Final Championship 28-6 at Wantland Stadium in Edmond, Oklahoma.

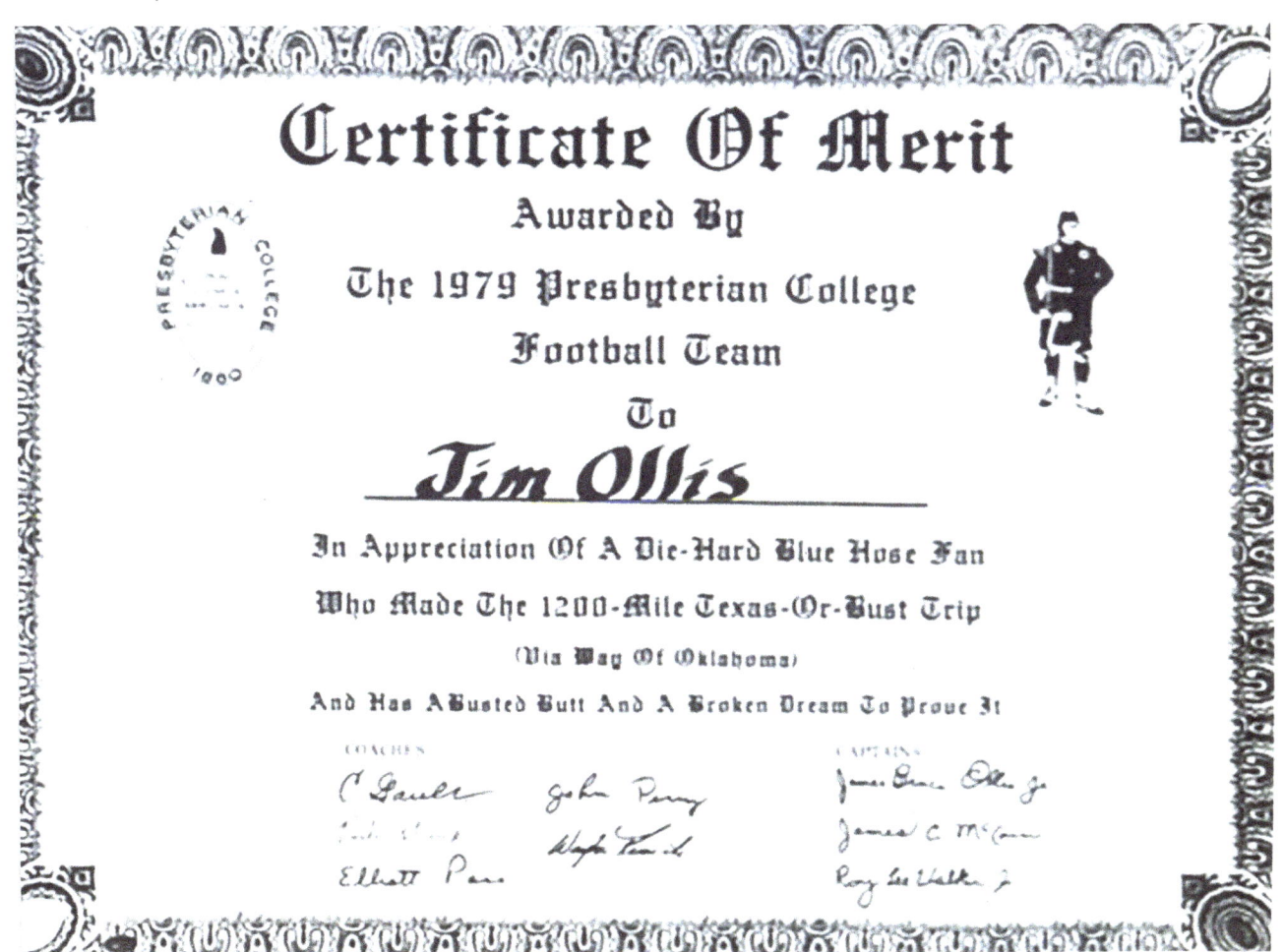

Bronchos **CENTRAL STATE UNIV.**

*

Blue Hose **PRESBYTERIAN COL.**

1979 NAIA Division I Football

SEMIFINALS

Wantland Stadium

Edmond, OK

December 8, 1979   1:30 p.m.

Official Program $1.00

Presbyterian College

The 1979 Presbyterian Blue Hose Football Team

Location: Clinton, SC
Enrollment: 900
Athletic Director: Calhoun F. Gault
Head Coach: Cally Gault
School Colors: Garnet and Blue
Nickname: Blue Hose
Sports Information Director: Hunter Reid

Dr. Kenneth Orr
President

Presbyterian College, owned by the Synods of South Carolina and Georgia, enjoys an established reputation for its educational product.

Here is a 99-year tradition spotlighted by the accomplishments of distinguished alumni in every field of endeavor. The rolls include college presidents, leaders of business and industry, churchmen by the scores, men of medicine and of law, scientists probing into outer space, the creative, and those who guard our creations as ranking officers of the armed forces.

They are the products of a distinctive program of Christian higher education which trains the mind and develops the physical and moral fiber necessary for future leadership.

The program features: Academic excellence in the liberal arts and sciences; pre-professional study for the ministry, medicine, dentistry, law, engineering, teaching; ROTC training toward reserve commissions; a self-governed student body, athletics and other varied extra-curricular activities.

Upon this solid tradition, Presbyterian College stands and points with enthusiasm toward the future. An expanded campus, selected student body, new facilities, enriched curriculum are the order of the day.

The President

DR. KENNETH B. ORR
President of Presbyterian College

Dr. Kenneth B. Orr assumed office in July as Presbyterian College's 15th president, successor to the retiring Dr. Marc C. Weersing.

He brought with him an unusual background that includes having been president of a religious graduate school, a pulpit minister, an All-City high school football player, an Air Force pilot, a salesman for Proctor & Gamble and the author of an award-winning doctoral dissertation.

Before stepping into the PC executive office, Dr. Orr earned distinction as president of Presbyterian School of Christian Education in Richmond, Va., where he served from 1974 to 1979. For ten years prior to that, he was assistant-to-the-presient and then vice-president of Union Theological Seminary in Virginia. His career also includes a three-year tenure as minister of the 400-member West End Presbyterian Church of Roanoke, Va.

Ken Orr is a 46-year-old Charlotte native who comes from a family of ministers, educators and lay leaders.

PC's new president is married to the former Janice Ann Jarrett of Tallahassee, Fla., and they have three sons - Kevin (14), Jeffrey (10) and Jonathan (6).

Southern Massacre

Dr. Bill J. Lillard
President

Central State University

Old North Tower

Location: Edmond, OK
Enrollment: 12,800
Athletic Director: Charles Murdock
Head Coach: Gary Howard
School Colors: Bronze and Blue
Nickname: Bronchos
Sports Information Director: Willard C. Pitts

During the last 15 years Central State University has been the fastest growing institution of higher education in the state of Oklahoma. From an enrollment of slightly less than 4,000 in 1964, CSU grew to nearly 13,000 students in 1979.

Much of Central's growth can be attributed to the keen concern for students which permeates the entire campus. Classes and programs are arranged and designed with student needs in mind. Degrees are sought by the students attending the university from early morning hours until late at night. Many students have found it possible to complete a degree while attending either in the morning, afternoon or during the night sessions.

Central State is the oldest institution of higher education in the state of Oklahoma, but the modern 200 acre campus provides comfortable life space conducive to academic pursuits in the more than 100 degree patterns offered on the bachelor's and master's levels.

While Central State is the third largest school in the state of Oklahoma, it hasn't been plagued with the problems that face some of the similar institutions across the nation. Central still maintains small classes in most instances, and instructors are easily accessible. Almost all classes are taught by regular faculty, of which over 50 per cent hold doctors degrees.

Central State is more than just people, buildings and cars; it is the hub of educational activity in Central Oklahoma where pride and progress go hand in hand as they have since before statehood.

CSU was established as the Territorial Normal School by the Territorial Legislature on December 24, 1890. The School was located in Edmond, OK under the following conditions; that Oklahoma County donate $5,000 in bonds; that Edmond donate 40 acres of land within one mile of town, the land to be divided into lots, except for ten acres for the campus; and these lots to be sold for the benefit of the school. Those conditions were met, and the land has long since been reclaimed by the school.

From an institution of twenty-three students in 1891, Central State University has grown to an enrollment of more than 12,800 students and a standard four year university. On April 13, 1971, the institution was officially redesignated "Central State University."

Athletic Director
Charles Murdock

Harry Fritz   **Al Meyer**   **W. C. (Red) Myers**

National Association of Intercollegiate Athletics

Approximately 240 NAIA football teams started 1979 in quest of a national title and the winners of today's two semifinal games will vie next Saturday (December 15) for the 24th NAIA Division I national football championship in the Palm Bowl in McAllen, Texas.

The eight teams that qualified for the NAIA Division I playoffs earned this distinction by their ranking in the final regular-season ratings conducted by the NAIA Football Coaches Association.

On behalf of the Association's more than 500 member institutions we thank those present today for your loyal support and for providing a vehicle for alumni and community involvement on campus while providing a robust and desireable activity for the students.

It is the strong feeling of the NAIA that football, one of 15 national championship events conducted by the Association, is an integral aspect of the total educational program.

HARRY FRITZ
NAIA Executive Director

Only four teams remain in contention for the NAIA Division I national football championship and the NAIA Coaches' Association extends its congratulations to those outstanding group of young men and coaches.

Members of the NAIA Football Coaches Association play an integral role in selection of the teams for the playoffs. Teams are selected on the basis of weekly ratings from the Division I and Division II football rating committees.

The NAIA Coaches' Association is the largest organization of college coaches in the world. This organization has made it possible for coaches to conduct their business on a professional basis and affords the opportunity for leadership within the profession.

AL MEYER
NAIAC President
Mayville State College ND

We offer our sincere congratualtions to the two teams assembled here today for this semifinal round of the NAIA Division I football playoffs.

Sponsorship of this event involves cooperation between college officials and community leaders and is a tribute to the importance of the young people being educated in our great colleges and universities.

The NAIA strives for a well-balanced and comprehensive program of activities — one that meets the needs of its total student population of 950,000 students. Currently, the NAIA conducts 15 national championships in 14 different sports.

We thank those present today for your loyal support in making this post-season game an outstanding athletic competition in the best tradition of American higher education.

W.C. (Red) MYERS
NAIA President
Erskine College SC

Southern Massacre

1979 BLUE HOSE ROSTER

No.	Name	Pos.	Ht.	Wt.	Class	Hometown
1	Chuck Bishop	K	5-11	148	Jr.	Lodge, S.C.
10	Ward Gatlin	QB	6-3	180	Sr.	Conway, S.C.
11	Donald Porter	QB	6-1	186	Jr.	Washington, D.C.
12	Jay Byars	FLK	6-1	172	Sr.	Cayce, S.C.
14	Paul Scott	QB	5-10	180	So.	Chamblee, Ga.
15	James Spence	QB	6-2	185	Jr.	Lexington, S.C.
23	Randy Morris	SE	5-9	143	So.	Marietta, Ga.
24	Jimmy Chupp	QB	6-½	172	Jr.	Doraville, Ga.
25	Lamar Roberts	P	5-11	160	Jr.	Greenwood, S.C.
26	Allan Gaston	DB	5-10	158	Sr.	Carrollton, Ga.
28	Erskine Reed	CB	5-10	185	Sr.	Orangeburg, S.C.
29	Mark Leverette	DB	5-11	170	So.	Simpsonville, S.C.
30	Dean Price	TE-FB	6-2	234	Jr.	Anderson, S.C.
31	Jo Nell	OB	5-9	180	Fr.	Charleston, S.C.
32	Ben Hood	OB	6-½	209	Jr.	Greensboro, Ga.
33	Joe Mooneyham	DB	5-10	177	So.	Pauline, S.C.
34	Heyward Hinton	DB	5-11	199	Jr.	Columbia, S.C.
36	Willie Cooper	DB	5-8	168	Jr.	Gable. S.C.
37	Ricky Kirkpatrick	FS	5-9	160	So.	Milledgeville, Ga.
40	Clayto Burke	OB	5-11	194	Sr.	Macon, Ga.
43	Marty Martin	LB	5-10	185	Fr.	Hopkins, S.C.
44	Mike Owens	DB	5-11	170	So.	Spartanburg, S.C.
46	Walter Atkins	OB	5-11	200	So.	Greenville, S.C.
47	Hal Brannen	DB	6-1	188	Jr.	Unadilla, Ga.
50	Leonard Howard	MG	6-2	219	Sr.	Doraville, Ga.
52	Larry Owens	LB	6-1	205	Jr.	Greenville, S.C.
53	Steve Stalvey	LB	5-10	197	So.	Waycross, Ga.
54	David Wise	LB	6-0	191	Fr.	Columbia, S.C.
55	Robert Hannah	LB	5-11	210	Sr.	Fairburn, Ga.
56	Jarrold Reeves	OG	6-1	204	Jr.	Avondale, Ga.
57	Frank Kube	C	6-0	205	So.	Orlando, Fla.
61	Larry Bridges	LB	6-0	200	Sr.	Greenville, S.C.
63	John D'Andrea	OG	6-0	225	Jr.	Fairburn, Ga.
64	Bruce Ollis	OG	5-11	206	Sr.	Laurinburg, S.C.
66	Barry Taylor	OG	5-11	212	Sr.	Durham, N.C.
67	Mark Wheless	DE	6-1½	205	So.	Clearwater, Fla.
70	Charles Yarborough	OT	6-½	202	So.	Clinton, S.C.
71	Robert Peterson	DT	6-1	218	Jr.	Duluth, Ga.
73	George Martin	DT	6-1	224	So.	Pickens, S.C.
74	Robbie Way	OG	6-3	225	Fr.	Lugoff, S.C.
75	Joe Grant	MG	5-11½	251	Jr.	Charleston, S.C.
76	Gene Harper	OT	6-4½	258	Jr.	Eatonton, Ga.
77	Roy Walker	OT	6-3½	232	Sr.	Clinton, S.C.
78	Chris William	DT	6-2	210	Jr.	Lawrenceville, Ga.
79	Reese Ammons	DT	6-2	230	So.	Darlington, S.C.
80	Jesse Cason	SE	5-9½	155	Jr.	Orlando, Fla.
81	Danny Thornton	TE	6-½	205	Jr.	Washington, Ga.
86	Hugh Bailey	DE	5-11	204	Jr.	Liberty, S.C.
88	Willie Mason	SE	510	158	Jr.	Laurens, S.C.
90	Mark Kay	DT	6-3	255	Sr.	Anderson, S.C.
95	Joe Lane	DE	6-0	187	Jr.	Tallahassee, Fla.
99	Jim McCoun	DE	6-2	209	Sr.	Decatur, Ga.

The 1979 Presbyterian Blue Hose Football Team

Reese Ammons
Walter Atkins
Hal Branner
Larry Bridges
Jay Byars

Jesse Cason
Jimmy Chupp
Willie Cooper
John D'Andrea
Allan Gaston

The Blue Hose Football Squad

 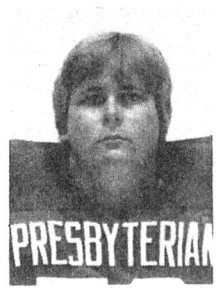   

Ward Gatlin
Gene Harper
Heywood Hinton
Been Hood
Leonard Howard

Mark Kay
Frank Kube
Joe Lane
Jim McCoun
Joe Mooneyham

Joe Nell
Larry Owens
Mike Owens
Donald Porter
Dean Price

Southern Massacre

Erskine Reed
Paul Scott
Jimmy Spence
Steve Stavley
Danny Thornton

Roy Walker
Robbie Way
Chris Williams

The Blue Hose Football Squad

National Association of Intercollegiate Athletics

NAIA-FOOTBALL COACHES ASSOCIATION

President: Don Larson, Illinois Wesleyan University, Bloomington IL
1st Vice President: Joseph Fusco, Westminster College, New Wilmington, PA
2nd Vice President: Thomas Parry, Central Washington University, Ellensburg, WA
3rd Vice President: Forrest Perkins, Wisconsin-Whitewater, Whitewater, WI
4th Vice President: Pat O'Neal, East Central Oklahoma State University, Ada, OK
Past President: Ron Randelman, Pittsburg State University, Pittsburg, KS
Coordinator: Division I: Clark Swisher, Northern State College, Aberdeen, SD
                Division II: Frank Waters, Saginaw Valley State College, University Center, MI
National Staff Liaison: Dr. Charles Morris, NAIA National Office, Kansas City, MO

Area Representatives

Area
1 Bob Shoup California Lutheran College, Thousand Oaks, CA
2 Ernest Hawkins, East Texas State University, Commerce, TX
3 Ted Kessinger, Bethany College, Lindsborg, KS
4 Ken Gibler, Missouri Valley College, Marshall, MO
5 Ralph Carpenter, Henderson State University, Arkadelphia, AR
6 Bill Ramseyer, Wilmington College, Wilmington, OH
7 Jack Huss, Lenoir-Rhyne College, Hickory, NC
8 Denny Creehan, Edinboro State College, Edinboro, PA

WHEN PRESBYTERIAN HAS THE BALL

BLUE HOSE OFFENSE

80 Jesse Cason, 5-9, 155, Jr ....SE
77 Roy Walker, 6-3, 232, Sr ....LT
64 Bruce Ollis, 5-11, 206, Sr ......LG
57 Frank Kube, 6-0, 205, So.........C
66 Barry Taylor, 5-11, 212, Sr ......RG
76 Gene Harper, 6-4, 258, Jr ....RT
81 Danny Thornton, 6-1, 205, Jr ....TE
15 James Spence, 6-2, 185, Jr .....QB
32 Ben Hood, 6-1, 209, Jr..........FB
40 Clayto Burke, 5-11, 194, Sr ......TB
12 Jay Byars, 6-1, 172, Sr. ....FL

BRONCHO DEFENSE

43 Ken Oleson, 6-3, 218, So ....LE
65 Gary Morgan, 6-1, 235, Sr ....LT
55 Ross Dodson, 6-0, 209, Sr ......NG
70 Terry Jones, 6-3, 274, Sr ....RT
45 Jay Jordan, 5-11, 203, Jr ....RE
33 James Bledsoe, 6-0, 231, Sr.....LB
89 Steve Perkins, 6-1, 213, Sr ......LB
16 Robert Hines, 6-0, 192, So ......SS
42 Mike Ciskowski, 6-0, 175, Jr ....WS
81 Danny Washington, 6-3, 199, Sr .CB
35 Sylvester Moore, 6-0, 186, Jr ....CB

PRESBYTERIAN BLUE HOSE DEPTH CHART

Offense

SE	80	Jesse Cason	12	Jay Byars
LT	77	Roy Walker	74	Robbie Way
LG	64	Bruce Ollis	63	John D'Andrea
C	57	Frank Kube	56	Jarrold Reeves
RG	66	Barry Taylor	63	John D'Andrea
RT	76	Gene Harper	74	Robbie Way
TE	81	Danny Thornton	30	Dean Price
QB	15	James Spence	14	Paul Scott
FB	32	Ben Hood	46	Walter Atkins
FL	12	Jay Byars	11	Donald Porter

Defense

LE	99	Jim McCoun	86	Hugh Bailey
LT	78	Chris Williams	79	Reese Ammons
MG	75	Joe Grant	50	Leonard Howard
RT	90	Mark Kay	79	Reese Ammons
RE	86	Hugh Bailey	84	Scott Hosch
LB	53	Steve Stalvey	54	David Wise
LB	61	Larry Bridges	55	Robert Hannah
LC	47	Hal Brennen	44	Mike Owens
RC	34	Heywood Hinton	26	Allan Gaston
FS	36	Willie Cooper	44	Mike Owens
SS	28	Erskine Reed	26	Allan Gaston

KO: 61 Larry Bridges
PAT: 1 Chuck Bishop
Punt: 84 Scott Hosch

Presbyterian	11-1
21 The Citadel	13
17 Furman	10
28 Lenoir-Rhyne	14
21 Wofford	23
21 Catawba	0
30 Elon	14
34 Mars Hill	6
48 Central Florida	0
21 Gardner-Webb	3
34 Carson-Newman	28
16 Newberry	14
36 Saginaw Valley	6

"The official NAIA football for 1979 is the Rawlings R-5, Rawlings Sporting Goods, Col, St. Louis, Missouri"

1979 BRONCHO FOOTBALL ROSTER

No.	Name	Pos.	Ht.	Wt.	Class	Hometown
4	Dannye Webb	DB	5-11	164	Fr.	Ponca City, OK
5	Morie Johnson	LB	6-1	210	Fr.	Anadarko, OK
6	Scott Burger	QB	6-4	215	Jr.	Okla. City, OK (PC West)
8	Johnny Scott	SE	6-2	177	Jr.	Fairfax, OK
10	Doug Shepherd	QB	6-3	210	So.	Tulsa, OK (Mason)
11	Kelley Hudson	FL	6-1	176	Fr.	El Reno, OK
13	Russ Wing	DB	6-1	178	So.	Broken Arrow, OK
16	Robert Hines	DB	6-0	192	So.	Owasso, OK
17	Marshall Goff	TB	5-10	161	So.	Bixby, OK
20	Jeff Jones	FL	5-6	155	Jr.	Crescent, OK
21	Otis McHenry	TB	5-11	166	So.	Haskell, OK
22	Jeff Jordan	DB	5-11	183	Jr.	Okla. City, OK (Southeast)
23	Bennie West	FL	5-7	179	Sr.	Okla. City, OK (Star-Spencer)
25	Steve Tate	TB	6-1	179	Jr.	Luther, OK
30	Lester Knauls	FB	5-11	196	Jr.	Roland, OK
31	Clifford Chatman	FB	6-3	218	Jr.	Clinton, OK
32	Kem Pipkins	DB	6-2	200	Jr.	Okla. City, OK (Millwood)
33	James Bledsoe	LB	6-0	231	Sr.	Choctaw, OK
35	Sylvester Moore	DB	6-0	186	Jr.	Amarillo, TX (Palo Duro)
39	Anthony Swanegan	FB	5-11	179	Fr.	Watonga, OK
40	Juan James	DB	6-2	185	Fr.	Okmulgee, OK
41	Thom Royce	DB	6-2	203	Sr.	Tulsa, OK (Rogers)
42	Mike Ciskowski	DB	6-0	175	Jr.	Medford, OK
43	Kenneth Oleson	DE	6-3	218	So.	Del City, OK
45	Jay Jordan	DE	5-11	203	Jr.	Okla. City, OK (Southeast)
50	Jeff Leader	C	6-1	228	So.	Perryton, TX
51	Raymond Pearce	OG	6-1	240	Sr.	Memphis, TN (Whitehaven)
52	Kirk Condry	C	6-2	242	Sr.	Tulsa, OK (Central)
53	Bill Green	DT	6-0	242	Fr.	Duncan, OK
54	Matt Armstrong	DT	6-4	250	Jr.	Edmond, OK
55	Ross Dodson	NG	6-0	209	Sr.	Stinnett, TX
56	Ken Sutton	LB	6-1	188	Fr.	Duncan, OK
60	Rod Chaney	OG	5-11	250	So.	Tulsa, OK (Edison)
62	Buddy Link	OG	6-2	219	Fr.	Amarillo, TX (Tascosa)
63	Jim Ford	OG	6-2	207	So.	Shawnee, OK
64	Joe Daniel	DE	5-10	204	Fr.	Okla. City, OK (Putnam City)
65	Gary Morgan	DT	6-1	235	Sr.	Duncan, OK
66	Brian Egan	OG	5-10	213	Sr.	Arlington, TX
67	Larkin Ryal	OT	6-1	230	Jr.	Okla. City, OK (John Marshall)
70	Terry Jones	DT	6-3	274	Sr.	Roland, OK
72	Brad Hall	OT	6-9	280	So.	Clinton, OK
74	Rod Davis	OT	6-1	248	Fr.	Okmulgee, OK
75	Larry Whatley	OT	6-3	244	Sr.	Yukon, OK
77	Robert Schwab	DT	6-2	230	Fr.	Okla. City, OK (W. Heights)
80	Bob Campo	TE	6-3	222	Fr.	Yukon, OK
81	Danny Washington	DB	6-3	199	Sr.	Grand Prarie, TX
83	Buck Abington	DE	6-0	190	Fr.	Ponca City, OK
84	Rick Leath	TE	6-3	232	Jr.	Altus, OK
85	Kenneth Howard	DE	6-2	217	Jr.	Okla. City, OK (Douglass)
87	Ron Dumas	TE	6-3	217	So.	Okla. City, OK (John Marshall)
88	Ben Young	TE	6-1	207	Sr.	Ponca City, OK
89	Steve Perkins	LB	6-1	213	Sr.	Tulsa, OK (Mason)

The 1979 Presbyterian Blue Hose Football Team

Buck Abington
Matt Armstrong
James Bledsoe
Scott Burger
Bob Campo

Rod Chaney
Clifford Chatman
Mike Ciskowski
Kirk Condry
Joe Daniel

The Broncho Football Squad

Rod Davis
Ross Dodson
Ron Dumas
Brian Egan
Jim Ford

Bill Green
Marshall Goff
Brad Hall
Robert Hines
Kenneth Howard

Juan James
Jeff Jones
Terry Jones
Jay Jordan
Jeff Jordan

Southern Massacre

Lester Knauls
Jeff Leader
Rick Leath
Buddy Link
Otis McHenry

Sylvester Moore
Gary Morgan
Kenneth Oleson
Raymond Pearce
Steve Perkins

The Broncho Football Squad

Kem Pipkins
Thom Royce
Larkin Ryal
Robert Schwab
Johnny Scott

Doug Shepherd
Ken Sutton
Anthony Swanegan
Steve Tate
Danny Washington

Dannye Webb
Bennie West
Larry Whatley
Russ Wing
Ben Young

The 1979 Presbyterian Blue Hose Football Team

WHEN CENTRAL STATE HAS THE BALL

BRONCHO OFFENSE

8 Johnny Scott, 6-2, 177, Jr. ......SE
67 Larkin Ryal, 6-1, 230, Jr ....ST
66 Brian Egan, 5-10, 213, Sr ....SG
52 Kirk Condry, 6-2, 242, Sr C
51 Raymond Pearce, 6-1, 240, Sr ...TG
75 Larry Whatley, 6-3, 244, Sr ......TT
88 Ben Young, 6-1, 207, Sr ....TE
 6 Scott Burger, 6-4, 215, Jr ....QB
31 Clifford Chatman, 6-3, 218, Jr ...FB
25 Steve Tate, 6-1, 179, Jr ....TB
23 Bennie West, 5-7, 179, Sr ....FL

BLUE HOSE DEFENSE

99 Jim McCoun, 6-2, 209, Sr ....LE
78 Chris Williams, 6-2, 210, Jr ......LT
75 Joe Grant, 5-11, 251, Fr ....MG
90 Mark Kay, 6-3, 255, Sr ....RT
86 Hugh Bailey, 5-11, 204, Jr ......RE
53 Steve Stalvey, 5-10, 197, So .....LB
61 Larry Bridges, 6-0, 200, Sr ......LB
47 Hal Brennen, 6-1, 188, Jr LC
34 Heyward Hinton, 5-11, 199, Jr ...RC
36 Willie Cooper, 5-8, 168, So ......FS
28 Erskine Reed, 5-10, 185, Sr .....SS

CENTRAL STATE BRONCHOS DEPTH CHART

Defense

DE 43	Kenneth Oleson	64	Joe Daniel
DT 70	Terry Jones	60	Ron Chaney
NG 55	Ross Dodson	53	Bill Green
DT 65	Gary Morgan	77	Robert Schwab
DE 45	Jay Jordan	85	Kenneth Howard
LB 33	James Bledsoe	5	Morie Johnson
LB 89	Steve Perkins	56	Ken Sutton
FS 42	Mike Ciskowski	13	Russ Wing
SS 16	Robert Hines	41	Thom Royce
CB 81	Danny Washington	40	Juan Price
CB 35	Sylvester Moore	32	Kem Pipkins

KO: 43 Ken Oleson
PAT: 6 Scott Burger
Punt: 6 Scott Burger

Offense

SE 8	Johnny Scott	20	Jeff Jones
ST 67	Larkin Ryal	74	Rod Davis
SG 66	Brian Egan	63	Jim Ford
C 52	Kirk Condry	50	Jeff Leader
TG 51	Raymond Pearce	62	Buddy Link
TT 75	Larry Whatley	72	Brad Hall
TE 88	Ben Young	84	Rick Leath
QB 6	Scott Burger	10	Doug Shepherd
FB 31	Clifford Chatman	39	Anthony Swanegan
TB 25	Steve Tate	21	Otis McHenry
FL 23	Bennie West	88	Ben Young

Central State   10-1
55 Evangel College 0
28 Southwestern State 0
49 Northwestern State 0
17 East Texas State 6
35 East Central State 28
20 Eastern New Mexico 0
35 Cameron University 14
48 Langston University 6
14 Northeastern State 22
30 Texas Lutheran 0
42 Kearney State 22

OFFICIALS:
Referee: Bill Abington
Field Judge: Bill Cullum
Head Linesman: Pete Musgrave
Umpire: Harold Bartlett
Back Judge: Jerry Hall
Clock Operator: Ed Owens

Game Officials for today's game provided by the Arkansas Intercollegiate
Larry Hall, Commissioner.

Southern Massacre

NAIA Tie Break Plan

If at the end of the fourth quarter, the teams have identical scores, the tie will be resolved in the following manner:
1. NAIA Game Committeeman will designate the end of the field on which the overtime period (s) will be played.
2. The Game Committeeman, the Game Officials, and the respective team captains shall assemble at the 50 yard line following a three minute intermission at the conclusion of the fourth quarter. The referee shall conduct a coin toss and the visiting team captain shall be given the privilege of calling the coin while it is in the air. The winner of the toss shall be given his choice of ball possession or defense for the first overtime period.
3. Each team shall put the ball in play from its opponent's 20 yard line, first down and 10 yards to go.
4. Teams shall alternate possession until the tie is broken following an equal number of possessions.

All Other Official NCAA Football Rules Apply Except:
1. Each team is allowed one (1) timeout for each overtime period. Any unused regulation game timeouts may be taken during any overtime period.
2. The same end of the field will be used for both possessions in order insure equal game conditions for both teams.
3. Each overtime period will include one possession by each team.
4. The loser of the coin toss for the first overtime period shall have the option of ball possession or defense to begin the second overtime period. Should there be additional overtime periods, the choice will be alternated between the teams.
5. There will be a one minute intermission between each overtime period. The team scoring the greater number of points in the overtime period (s) shall be declared the winner. The final score shall be determined by totaling all points scored by each team during the regulation and overtime period (s).

National Association of Intercollegiate Athletics

NAIA FOOTBALL

Established in 1940 as the National Association of Intercollegiate Basketball, the NAIA emanated from a "National Small College Basketball Tournament" inaugurated in 1937.

Football, one of 15 national championship events conducted by the NAIA, became part of the NAIA championship program in 1956. The first two years, only two teams were selected for the championship, but in 1958, the NAIA inaugurated a playoff system to determine which teams would advance to the championship game.

NAIA football teams were lumped together in one division for 13 years — from 1956 to 1969. Division II became a reality in 1970 following a year-long study of the membership and an endorsement by the NAIA Football Coaches Association.

Four teams made up the playoff field in each division until 1978 when the championship series was expanded to include eight teams and went from two weekends and seven playoff games to three weekends and 14 playoff games.

The first championship game was played in 1956 with St. Joseph, Ind. and Montana State battling to an 0-0 tie in the mud in the Aluminum Bowl in Little Rock, Ark. Moving to St. Petersburg, Fla., in 1957 until 1961, the championship game was called the Holiday Bowl. In 1961 the title game moved to Sacramento, Calif., became known as the Camellia Bowl and remained on the West Coast until 1964.

The Champion Bowl became the official name in 1964 and held that title through the 1976 championship game. The last two championship games have been played at neutral sites — Seattle (Apple Bowl, 1977) and McAllen, Tex. (City of Palms Bowl, 1978).

All nine of the Division II championship games have been played at either on-campus sites or nearby locations.

Texas A&I University, holders of the NAIA record for consecutive victories (42) and the longest unbeaten streak (46 games) has captured six of the previous 23 national championship title games.

Westminster PA has won three national titles and Texas Lutheran has taken two crowns since Division II was formed in 1970.

The 1979 Presbyterian Blue Hose Football Team

HEAD FOOTBALL COACHES

Cally Gault
Blue Hose Head Coach

Gary Howard
Broncho Head Coach

Presbyterian College Head Coach Cally Gault is the dean of active South Carolina college coaches. He's now in his 17th season as head coach of the Presbyterian College Blue Hose, and this year guided the team to the school's best regular season record, 10-1, and the No. 1 NAIA national ranking.

A 1948 graduate of Presbyterian College, Coach Gault had an outstanding high school coaching career prior to returning to P.C. as head coach. At North Augusta High School his teams won 88, lost 13 and tied seven. That included three state championships and a four-year undefeated streak of 43 straight games (1954-58).

The 51-year-old coach has been "South Carolina College Coach of The Year" four times and has won the conference honor three times.

Gault is married to the former Joy Godfrey of Clinton, SC, and they have two daughters, Mrs. Stanley (Joy) Gruber and Mrs. Bob (Emmie An) McLean, and a son, Cal, who is a student at the University of South Carolina.

In three short years head football coach Gary Howard has returned Central State to prominence in Oklahoma College football. His first squad finished 5-5-1 after dropping the first five games. His last year's squad lost the opening contest before rolling off seven straight victories and climbing to the number three spot on the NAIA charts.

This year his team has already equalled that mark; the 7-0 mark posted by the Bronchos again have them situated in the number three spot of NAIA national poll.

His coaching experience includes a year at Del City High School, a year at the University of Arkansas and a year at Northeastern A&M Junior College where he helped to guide the Norsemen to a National Junior College Championship.

During his first nine years with the Bronchos he served as an assistant coach and defensive coordinator. This year he works primarily with the offensive line.

Code of Officials Signals

Touchdown or Field Goal

Helping the Runner, or Interlocked Interference

Ball Ready for Play

Grasping Face Mask

Delay of Game

Roughing the Kicker

Ball Dead; If Hand is Moved from Side to Side: Touchback

Illegally Passing or Handling Ball Forward

Incomplete Forward Pass, Penalty Declined, No Play, or No Score

Touching a Forward Pass or Scrimmage Kick

Safety

Non-contact Fouls

Loss of Down

Substitution Infractions

Clipping

Illegal Procedure or Position

Blocking Below the Waist

Offside (Infraction of scrimmage or free kick formation)

Illegal Shift

Player Disqualified

Illegal use of Hands and Arms

Illegal Motion

Personal Foul

First Down

Ineligible Receiver Down Field on Pass

Ball Illegally Touched, Kicked, or Batted

Time out; Referee's Discretionary or Excess Time Out followed with tapping hands on chest.

Forward Pass or Kick Catching Interference

Start the Clock

Intentional Grounding

The 1979 Presbyterian Blue Hose Football Team

The Laurens County Advertiser December 5, 1979

Blue Hose face formidable foe in semis

By SAM REGISTER

Presbyterian will enter the semifinals of the NAIA Division I playoffs Saturday against power-offense based Central State, Okla., a team whose coach describes as looking much like the Blue Hose.

Central State coach Gary Howard said the two teams have similar ability, size, and speed. The Broncos are 10-1 and have outscored their opponents this year 331 to 76. They defeated Kearney State 42-22 in the quarterfinals Saturday at Kearney, Neb. Kearney State was ranked third in the NAIA going into that game.

According to Coach Cally Gault, the Hose are treating Saturday's game the same way they have all season.

"Right now we're getting ready for a football game just like any other," said Gault.

"They are better than Saginaw and I understand they were ranked number one at one time this season. They're a big football team.

"We respect everyone but fear no one," said Gault. "We can get our ears pinned back and vice-versa."

The Broncos return 12 seniors from a team that went 7-3 last season. According to Howard the interior line is the strength of the Central defense, which is composed of 6-3, 274-pound Terry Jones, Gary Morgan

> "We respect everyone but fear no one. We can get our ears pinned back and vice-versa." —Cally Gault

(6-1, 235) and Ross Dodson (6-0, 209). All are seniors.

The offense operates around the junior-oriented backfield. Quarterback Scott Burger, a 6-4, 215-pound junior, has run for 12 touchdowns and 420 yards. He has completed 59 of 121 passes for 1,216 yards and 11 TDs.

The team's leading rusher is fullback Clifford Chapman, a 6-3, 218-pound junior. Chapman has rushed for 892 yards on 177 carries for a 5.0 yards-per-carry average. He has scored seven times. Rounding out the backfield is Steve Tate, who has carried 141 times for 813 yards. The 6-1, 179-pound junior back has scored five touchdowns.

Although Gault is happy about reaching the semifinals, he is not particularly happy that his team has to travel. He seemed to have mixed emotions Saturday following the announcement.

"Yes, I was a bit peeved because I felt we were well prepared," he said. "I feel like if Kearney State had won we would have hosted Central State had already traveled once.

"We were entirely pleased with the cooperation of Laurens and Clinton. These two communities joined together and did a good job of backing us."

Gault's biggest concern is probably Jimmy Spence, who reinjured his knee Saturday against Saginaw but the Blue Hose mentor said that he plans to start Spence this Saturday.

"We'll go with Spence," he said. "But it's good to know you've got another player behind him with experience."

That other player is Paul Scott, who came off the bench as a replacement for the wounded Spence and completed 14 of 15 passes for 168 yards and two touchdowns and was named the offensive player of the game.

"He had been throwing well in practice," said Gault, "but in practice you know who you're throwing against. He was very calm. I was surprised at his passing ability but not that he quarterbacked a good game. Some people can just go in and take over a huddle and that's what he did. He's as at home in the huddle as he is eatin' chitlins with Roy Walker."

The Hose got off to a rather slow start against the Fighting Cardinals Saturday, coughing up a fumble on the second play of the game that resulted in Saginaw's lone score. Gault was admittedly unhappy with that but said it could have also been a blessing. "We were very tight early and I was upset we didn't start off the way I wanted to. But maybe it's good we didn't because at times we have and it's caused us trouble."

The team will be departing from Greenville at 9 p.m. Thursday and will return Sunday. The game, which will be carried on WPCC beginning at 1:30 will be played in Central's 5,000 seat stadium on campus.

Clayto Burke takes a Paul Scott handoff

Burke was named SAC-Eight offensive player of the year last week.

"The Vista," an Oklahoma newpaper predicts a 35-17 win for Central State Oklahoma over the Presbyterian College Blue Hose.

CSU vs. Blue Hose, A Game of Speed

By Tim Chavez
The Vista Sports Editor

It will be speed versus speed this Saturday afternoon at Wantland Stadium when the Central State Bronchos host thte Presbyterian Blue Hose in a semifinal matchup of the NAIA Championship Playoffs.

The South Carolinians bring a No. 1 rating to Edmond and a 10-1 record. The Blue Hose blasted their quarterfinal opponent Saginaw Valley, 36-6, in quarterfinals action.

The Bronchos and Presbyterian look almost like a carbon copy of each other on offense. Both squads like to run to the outside and the two schools possess the speed to accomplish the task. Like Steve Tate, CSU's record breaking tailback, the Blue Hoses also have a talented I-Back with tremendous speed and moves.

At the quarterback position, Presbyterian will feature a signal-caller who has passed for over 1,000 yards on the year. The visitors speed and talent at the quarterback and tailback position could pose problems for the Bronchos.

However, if there is a difference in both squads it might lie in the defense. The strong unit for the Blue Hose is their offense, for the Bronchos both units are solid and strong.

Head coach Gary Howard cited the key to the game would be the ability of the Bronchos to stop the outside Presbyterian offense and its outside game. Offensively for the Bronchos, quarterback Scott Burger said CSU would come out running and pass if the going got difficult on the ground.

When asked whether he preferred the Bronchos run or pass the ball, the coach of the Blue Hose said he would rather have Central State fumble the ball.

Neither the Bronchos or the Blue Hose have played common opponents this season, but the Presbyterian mentor called the Bronchos the best team they've faced this year.

Saturday's semifinal clash should be a high-scoring contest in the first half. However, like they did against Kearney State last week, the CSU defense should come out in the second half and shut the visitors down.

Although they scored 20 first half points last week, the CSU offense still had a little rough going due to the poor footing on the Kearney field. Mother Nature has blessed Edmond with dry and warm weather which will help the CSU offense.

Look for the Bronchos to advance to the NAIA championship game with a 35-17 win over the Presbyterian Blue Hose.

Week 13

#1 Presbyterian College
Blue Hose

6

#4 Central State University
Fighting Cardinals

28

Edmond, Oklahoma
PC Final Record 11-2

December 8, 1979   2:00 PM

NAIA Division 1 Semi Final Championship

Statistics	PC	CSU
First Downs	16	12
Rushes / yards	41 / 57	41 / 231
Passing yards	152	87
Passes	17-36-1	3-10-1
Fumbles / lost	7-4	3-1
Penalties / yards	1-15	13-121
Punts / average	7-34	7-36

Scoring Summary

Q1 CSU .... PC 0 - CSU 7 .... 60 yard drive .... QB Burger 1 yard run .... Burger PAT .... 03:29 remaining

Q2 CSU .... PC 0 - CSU 14 .... 9 yard drive .... QB Burger 5 yard .... Burger PAT .... 8:33 remaining

Q2 CSU .... PC 0 - CSU 20 .... 45 yard drive .... QB Burger 44 yard pass to TE Young .... PAT failed ... 0:48 remaining

Q3 CSU .... PC 0 - CSU 28 .... 41 yard drive .... QB Burger 5 yard run .... RB Chatman 2 pt conversion good .... 12:38 remaining

Q3 PC .... PC 6 - CSU 28 .... 34 yard drive .... QB Spence 11 yard pass to RB Atkins .... 2 pt conversion failed .... 7:33 remaining

Highlights
Presbyterian College Blue Hose vs CSU Bronchos

- Was it nerves? Was it the cold weather? The Presbyterian College Blue Hose simply had a case of the drops. Balls, interceptions, punts and passes were difficult to handle in Edmond, Oklahoma.
- The Presbyterian College Blue Hose fumbled 7 times, turning the ball over 5 times for the game, including one interception.
- Playing from behind was something the Blue Hose was not familiar with.
- In the first quarter, CSU had to punt from deep in their territory. The punt was fumbled resulting in a PC turnover. CSU then went 60 yards in 7 plays to take a 7-0 lead late in the first quarter.
- The next 3 possessions by the Presbyterian College Blue Hose resulted in fumbles. CSU scored in the mid second quarter on a 3 play 9 yard drive. CSU took a 14-0 lead.
- Near the end of the half, with 40 seconds left, CSU had a 4th and 17 at the PC 32. CSU QB Burger went for it all and hit TE Young for a 32 yard touchdown pass. The PAT failed. CSU went to the locker room at halftime with a 20-0 lead.
- With the exception of the last minute touchdown by CSU, PC Head Football Coach Cally Gault was elated by the way the defense played in the first half. The unfortunate ball position the turnovers had caused did not reflect the effort made by the Blue Hose defense.
- Early in the third quarter, CSU drove 41 yards on 4 plays for a 5 yard touchdown by QB Burger. CSU then converted a 2 point conversion to make the score 28-0
- The Presbyterian College Blue Hose defense then shut down the CSU Bronchos for the rest of the game.
- Midway through the third quarter, PC RB Walter Atkins was on the receiving end of an 11 yard pass from QB Jimmy Spence. The 34 yard drive took only 4 plays. The attempted 2 point conversion failed. The resulting 28-6 score prevailed

- There was no scoring in the final 20 minutes of the game.
- The touchdown pass from PC QB Jimmy Spence to PC RB Walter Atkins was the first touchdown scored on CSU on their own home field in 1979.
- Backup Presbyterian College Blue Hose QB Paul Scott started the game. Early in the second quarter, he was hit, resulting in a fumble. "I don't remember anything about the game from that point on." PC QB Jimmy Spence came in and finished the game.
- This was the first game in 2 years that Presbyterian College Blue Hose QB Jimmy Spence had not started.
- CSU QB Burger defined what "Punt, Pass and Kick" was all about, as he did it all.
- PC quarterbacks were sacked 7 times in the game.
- CSU Burger was named the Offensive Player of the Game.
- The NAIA Division 1 Championship (The Palm Bowl) in McAllen Texas will feature the CSU Bronchos (Edmond, OK) versus the Texas A&I Javelinas (Kingsville, TX)
- On December 15, 1979, the Texas A&I Javelinas defeated the CSU Bronchos 20-14 to win their 6th NAIA National Title

THE SUNDAY OKLAHOMAN Sports

SUNDAY, DECEMBER 9, 1979

Burger Fuels Broncho Triumph, 28-6

By Kathy Perovich
Staff Writer

EDMOND — Once Central State made its way into the NAIA playoffs, coach Gary Howard quit paying attention to how the teams were ranked, saying that any squad who had come this far was worthy of No. 1 status.

Saturday afternoon, after CSU quarterback Scott Burger scored three touchdowns himself and threw for one more, propelling the Bronchos past Presbyterian College, 28-6, and into the City of Palms Bowl, the unflappable Howard remained nonchalant about beating the No. 1 ranked team in the nation.

"Of course we're happy about being in the championship game," Howard said. "It's been our goal all year. Being ranked No. 1 in the playoffs doesn't mean anything. The No. 8 team has just as good a chance."

Included in the 5,000 spectators at Wantland Stadium Saturday was Oklahoma governor George Nigh.

Central State will meet Texas A&I next Saturday in McAllen, Texas for the national NAIA championship. The Javelinas defeated Angelo State, 22-19, Saturday night in Kingsville, Texas.

"I feel good about being in the playoffs," Howard said. "I don't care which team we'll be playing."

The CSU defense squeezed the life out of Presbyterian's running game. The team from Clinton, S.C., netted only 57 yards. Tailback Clayto Burke, who was averaging 127 yards a game before Saturday and who is PC's all time leading rusher, ground out 52. The CSU defense knocked the ball loose seven times and then recovered four of those fumbles. Three were scooped up by defensive end Jay Jordan.

Jordan and Burger, who are roommates, were named the outstanding defensive and offensive players of the game.

"Central State has got to be one of the best teams in the country or they wouldn't have beaten us," cracked Presbyterian coach Cally Gault. "We played 1,200 miles from home, and some of our kids had never been on an airplane before."

CSU tight end Ben Young, who caught a 32-yard touchdown pass from Burger while squeezed between two Presbyterian defenders, was leery of Gault's explanation.

"At the first of the game, I was checking them out," Young said. "They didn't seem up to me. Playing right has nothing to do with traveling."

Reserve quarterback Paul Scott started for Presbyterian but was relieved by a wobbly James Spence after Scott showed a tendency to fumble. Spence, who had been the starting quarterback all year, was forced from the last two games with a knee injury. He never moved smoothly Saturday but Gault defended his decision to play Spence.

"He'll (Spence) pull himself out if he can't play," Gault said.

The Bronchos led 20-0 at halftime and while Presbyterian's offense looked livelier in the second half, that 20-point deficit was psychologically as well as physically more than the Blue Hose could rally up against.

Burger's longest pass, a 44-yarder to Johnny Scott, came late in the first quarter and midway through the Bronchos' first scoring drive. CSU started at its own 12 and ran out of downs on the 18. Burger's subsequent punt

See Page 3C, Column 1

Scott Burger gets slammed just after making a pitchout Saturday during Central State's 28-6 playoff victory over Presbyterian College. Burger scored three touchdowns, passed for another and kicked two extra points.

Statistics

Presbyterian
RUSHING

Player	C	Yds.
Clayto Burke	14	57
Ben Hood	6	28
Walter Atkins	5	10
Paul Scott	5	7
James Spence	11	11

PASSING

Player	A	C	Yds.
James Spence	30	14	106
Paul Scott	5	3	46
Donald Porter	1	0	0

PASS RECEIVING

Player	C	Yds.
Jesse Cason	5	48
Clayto Burke	3	26
Denny Thornton	3	26
Donald Porter	3	25
Jay Byars	1	10
Ben Hood	1	7
Walter Atkins	1	11

PUNTING

Player	K	Avg.
Scott Hoech	7	33.6

Central State
RUSHING

Player	C	Yds.
Steve Tote	21	116
Clifford Chatman	20	88
Scott Burger	11	42
Ben Young	1	0

PASSING

Player	A	C	Yds.
Scott Burger	10	3	87

PASS RECEIVING

Player	C	Yds.
Johnny Scott	1	44
Ben Young	1	32
Clifford Chatman	1	11

PUNTING

Player	K	Avg.
Scott Burger	7	35.9

Central State 28
Presbyterian 6

Presbyterian 0 0 6 0 — 6
Central St.   7 13 8 0 — 28

CSU—Scott Burger 1 run (Burger kick)
CSU—Burger 8 run (Burger kick)
CSU—Ben Young 32 pass from Burger (kick failed)
CSU—Burger 6 run (Clifford Chatman run)
PC—Walter Atkins 11 pass from James Spence (run failed)

Game in Figures

Presbyterian		Central State
18	First downs	12
57	Rushing yardage	231
152	Passing yardage	87
17-36	Passes completed	3-10
1	Interceptions by	1
7-34	Punts, average	7-36
4	Fumbles lost	1
5-15	Yards penalized	13-121

The 1979 Presbyterian Blue Hose Football Team

What the hell is a Blue Hose?

Bronchos Win, Hit NAIA Title Game

From Page 1C

proved too slick for PC and Danny Washington recovered the resulting fumble at the CSU 40. Two plays later, Burger's pass to Scott brought the ball down to the Blue Hose 14. Short gainers by tailback Steve Tate and fullback Clifford Chatman took the ball down to the one and Burger stepped in for the score. His PAT at 3:29 put the Bronchos up 7-0.

Jordan's third fumble recovery came in the second quarter at the Blue Hose 10-yard line and set up Burger's second score. An illegal motion penalty against PC and a two-yard loss by Burger pushed the ball back to the 16. Then Burger passed to Chatman at the five, and on the next play used a block by the fullback from Clinton to gain entrance into the end zone. Burger's PAT was good and the Bronchos led 14-0.

CSU's next scoring drive encompassed 56 yards in nine plays. Penalties for holding and delay of game pushed the Bronchos back from the 20 to the PC 32. On third down, Burger threw an incomplete pass intended for Young in the end zone. Then with :48 seconds remaining in the half, he hit Young on the same play for the touchdown. The extra point was wide.

The Bronchos' final touchdown came on their first possession of the second half. A 26-yard punt by Scott Hosch gave CSU the ball on the PC 41. Runs of 10 and 17 yards by Tate and a nine-yard gain by Burger set up Burger's five-yard scoring blast. Chatman ran across the two-point conversion.

Steve Tate led all rushers with 111 yards on 21 carries while Chatman finished with 83 on 20 totes.

Presbyterian's only score came early in the third period, when Spence hit Walter Atkins on an 11-yard touchdown strike, capping an 80-yard, 11 play drive. That drive was kept alive by a fumbled punt by Bennie West on the CSU and a clipping penalty against the Bronchos two plays later put the ball on the 15.

Spence completed 17 passes of 36 attempts for 152 yards. The Bronchos were penalized 121 yards while the Blue Hose were caught once for holding.

The Palm Bowl will be televised Saturday, December 15 at 1:30 p.m and repeated Sunday, December 16, at 12:30 on cable television.

Broncho Defense Earns The Right To Be Noticed

By Rob Wiley
Staff Writer

EDMOND — The Central State University hierarchy put up one sign on one end of Wantland Stadium that said "Welcome Presbyterian College."

Unconfirmed reports said the Central State defensive unit put up the sign on the other end, the one that said "What in Hell is a Blue Hose?"

After 60 minutes of football Saturday, the 5,000 fans in Wantland knew what a Blue Hose was — a highly publicized offensive machine that ran into a Broncho defensive unit hungry for some attention.

When the Central State defenders sent the Hose home, the visitors from North Carolina were definitely blue from a 28-6 defeat, probably black with bruises from the pounding they received and assuredly red from embarassment as the Bronchos advanced to the City of Palms Bowl for the NAIA championship.

The sagging Hose went home for the winter, glad they won't have to face a defense the likes of Central State again this year.

"I think we got 'em down early and that made a lot of difference," said senior end Jay Jordan, named the defensive player of the game by probably the most media to see the Bronchos since their 1972 semifinal loss to East Texas. "They have a good and hard-hitting ball club."

Not quite as hard-hitting as the Bronchos were Saturday, however. Central State caused seven Hose fumbles and recovered four of them, all in the first half when Scott Burger was putting 20 CSU points on the boards. Jordan recovered three of them, the last one leading to Burger's and CSU's second touchdown.

The other one ended up in Danny Washington's grasp and led to Burger's first score.

"I was just lucky to be at the right place at the right time," said the former Southeast all-stater as the teams trudged off the windswept, dyed-green field. "We had to shut 'em down outside and we did."

While Burger and his offensive mates were methodically taking the early lead, Jordan and the defense were acting as if gentlemen truly do prefer Haines. The Blue Hose had romped to an 11-1 record mostly on its offense, which was held under three touchdowns only twice.

Hose tailback Clayto Burke gained 1,518 yards through the year and scored 16 touchdowns. He had 52 yards Saturday and nothing even close to a touchdown.

The only Hose score came courtesy of a Bonnie West fumble on a punt that Dean Price recovered on the CSU 34. It was the first touchdown the Broncho defense has allowed at Wantland all season and kept Central State from its sixth shutout of the year.

"That's all we talked about, getting that shutout," said senior tackle Gary Morgan, who had one of the Bronchos' 10 quarterback sacks. End Ken Oleson, who wasn't even assigned a number in the preseason brochure, had four and Ross Dodson three.

"All year long, nobody has scored on us here, but we're happy to keep them to six," said Morgan. "As long as the offense scores more than they do."

Morgan is one of six seniors on the starting defense, so Saturday was his last day to shine at Wantland. With the chilly wind blowing out of the northeast, however, it didn't take long for his thoughts to turn to palms.

"We're ready, you bet," The Duncan native said. "One more to go. This was the last home game for me, and it made it all worth while. We're all looking forward to getting a suntan."

The Broncho defense was relentless on sophomore Paul Scott, who started for injured James Spence. The Hose's leading passer relieved Scott in the second quarter, but he received the same rough treatment.

"We were looking for them to run that No. 40 (Burke), so we shut him down there at first," said Morgan. "Their quarterback (Spence) had been hurt and I don't think he really wanted to be in there. In the second half he just gave up and threw it up for grabs a lot."

A neutral observer, back judge Jerry Hall from the Arkansas Intercollegiate Conference, perhaps said it best.

"They (Central State) have a hell of a team," he said. "They're as good as the best team in the AIC and have a good shot at the title."

And there probably won't be any signs asking "What in Hell is a Broncho?"

Southern Massacre

The late season turnover trend by the 1979 Presbyterian College Blue Hose caught up with them in Edmond, Oklahoma. If a first half could be replayed, this game was the season candidate.

Although Central State rolled up 28 points against Presbyterian, the Blue Hose defense wasn't lacking

Advertiser SPORTS

Turnovers bury Presbyterian

By SAM REGISTER

Quote 'em

"We haven't had too much trouble with turnovers this year. It's a shame we had to have that kind of trouble today."—CALLY GAULT, Presbyterian football coach, after his team's 28-6 loss in the NAIA playoffs.

"I have nothing to say, and I'm only going to say it once."—FLOYD SMITH, Coach of the Toronto Maple Leafs, after his team was tied by the Edmonton Oilers.

"There are two things not long for this world—dogs that chase cars and pro golfers who chip for pars."—LEE TREVINO.

Coach Cally Gault learned a valuable lesson during his team's trip to the NAIA playoffs: "If you're going to McAllen, Texas, you don't go by way of Oklahoma."

Despite Presbyterian's 28-6 loss to Central State Saturday plus a fever of 101 degrees and a touch of the flu, Gault was his usual silver-tongued self Sunday evening.

"It was one of those games," he said. "It's hard to come back in the second half when you're 20 points down and facing a tough wind—and a tough football team. They didn't beat us as much as we beat ourselves. It wasn't a lack of effort or preparation, it was just one of those days. We can blame it all on our mistakes and their middle guard."

Momentum seemed to be with the Hose at outset of the game when Central State was forced to punt from deep in their own territory. Joe Monneyham attempted to field the punt at the Bronco 40 yard line but the ball slipped through his hands and Central recovered. Quarterback Scott Burger punched it in from the one seven plays later.

On PC's next possession, they moved the ball from their 23 to the Bronco 41. But Paul Scott, who started the game in place of the injured Jimmy Spence, fumbled and Central State's Jay Jordan pounced on the ball, ending the Hose' scoring threat.

Scott again fumbled early in the second period and was relieved by Spence. But on his second play from scrimmage Clayto Burke fumbled a pitch and Burger scored again, this time from the five.

It looked as if the Hose would go to the lockerroom trailing 13-0, but with 48 seconds remaining in the first half, the Broncos were fourth-and-17 from the Presbyterian 32. Burger fired a pass over the middle to Ben Young and he caught it between two Hose defenders in the end zone. That play took PC out of the playoff picture.

"We did not execute well. But it wasn't that as much as we just didn't catch the football," said Gault. "The big thing was we were tight. We haven't even traveled that far and stayed overnight. I'm not blaming it on that, but we seemed to go down a little easier. Or maybe they just had good tacklers."

There were reports that the Presbyterian team was not treated in the most hospitable manner and that Central State was a cocky football team. "The people from Saginaw might have thought we were cocky, I don't know," replied Gault. "When you get in the top four you'd better be cocky because you're good. And they (Central State) had to be good, because they beat a good football team."

Gault, whose team finished the season with an 11-2 mark and won the conference championship and numerous individual awards, said the best thing to come out of the season was the coooperation between Laurens and Clinton. "The way both towns backed our football team was the best thing to come out of the season," he said. "People speak about a breech between the two towns. If there is one, it wasn't noticeable."

He also praised the city of Clinton and some 400 PC students which met the team upon their arrival in Clinton around 11:30 Saturday night. "After we got beat it took a little of our class away, but those people gave it back. They helped us lose with class," he said.

"I'm just sorry it had to end on a losing note," said Gault. "But if I hadn't blown so much smoke, people wouldn't have expected so much. But we reached more than the majority of goals we set."

Statistics

	PC	Central
First downs	13	12
Rushes-yards	41-57	41-231
Passing yards	152	87
Passes	17-36-1	3-10-1
Punts-avg.	7-35.6	7-35.9
Fumbles-lost	7-4	3-1
Penalties-yards	1-15	13-121

Presbyterian 0 0 6 0—6
Central State 7 13 8 0—28
A-5,000 (est.)

Individuals

Rushing, Presbyterian: Burke 14-52, Hood 6-22, Atkins 5-8, Scott 5-(9), Spence 11-(22); Central State: Tate 21-111, Chatman 20-83, Burger 11-40, Young 1- (-3).

Passing, Presbyterian: Spence 14-30-1, 106, Scott 3-5-0 46, Porter 0-1-0 0; Central State: Burger 3-10-1 87.

Receiving, Presbyterian: Cason 5-48, Burke 3-26, Thornton 3-28, Porter 3-25, Byars 1-10, Hood 1-7, ATkins 1-11; Central State: Scott 1-44, Young 1-32, Chatman 1-11.

Over 20,000 buyers read Classifieds weekly! Dial 984-2586

Jimmy Spence unloads against the Broncos
...The junior signal-caller replaced Paul Scott in the second quarter

Notable Quotes Regarding NAIA Semi Final Game

"When you get in the top four, you'd better be cocky, because you're good. And they (Central State Oklahoma) had to be good because they beat a good football team."
    - Presbyterian College Head Football Coach Cally Gault, 1979

"I remember hearing that Erskine Reed, mid-week prior to the Central Oklahoma game, went by Coach Renwicks' office and asked him to borrow the keys to his car. Coach Renwick asked Erskine why he needed his car, and Erskine replied, "Coach, if I leave now (as Erskine had never flown before), I can meet you and the team when you land in Oklahoma."
    - Andy Forrest OG, 2023

"Erskine Reed had never been on a plane flight. When he got on the plane, he walked past my wife and I. We asked him where he was sitting on the plane, and he replied, "I'm sitting in the back Coach. Have you ever heard of a plane backing into a mountain?"
    - Presbyterian College Assistant Coach Wayne Renwick, 2023

"In my defense, I mentioned my concern about flying to someone the week of the game. That story blew up! I do remember arriving on the field in Oklahoma and they had a grass bank where spectators could sit. There was a banner that said, "What the Hell is a Blue Hose?"
    - Erskine Reed CB, 2023

"Central Oklahoma was a feeder school. We were outsized."
    - Leonard Howard MG, 2023

"The cheerleaders drew straws in Greenville Dining Hall as there was not enough room on the plane for all of us. Half of us went on the plane, the other half went on the bus. The game was a battle in Oklahoma."
    - Mitchell Poe Presbyterian College Cheerleader, 2023

"Like all of our games prior to the semifinal game, on defense, we wanted to beat the opponent's best player, as we could demoralize the defense for the rest of the game."
- Presbyterian College Assistant Coach Wayne Renwick, 2023

"There was a cold wind in Oklahoma. The field was the worst field we played on in 1979. The brown grass on the field was painted green."
- Jay Byars WR, 2023

"Joe Mooneyham mishandled a punt. I remember he took it very hard."
- Presbyterian College Assistant Football Coach Bob Strock, 2023

"I remember that Central State Oklahoma was known for their Mortuary Science programs. They were the better team that day."
- John D'Andrea OG, 2023

"I started the game and got hit early. I came out of the game. Jimmy finished the game. That's all that I remember."
- Paul Scott QB, 2023

"The wind was incredible and was a factor. We were the only team to score on their home field in 1979."
- Presbyterian College Assistant Coach Wayne Renwick, 2023

"We haven't had too much trouble with turnovers this year. It's a shame we had to have this kind of trouble today."
- Presbyterian College Head Football Coach Cally Gault, 1979

"The landscape and the way the stadium was situated created an optical illusion for me."
- Jimmy Spence QB, 2023

"We just didn't play as well as we could have played."
- Bruce Ollis OG, 2023

The 1979 Presbyterian Blue Hose Football Team

Presbyterian College Assistant Coach John Perry consoles Captain Bruce Ollis after the Semi Final loss to Central State Oklahoma.

"Central State Oklahoma was a bigger and better team. We lacked emotion. It was the first game I wished I had done a better job in the weight room. It was the first game of my career I tackled a running back three yards in the backfield and he made a one yard gain!"
 - Joe Grant MG, 2023

"The wind was brutal. The size of their team caused us problems."
 - Chris D'Andrea DE, 2023

"The temperature was in the 40's, but with the wind, it felt like it was in the 20's. The field was painted green."
 - Frank Kube C, 2023

"I remember the banquet for both teams on Friday night before the game. A question was asked to Dr. Orr, Presbyterian College President, as to why his wife did not travel to Oklahoma. He replied, "She is going to be at the next game." A Central State Oklahoma player immediately responded yelling out, "There's not going to be a next game!"
 - Jim McCoun DE, 2023

"We were in Oklahoma. One half of the cheerleading squad went on the plane, and the other half traveled by bus."
 - Jane (Bell) Ollis, Presbyterian College Cheerleader, 2023

"Players, parents and students attended the game in Oklahoma at their own expense. When we got on the bus to return home, the coaches knew that we had Coors beer in our suitcases to bring back (Coors was not sold east of the Mississippi River in 1979). We were reminded not to be seen drinking a beer. The bus was quiet, and the sound of cans being opened on the way to the airport could be heard."
 - Chris D'Andrea DE, 2023

"I was humbled at the reception we received at 11:00 PM when we returned to school after our plane trip from Oklahoma. I will never forget the crowd that was waiting for us."
   - Joe Mooneyham DB. 2023

"When we returned from Greenville after our plane trip from Oklahoma, we were tired and wanted to get home. We were greeted in Clinton by students and PC supporters with banners showing appreciation of our season."
   - Leonard Howard MG, 2023

"We were instrumental in providing and organizing a bus for students, parents and Presbyterian College supporters to travel to Oklahoma to see the semifinal football game. It was a long ride. We arrived, saw the game, and immediately returned to South Carolina."
   - Ginger Crocker, 1979 Presbyterian College Admissions Counselor, 2023

"I realized after returning to school and seeing the reception just how much our team was appreciated."
   - Mark Kay DT, 2023

"In Oklahoma we were outmanned and out schemed."
   - David Neisler LB, 2023

"After the quarterfinal win over Saginaw Valley, WSB TV in Atlanta contacted Coach Gault. If Presbyterian hosted the semifinal game, WSB TV wanted to televise the game to the Atlanta metro area. Coach Gault contacted the NAIA, and the NAIA determined that televising the game would be an unfair recruiting advantage for Presbyterian College. In addition, Coach Gault was upset regarding the NAIA's decision to have nationally ranked #1 Presbyterian College going on the road to Edmond, Oklahoma to play Central State Oklahoma."
   - Presbyterian College Assistant Coach Wayne Renwick, 2023

The 1979 Presbyterian College Blue Hose Football Cast of Characters

The 1979 Presbyterian Blue Hose Football Team

Notable Quotes Regarding Presbyterian College

"Presbyterian College gave me the opportunity to extend my football career and it resulted in lifelong friendships."
- David Waldkirch QB, 2023

"Presbyterian College gave me an excellent education."
- Leonard Howard MG, 2023

"Presbyterian College gave me the opportunity to play football in a small community."
- Ricky Kirkpatrick DB, 2023

"Presbyterian College enabled me to study pre-law and continue my football career."
- Jimmy Spence QB, 2023

"Presbyterian College, nothing like a small school experience!"
- Tom Steele TE, 2023

"Presbyterian College is a place I didn't get lost in the crowd."
- Robbie Way OG, 2023

"Presbyterian College was best for me as it was a small school in a small town. Our faculty supporting us in the stands helped make it a family atmosphere."
- Jay Byars WR, 2023

"Presbyterian College experience is the same, year after year."
- Randy Randall Presbyterian College Head Women's Basketball Coach, 2023

"Presbyterian College was the best fit for me. I enjoyed going to PC."
 - Walt Atkins RB, 2023

Presbyterian College Assistant Football Coach Wayne Renwick reunited with the 1979 Bronze Derby football.

Southern Massacre

Blue Hose Coaches

CALLY GAULT
Head Coach
Athletic Director

The dean of active South Carolina college coaches, Calhoun Folk "Cally" Gault, begins his 17th season as Athletic Director and Head Coach at Presbyterian College. Gault has more total years of service at PC than all of the present state college football coaches combined. He also has the distinction of having been selected either state or conference coach of the year in seven of his sixteen years. His 89 wins, 73 losses and 6 ties against the toughest of small college schedules represents the best winning percentage of PC coaches. An 8-2-1 record, a tie for the South Atlantic Conference championship and a high national ranking gave the 1979 Blue Hose team PC's best record in nearly twenty years.

Gault returned to his Alma Mater in 1963 after an outstanding high school record to become the second PC alumnus to serve as Head Football Coach, and just the fourth athletic director in the then 49 years of Blue Hose football. A spirited and exciting team posted a 5-5 record in 1964, and Gault was selected South Carolina "Coach of the Year," an achievement that has been voted him three other times in 1966, 1968, and 1972. In addition, he has been voted Conference Coach of the year in 1969, 1970, and 1977. The three years of 1970, 1971, 1972 established Gault as one of the premier football coaches in the South as PC teams posted 8-3, 8-3, and 7-2-1 records, respectively, over those years. This represented the best three years in the state and the best ever in Blue Hose football.

Presbyterian College was a member of the Carolina Conference for eight years, 1965-1972, sharing the conference championship in 1966, 1968, and 1972, and winning it outright in 1970 which represented another peak in Gault's coaching career as the Blue Hose posted a 5-0 conference mark in clinching the Carolinas Conference crown, the only ever in South Carolina.

Gault was called to his Alma Mater after one of the most success-

COACH STROCK AND WIFE, BETTY

COACH GAULT AND WIFE, JOY

ful coaching stints in S.C., at North Augusta High. While there, he watched his teams win 88 games, lose but 13, and tie 7, including three state championships and a four year undefeated streak of 43 consecutive games (1954-58) which is still a South Carolina record. Gault coached at Mullins, S.C., early in his career, was an assistant at North Augusta before serving in the army and returned there to direct the program until moving to Presbyterian.

A native of Bamberg, S.C., who grew up in Greenville, S.C., Gault received his Bachelor's Degree in History from Presbyterian College in 1948 at the age of 20. As a student, he earned letters in football, basketball and baseball. He ran halfback for three years under S.C. Hall of Famer Coach Lonnie McMillian, the man who introduced T-formation football to the Southeast and the only other alumnus to serve as PC Head Coach. Gault holds a Masters Degree in Education from the University of South Carolina, awarded in 1956.

A highly sought after speaker, the 51 year old coach has given well over 1600 talks in 16 years at high schools, civic clubs, churches, and other affairs.

Gault is married to the former Joy Godfrey of Clinton. They have two daughters, Mrs. Stanley (Joy) Gruber and Mrs. Bob (Emmie An) McLean, and a son, Cal, who is a student at the University of South Carolina.

Gault has always held that PC presents South Carolina's most exciting football and past history shows his claim to be true as the Blue Hose year after year meet one of the nation's toughest small college schedules.

The 1979 Presbyterian Blue Hose Football Team

Blue Hose Coaches

BOB STROCK
Defensive Backfield Coach

Bob Strock, defensive backfield coach and physical education co-ordinator will begin his eleventh season as a member of the Presbyterian College staff. Strock, a native of Hamlet, N.C., received his B.S. degree from Erskine College in 1955 and his M.Ed. from Western Carolina University in 1965.

After his graduation from Erskine, Strock began his high school coaching career which spanned 12 years until he came to Presbyterian in 1969. During eight of those years Coach Strock served as Athletic Director and Head Football coach at the Walterboro (S.C.) High School. At Walterboro Coach Strock experienced only one losing season and in 1968 was chosen as the head coach in The S.C. Coaches Association All Star Game in Columbia. Strock gained recognition as one of the state's leading high school coaches as he led the definite underdog South Team to a 22-14 win.

Strock's first year at Presbyterian was a dismal start as the Hose posted a 5-6 record, but during his ten years as defensive back-field coach he has gained a 58-45-3 record. His defensive secondary teams have produced numerous interceptions each season and has had several members of his team to make the All-district and the All-American honor rolls. His 1977 secondary set a school record of 27 interceptions.

Coach Strock served as head track coach at P.C. for seven years. During that seven-year tenure, his Blue Hose teams won 39 and lost 12 in dual and tri-meet competition. Eight school records were broken while he was coach.

Strock has been active in the Broad St. Methodist Church in Clinton. He has served on the Council of Ministries for a period of six years and has taught in the High School Division Sunday School Class for five years and the Adult Division for three years.

Strock is married to the former Betty Byrd of North Charleston, S.C. and they have a daughter and a son. Coach Strock's favorite hobby is playing tennis.

From left to right, Coach Wayne Renwick, daughter Allison and wife Sherry; Coach John Perry and wife Cindy; Coach Elliott Poss and wife Kathy.

ELLIOTT POSS
Defensive Line Coach

Elliott Poss, a 1971 P.C. graduate, will be starting his fifth season as a member of the Blue Hose coaching staff. Poss comes to Presbyterian from Washington-Wilkes High School where he served in two capacities as both a football coach and an assistant principal.

Poss, who was graduated from Presbyterian with a B.A. in economics and a M.Ed. degree from the University of Ga., will serve as track coach. Coach Poss will also be an instructor in freshmen physical education courses.

In 1970 Coach Poss was selected the Blue Hose captain along with quarterback Allen McNeill. Poss played as a defensive back for three years at Presbyterian and started each year after his freshman year. In his senior year the 30-year-old coach had his best season as he was selected to the All-Carolinas Conference team and the All-District team as defensive back. He received the academic honor as he made the Who's Who list of campus leaders.

After his graduation in 1971 Poss returned to his native town of Washington, Ga. and assumed coaching duties at Washington-Wilkes High School. While an assistant at Washington, Poss watched his team post a 29-13 record. Poss was the assistant in charge of the defensive backs during his tenure at his former high school.

Coach Poss was married in December 1975 to the former Kathy Wallace of Washington, Ga.

JOHN PERRY
Offensive Line Coach

John Perry begins his fifth year as offensive line coach for the Blue Hose. A 1972 graduate of P.C., he came to the athletic department after 2½ years with the admissions office at the college. He began his
(Cont'd. on Page 7)

171

(Cont'd. from Page 6) coaching duties in January 1975.

Perry's duties range from golf coach in the spring months to a physical education instructor in the other months. One of Perry's chief responsibilities will be the job of recruiting future football players for the Blue Hose. Perry gained this most valuable experience while serving as assistant admissions director for the past two years until his appointment to the athletic department staff.

While a student-player at Presbyterian, Perry was a key figure in the development of one of the best football teams in the school's history. In his senior year, the team took a co-championship with Elon in the old Carolinas Conference and he was the team captain for the season. As a player Perry was both an offensive tackle and a defensive middle guard. In the latter position he was chosen to the NAIA All-District Six team. Perry was also president of the P.C. Chapter of the Fellowship of Christian Athletes.

Perry, a native of Eufaula, Ala., is married to the former Cynthia Cauble of Columbia. A member of Broad Street United Methodist Church, his hobbies include tennis, hunting, fishing, camping and hiking.

WAYNE RENWICK
Offensive Back Coach

Wayne Renwick begins his fourth year at P.C. working with the offensive backs and receivers. He came here following three highly successful years at Spring Valley High School in Columbia, S.C. During this time, his teams won three straight AAAA football championships, an accomplishment which has never been duplicated in AAAA football in S.C. while posting an impressive 37-4 record.

Renwick is a 1973 graduate of Presbyterian College and holds a Masters degree from South Carolina State in Guidance and Counseling. While at P.C., Wayne enjoyed four successful years on the football team, the first two years as a place kicker and the last two years as the starting quarterback for the Blue Hose. During his junior and senior years, Wayne was honored by being named to the NAIA All-District Six teams and was selected by the coaches of the Carolinas Conference as the quarterback on the All-Carolinas Conference team both years. His senior year saw Renwick named by his teammates as their captain. Wayne was also honored by the KA fraternity as the Outstanding Athlete for 1973.

The 1977 football campaign produced a new look for the P.C. offense as Renwick along with fellow assistant John Perry incorporated the Veer attack with the 'I' offense to give the Hose its most consistent ground game in years.

Wayne is married to the former Scheryl Croxton of Winnsboro, S.C. and they have a daughter, Allison Michelle.

YOU COULDN'T PICK A BETTER PLACE FOR BANKING.

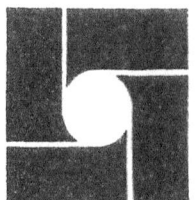

First National Bank of South Carolina

POST OFFICE BOX 210, CLINTON, S. C. 29325

Notable Quotes Regarding the 1979 Presbyterian Coaching Staff

"In 1979, it was an honor and a great learning experience to chart the plays. I love those guys! Coach Renwick loved to repeat successful plays. I would have taken a bullet for Coach Gault."
  - Ronnie Hollier WR, 2023

"Coaches were always thinking ahead. The week of practice prior to the Saginaw Valley game, Coach Renwick made sure I was ready."
  - Paul Scott QB, 2023

"Our coaching staff was our extended family. The Renwick offensive system clicked."
  - Jimmy Spence QB, 2023

"Coach Renwick was ahead of his time and cannot be underestimated. He was always testing plays to see what would work. Coach Gault was a classy individual and big hearted."
  - David Neisler LB, 2023

"Coach Gault was most disciplined. He stressed to not allow the moment to get to the player's heads."
  - Bentley Anderson Athletic Training Staff, 2023

"Coach Gault fired me so many times, then we'd make our peace and he'd rehire me."
  - Presbyterian College Assistant Football Coach Bob Strock, 2019

"The coaches truly loved us."
  - Jim McCoun DE, 2023

"We had motivated coaches. They were better human beings!"
 - Frank Kube C, 2023

"I would eat a brick for Coach Gault. A Cob or rostered player, it did not matter. We were all part of the team. Coach Poss was a genius."
 - Tom Steele DE, 2023

"Coach Gault was the ultimate Ambassador for Presbyterian College."
 - Robbie Way OG, 2023

"Coaches were fun loving. There were no fights or animosity. We all cared about each other which resulted in a special chemistry and a jovial spirit. The coaches had different personalities. Perry was calming, Poss was smart, Renwick was talkative. Gault and Strock let the coaches do their thing!"
 - Andy Forrest OG, 2023

"Coach Gault had such a competitive spirit. He hates to lose. Coach Renwick, if he stayed in the coaching profession, would have been a Division 1 Head Coach."
 - Claude Crocker Captain, 1977 Presbyterian College Football Team, 2023

"Players appreciated the coaches' experience. The coaches wanted to help and wanted to make the team better. Coach Perry loved the game of football. The coaches truly cared."
 - Chip Cross OG, 2023

"There was no discipline prior to the mid 70's. Coaches Poss, Perry and Renwick introduced more team rules with structured days and nights."
 - Bob Peterson DT, 2023

"The Coaches were family. Years later, they still touch base with players. Coach Poss was not only a good coach but was also a good person. Coach Gault was a father figure. His door was always open. The coaches genuinely cared."
- Leonard Howard MG, 2023

"Coach Gault and Coach Strock were joined at the hip."
- John Cann OG, 2023

"Coach Gault told me to call him Cally. I replied that I always thought that his first name was Coach! The team had a family atmosphere. The players and coaches developed a close relationship due to their proximity in age."
- Kathy Poss wife of Assistant Football Coach Elliot Poss, 2023

"The coaches were gracious. They always acknowledged all the student athletes on campus."
- Mitchell Poe Presbyterian College Cheerleader, 2023

"Coach Gault was PC. He still is. When I think of things, I think of people. I don't think of buildings. When I think of PC, I think of Cally Gault."
- Presbyterian College Head Football Coach Tommy Spangler, 2019

"The coaches were like family. I was married while attending PC and all the coaches were at my wedding."
- Hank Mason Athletic Training Staff, 2023

"The coaching staff worked so well together. Coach Gault was a people person. They all loved Presbyterian College! We played hard for the coaches as they worked hard for us."
- Bruce Ollis OG, 2023

"Coach Poss was the finest man I ever met."
- Mark Kay DT, 2023

"Coach Renwick was a smart guy. He trusted me. He provided a lot of energy. I learned a lot from him."
    - Jesse Cason WR, 2023

"Coaches were smart, teaching fundamentals and individual techniques. Both Coach Poss and Strock were creative individuals with attention to detail. Coach Renwick was a master of plagiarizing other teams plays."
    - Joe Mooneyham DB, 2023

"Regarding Coaches Poss, Perry and Renwick, these coaches knew Coach Gault's' philosophy and the PC tradition continued."
    - Presbyterian College Assistant Football Coach Bob Strock, 2023

"Presbyterian College was a special place. Coaches knew how to lead younger men. Other than the immediate family, the PC family is the next closest thing."
    - Jeff South DB, 2023

"The coaches reminded us that we were not the only student athletes on campus and encouraged the football players to support the other student athletes on campus."
    - Ronnie Hollier WR, 2023

"The coaches kept us focused. They were humble and the salt of the earth."
    - Chris D'Andrea DE, 2023

"Coach Poss always had a tremendous game plan. We had tremendous talent in our secondary."
    - Willie Cooper DB, 2023

"The coaches worked their tails off to reward the players with scholarships when and where they could."
    - David Waldkirch QB, 2023

"In retrospect, when looking back at the 1979 team, we had multiple players that could have played in either the Southern Conference, South Carolina or Clemson."
    - Bruce Ollis OG, 2023

"Coach Renwick was a teacher on the field. His offense always included various formations."
    - Jay Byars WR, 2023

"Prior to game day, Coach Renwick and Gault would bring me into an office and challenge me on the opponent's defensive schemes. They would add and subtract situations, sometimes trying to confuse me. They went on and on and would ask me what I would do next. I paused and finally looked at them and said, "Call time out!"
    - Jimmy Spence QB, 2023

"Prior to home games, Coach Renwick would cut and manicure the field."
    - Randy Randall Presbyterian College Head Women's
    Basketball Coach, 2023

Southern Massacre

1979 PRESBYTERIAN COLLEGE ROSTER

NO.	NAME	POS.	HT.	WT.	YR.	LET.	HIGH SCHOOL	HOMETOWN
1	Bishop, Chuck	K	5-11	148	3	1	Andrew Jackson Ac.	Lodge, S.C.
10	Gatlin, Ward	QB	6-3	180	4	0	Conway	Conway, S.C.
11	Porter, Donald	QB	6-1	186	3	1	Eastern	Washington, D.C.
12	Byars, Jay	flk-SE	6-1	172	4	3	Airport	Cayce, S.C.
14	Scott, Paul	QB	5-10	180	2	0	Chamblee	Chamblee, Ga.
15	Spence, James	QB	6-2	185	3	1	Lexington	Lexington, S.C.
16	Cross, Chip	LB	5-11½	195	1	0	McDowell	Marion, N.C.
17	Hollier, Ronnie	QB	6-2	185	2	0	Cardinal Newman	Columbia, S.C.
20	Barker, Mike	OB	5-10	185	2	0	Episcopal	Jacksonville, Fla.
22	Neisler, David	LB	5-11	187	2	0	Oak Ridge	Orlando, Fla.
23	Morris, Randy	SE	5-9	143	2	0	Osborne	Marietta, Ga.
24	Chupp, Jimmy	OB	6-½	172	3	1	Sequoyah	Doraville, Ga.
25	Lamar Roberts	P	5-11	160	3	0	Greenwood	Greenwood, S.C.
26	Gaston, Allan	OB	5-10	158	4	2	Carrollton	Carrollton, Ga.
28	Reed, Erskine	CB	5-10	185	4	2	Wilkinson	Orangeburg, S.C.
29	Leverette, Mark	DB	5-11	170	2	0	Hillcrest	Simpsonville, S.C.
30	Price, Dean	TE-FB	6-2	234	3	1	Hanna	Anderson, S.C.
31	Nell, Jo	OB	5-9	180	1	0	Bishop England	Charleston, S.C.
32	Hood, Ben	OB	6-½	209	3	1	Green County	Greensboro, Ga.
33	Mooneyham, Joe	DB	5-10	177	2	0	Dorman	Pauline, S.C.
34	Hinton, Heyward	DB	5-11	199	3	2	Columbia	Columbia, S.C.
36	Cooper, Willie	DB	5-8	168	3	0	Mayewood	Gable, S.C.
37	Kirkpatrick, Ricky	DB	5-9	149	2	0	Gatewood	Milledgeville, Ga.
40	Burke, Clayto	OB	5-11	194	4	3	Southwest	Macon, Ga.
44	Owens, Mike	DB	5-11	170	2	0	Liberty	Spartanburg, S.C.
45	Fowler, Christopher	DE	5-11	175	1	0	Greer	Greer, S.C.
46	Atkins, Walter	RB	5-11	200	2	1	Southside	Greenville, S.C.
47	Brannen, Hal	DB	6-1	188	3	1	Fullington Ac.	Unadilla, Ga.
50	Howard, Leonard	MG	6-2	219	4	2	Sequoyah	Doraville, Ga.
51	Gallman, Todd	LB	5-11	190	1	0	Gaffney	Gaffney, S.C.
52	Owens, Larry	LB	6-1	205	3	1	Carolina	Greenville, S.C.
53	Stalvey, Steve	LB	5-10	197	2	1	Ware County	Waycross, Ga.
54	Wise, David	LB	6-0	191	1	0	Richland Northeast	Columbia, S.C.
55	Hannah, Robert	LB	5-11	210	4	0	Campbell	Fairburn, Ga.
56	Reeves, Jarrold	OG	6-¾	204	3	0	Avondale	Avondale Estates, Ga.
57	Kube, Frank	C	6-0	205	2	0	Edgewater	Orlando, Fla.
58	Godley, Tommy	MG	5-11	218	2	0	And. Jackson Ac.	Islandton, S.C.
59	Riner, Garland	C	6-2½	222	2	0	Baldwin	Milledgeville, Ga.
60	Bowen, Johnny	OG	5-9	227	2	0	Dodge County	Chester, Ga.
61	Bridges, Larry	LB	6-0	200	4	2	Carolina	Greenville, S.C.
62	Albright, Glenn	OT	6-4	210	1	0	Hardaway	Columbia, S.C.
63	D'Andrea, John	OG	6-0	225	3	1	Westwood	Fairburn, Ga.
64	Ollis, Bruce	DE	5-11	206	4	2	Scotland	Laurinburg, N.C.
65	Forrest, Andy	OG	5-9	182	3	0	Mauldin	Mauldin, S.C.
66	Taylor, Barry	OG	5-11	212	4	2	N. Durham	Durham, N.C.
67	Wheless, Mark	DE	6-1½	205	2	0	Clearwater	Clearwater, Fla.
69	Cann, John	OG	6-1	210	2	0	Chester	Chester, S.C.
70	Yarborough, Charles	OT	6-½	202	2	0	Clinton	Clinton, S.C.
71	Peterson, Robert	DT	6-1	218	3	0	Duluth	Duluth, Ga.
72	Finley, Hank	OT	6-2	220	2	0	Laurens	Laurens, S.C.
73	Martin, George	DT	6-1	224	2	0	Pickens	Pickens, S.C.
74	Way, Robbie	OG	6-3	225	1	0	Lugoff-Elgin	Lugoff, S.C.
75	Grant, Joe	MG	5-11½	251	3	1	James Island	Charleston, S.C.
76	Harper, Gene	OT	6-4½	209	3	1	Gatewood	Eatonton, Ga.
77	Walker, Roy	OT	6-3¼	232	4	3	Clinton	Clinton, S.C.
78	Williams, Chris	DT	6-2	210	3	0	Central Gwinnett	Lawrenceville, Ga.
79	Ammons, Reese	DT	6-2	230	2	0	St. Johns	Darlington, S.C.
80	Cason, Jesse	SE	5-9½	155	3	2	Oak Ridge	Orlando, Fla.
81	Thornton, Danny	TE	6-½	205	3	2	Washington-Wilkes	Washington, Ga.
82	Ingram, Otis	DE	6-0	206	1	0	Dunwoody	Dunwoody, Ga.
83	Reeves, Cliff	TE	6-2	205	2	0	Riverview	Arlington, Ga.
84	Hosch, Scott	DE	6-0	202	1	0	N. Gwinnett	Buford, Ga.
85	Rabun, Dan	DT	6-2	200	2	0	Thomson	Thomson, Ga.
86	Bailey, Hugh	DE	5-11	204	3	0	Liberty	Liberty, S.C.
87	Gruber, Richard	DE	6-0	176	2	0	Dorchester Ac.	St. George, S.C.
88	Mason, Willie	SE	5-9	158	3	1	Laurens	Laurens, S.C.
89	D'Andrea, Chris	DE	6-1	201	2	0	Westwood	Fairburn, Ga.
90	Kay, Mark	DT	6-3	255	4	2	Hanna	Anderson, S.C.
91	Steele, Tommy	TE	6-1	190	2	0	Buford	Lancaster, S.C.
92	Shamrock, Greg	OT	5-11½	187	1	0	Eustes	Eustes, Fla.
93	Addison, Eddie	DT	6-1	223	2	0	Stevens Co.	Toccoa, Ga.
95	Lane, Joseph	DE	6-0	187	3	0	Rikards	Tallahassee, Fla.
99	McCoun, Jim	DE	6-2	209	4	3	Lakeside	Decatur, Ga.

The 1979 Presbyterian Blue Hose Football Team

TRI-CAPTAINS - Coach Cally Gault is shown with 1979 Tri-Captains Bruce Ollis, Roy Walker and Jim McCoun.

Notable Quotes Regarding Team Leadership

"The 1977 leadership by Captains Claude Crocker and Porky (Alan Smith) were instrumental in the 1979 team."
    - Presbyterian College Assistant Football Coach Bob Strock, 2023

"In 1977, we flipped culture. There were rules that every team member had to follow. Players were held accountable. Summer conditioning was stressed and challenged when reporting to campus. The quality of our talent improved. Our methods improved performance on the field and the new culture at PC was accepted."
    - Allan Smith Captain, 1977 Presbyterian College Football Team

"In 1977, there was a buy-in by the whole team regarding a new culture. Allan and I stepped forward. We were sick and tired of losing."
    - Claude Crocker Captain, 1977 Presbyterian College Football Team

"I had played in 4 High School State Championships prior to coming to PC. In 1976, PC only won 3 games. I didn't like to lose. The program momentum began in 1977."
    - Roy Walker, OT, 2023

"Leadership and their roles were demonstrated by both players and Coaches."
    - Bentley Anderson Athletic Trainer, 2023

"The year was a culmination of upper class leadership of what was possible."
    - Jim McCoun DE, 2023

"'We had a core group with Senior Leaders. During the summer prior to the 1979 season, there were letters sent to the players. Summer conditioning

was stressed. The Seniors worked hard."
    - Jay Byars WR, 2023

"Throughout the 1970's, the teams built a tempo and a culture. The 1979 season resulted in a winning culture."
    - Presbyterian College Assistant Football Coach John Perry, 2023

"The leadership of the team came from the Seniors and Captains."
    - John D'Andrea OG, 2023

"When I look back in my second year there was a cultural change in 1977. It was a great change."
    - Erskine Reed CB, 2023

"We had great leadership. The leaders set the tone."
    - Chip Cross OG, 2023

"In both 1978 and 1979, we had outstanding Seniors and Senior Leadership. PC developed a culture of winning."
    - Bob Peterson DT, 2023

"We had 5th year Seniors. The team concept of camaraderie developed. Bruce Ollis was a great leader."
    - Leonard Howard MG, 2023

"The Captains were incredible leaders."
    - John Cann OG, 2023

"The year was very special. Our Senior Leadership was incredibly key. They were a special group of people."
    - Jeff South DB, 2023

"We had an incredible group of leaders."
    - Paul Scott QB, 2023

"The older players were not used to losing as we had come from successful high school programs. The 1978 Seniors and team were the catalyst for the 1979 team. The 1978 team put Presbyterian College football on the map. Winning just happened as the Coaches put no emphasis on anything. There was a loose atmosphere with no pressure to win."
    - Bruce Ollis OG, 2023

"Leadership has a purpose. Jim McCoun was an outstanding leader. Jim led with passion."
    - Tom Steele TE, 2023

"Jim McCoun and Senior Leadership was revered by the players."
    - Chris D'Andrea DE, 2023

"1977 leaders including Alan Smith aided in developing a culture which included good football players on the 1979 team."
    - Randy Randall Presbyterian College Women's Head
      Basketball Coach, 2023

"Our confidence was a result of our strong leadership."
- David Neisler LB, 2023

"We had a strong group of Seniors and Captains."
    - David Waldkirch QB, 2023

"The Captains led by example. They were great leaders. They all demonstrated a high level of character, drive and hard work."
    - Jane (Bell) Ollis, Presbyterian College Cheerleader, 2023

The 1979 Presbyterian Blue Hose Football Team

Walt Atkins RB reunited with 1979 Bronze Derby football.

Southern Massacre

OFFENSIVE LINE---Front row, Frank Kube, Greg Shamrock, Andy Forest, Bruce Ollis, Johnny Bowen, John D'Andrea; Middle row, Charles Yarborough, Barry Taylor, Jarrold Reeves, Larry Owens, John Cann, Danny Thornton; Top row: Dean Price, Tommy Steele, Hank Finley, Gene Harper, Roy Walker, Robbie Way and Rob Hobby (no longer on team).

DEFENSIVE LINEMEN—Front row, Dan Rabun, Hugh Bailey, Joe Grant, Garland Riner, Bob Petersen, George Martin; Middle row, Joe Lane, Eddie Addison, Chris Williams, Jim McCoun, Tommy Godley, Richard Gruber; Top row, Mark Kay, Leonard Howard, Mark Wheless, Reece Simmons, Chris D'Andrea and Scott Hosch.

The 1979 Presbyterian Blue Hose Football Team

OFFENSIVE BACKS---Front row, D. Porter, R. Morris, P. Scott, Jo Nell, J. Byars; Middle row, R. Hollier, M. Barker, J. Cason, C. Burke, W. Atkins, B. Hood; Top row, J. Spence, C. Bishop, J. Chupp and W. Gatlin.

DEFENSIVE BACKS, LINEBACKERS---Front row, David Neisler, Larry Bridges, Steve Stalvey, Chip Cross, Robert Hannah; Middle Row, Ricky Kirkpatrick, Willie Looper, Jeff South, Mike Owens, Joe Mooneyham; Top row, Alan Gaston, Erskine Reed, Hal Brannen, Heyward Hinton, and Mark Leverette.

Southern Massacre

FRESHMEN BACKS—Front row, G. Patton, C. Fowler, C. Hensley, L. Roberts, J. Breazeale, J. Thomas; Middle row, S. Teat, M. Shea, M. Martin, G. Glaspy, L. Buckner, B. McKean; Top row: S. Gonyea, D. Waldkirch, D. Cheek, B. Shaver, R. Bates and R. Maddox.

FRESHMAN LINEMEN—Front row, Asbell (no longer on team), Jerry Goodwin, Jay Finella, Jack Lee, Steve McCall, David Wise; Middle row, Otis Ingram, Hugh McClellan, Neal Barber, Greg Bolton, Todd Gallman, Dillard (no longer on team); Top row, Tim Wilson, John Gates, Glenn Albright and Bill Atkins.

Notable Quotes Regarding The 1979 Team

"We all were very close. There was camaraderie throughout the team and bonds were created that still exist today."
- Ricky Kirkpatrick DB, 2023

"The momentum had been growing since 1976, and we reached the pinnacle in 1979."
- Mitchell Poe Presbyterian College Cheerleader, 2023

"We had a remarkable set of talent on the team."
- Presbyterian College Assistant Coach Wayne Renwick, 2023

"We had a fun time and enjoyed the moment. The team had respect for one another. We loved one another. We had a special type of swag. We were confident and playing to win."
- Walt Atkins RB, 2023

"We had athletes on the team. Many could play different positions. We were a special group. The lines and backs (both offensive and defensive), receivers and special teams developed (lifelong) relationships."
- Jimmy Spence QB, 2023

"There was a great feeling of excitement and togetherness. I was surrounded by great athletes. There was no bickering as we were all friends with each other."
- Hank Mason Athletic Training Staff, 2023

"We had a lot of role players. Everyone had a part. We had no prima donnas."
- Andy Forrest OG, 2023

"We played as a smart team."
    - Jay Byars WR, 2023

"Our structured practices made so much of a difference. We played together and we were family. Our talent was unbelievable."
    - Tom Steele TE, 2023

"There were no egos on the team. All of the players handled football in a professional manner."
    - Bentley Anderson Athletic Training Staff, 2023

"In the 17 years I have been at Presbyterian College, we've always tried to be optimistic. I can say that this year I am more optimistic than I've ever been. Our biggest weakness was that we had a cheerleading squad with six cheerleaders, three blondes and three brunettes, and I've never seen a good cheerleading squad without a redhead. So we got one and now we're fixed up!"
    - Presbyterian College Head Football Coach Cally Gault, 1979

"We played as a seasoned team and stayed healthy."
    - Erskine Reed CB, 2023

"We were a team with no egos. We were good friends with the right chemistry. I liked them all."
    - Jo Nell RB, 2023

"We developed a brotherhood. Our football brotherhood overrode our fraternal bond. We developed a culture of winning."
    - Bob Peterson DT, 2023

"The 1979 season was a fatalist year for Presbyterian College football. It happened for a reason."
    - Leonard Howard MG, 2023

"The team had belief and support in each other. All the players were treated the same. We developed relationships and camaraderie. There were no egos. The talent level was high and there were great expectations at the level of talent on the team."
    - Chip Cross OG, 2023

"We had superstars. Our players jelled and nobody was worried about standing out. Winning just happened."
    - Bruce Ollis OG, 2023

"The starters were well focused, mature and beyond their years."
    - Jeff South DB, 2023

"I saw Clemson play Ohio State in the Orange Bowl, and the Tigers were terrific. With all due respect to the Tigers, if they had two of our players (Heyward Hinton and Erskine Reed), there were two of their defensive backs that wouldn't have started. Our two men are better."
    - Presbyterian College Assistant Football Coach Bob Strock, 1979

"The offense and defense complimented each other throughout the year. Our team was synergistic."
    - Joe Mooneyham DB, 2023

"Looking back, I didn't realize how special we had it."
    - John Cann OG, 2023

"We were an unselfish group. We stuck our nose in the ground and went after it. We became lifelong friends."
    - John D'Andrea OG, 2023

"We had success beyond my wildest dreams. We were a true band of brothers. There wasn't anyone you wouldn't fight for!"
    - Frank Kube C, 2023

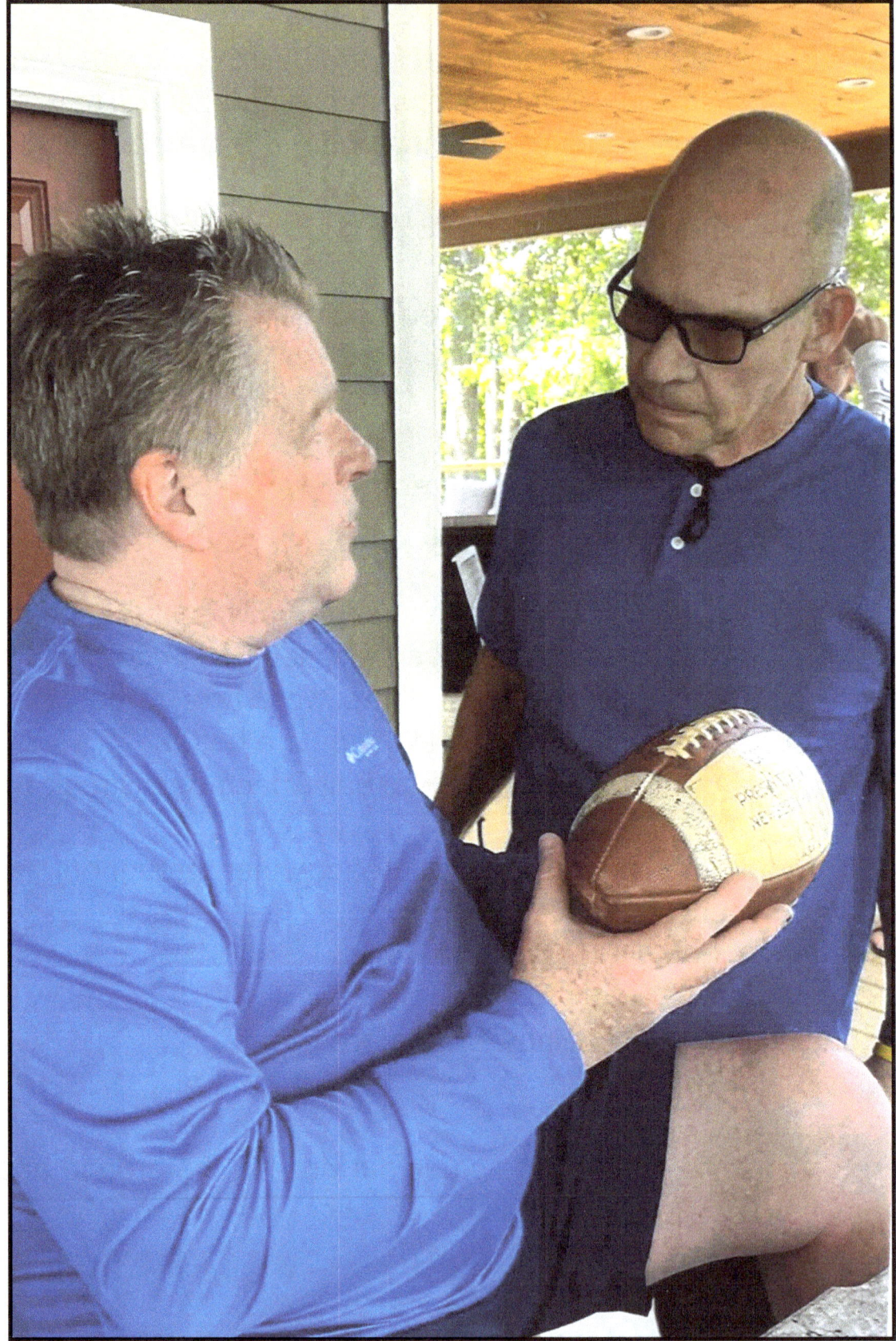
Bob Peterson OT and Bruce Ollis OG reunited with the 1979 Bronze Derby game ball.

The 1979 Presbyterian Blue Hose Football Team

STUDENT ASSISTANTS—Presbyterian College student assistant coaches are, kneeling, left to right, Mark Padgett and Ricky Rentz; standing, Tony Grove and Paul Moye.

MANAGERS, TRAINERS—Standing, left to right, Tommy Wade, Bryon Rucker, Bentley Anderson; kneeling, Reno

Notable Quotes Regarding Athletic Training Staff

"We started our regular season with 22 starters, 11 on offense and 11 on defense. We ended the regular season with the same starters."
    - Presbyterian College Assistant Coach Wayne Renwick, 2023

"Many don't know, but I broke my wrist in The Citadel game. Reno (Wilson) and the staff took care of me throughout the season. Ironically, I had a couple interceptions the next week in the Furman game."
    - Willie Cooper DB, 2023

"You cannot say enough about that group of men. Hank (Mason) had the military discipline within the group, and it worked."
    - Andy Forrest OG, 2023

"If Reno (Wilson) was a woman, I would have married him! He and the staff would check the players not only in the athletic center, but also in the dorms after hours."
    - Frank Kube C, 2023

"The trainers put us in a position to heal. They were a tremendous part of our success. They held us together."
    - David Neisler LB, 2023

"Although I was not hurt and hated to be taped, the staff was very vital to keep us going!"
    - Randy Morris WR, 2023

"I received a call from my daughters' school. She was ill and had to come home. Elliot was on the practice field with the team and I was on the other side of the county. Elliot sent Reno (Wilson) to pick up our daughter. We were all family!"
    - Kathy Poss wife of Assistant Football Coach Elliot Poss, 2023

"Bentley (Anderson) took his job very seriously and it was much appreciated"
	- Jay Byars WR, 2023

"I appreciated Reno (Wilson) and his compassion."
	- Chip Cross OG, 2023

"The staff deserves so much credit!"
	- John D'Andrea OG, 2023

"The training staff was serious and kept us healthy."
	- Erskine Reed CB, 2023

FIELD AND GYM SUPERVISORS--Willie Byrd, left, and Gene Murphy.

P.C. CHEERLEADERS--Leading the cheers for the football Blue Hose this season are, front, alternate Deborah Campbell; kneeling, Dave Torrey, Mitchell Poe, Gerald Martino, co-captain, Steve Odum; standing, Elaine Odum, Jeannie Epting, Carol Fulton, Karen Wessinger, captain, Jane Bell, Gayla McSwain.

1979 Presbyterian College Blue Hose Achievements

Conference, State and National Awards

Wait 'till next year NAIA.

1979 Presbyterian College Football Results

SAC 8 Champions (7-0)
Overall (11-2)

September 8	Presbyterian	21	Citadel	13	Charleston, SC
September 15	Presbyterian	17	Furman	10	Greenville, SC
September 22	Presbyterian	28	Lenoir Rhyne	14	Hickory, NC
September 29	Presbyterian	21	Wofford	23	Clinton, SC
October 6	Presbyterian	21	Catawba	0	Salisbury, NC
October 13	Presbyterian	30	Elon	14	Clinton, SC
October 20	Presbyterian	34	Mars Hill	6	Clinton, SC
October 27	Presbyterian	48	UCF	0	Clinton, SC
November 3	Presbyterian	21	Garner Webb	3	Boiling Springs, NC
November 10	Presbyterian	34	Carson Newman	28	Clinton, SC
November 22	Presbyterian	16	Newberry	14	Newberry, SC

NAIA Quarter Finals

| December 1 | Presbyterian | 38 | Saginaw Valley | 6 | Clinton, SC |

NAIA Semi Finals

| December 8 | Presbyterian | 6 | Central State OK | 28 | Edmond, OK |

1979 SAC 8 Football Standings

School	SAC 8 Record	Overall Record
Presbyterian College	7-0-0	11-2-0
Mars Hill	5-1-0	7-2-1
Carson Newman	4-3-0	6-4-0
Elon	3-4-0	5-5-0
Newberry	3-4-0	5-5-0
Lenoir Rhyne	2-4-0	5-5-0
Catawba	2-5-0	3-8-0
Gardner Webb	1-6-0	4-7-0

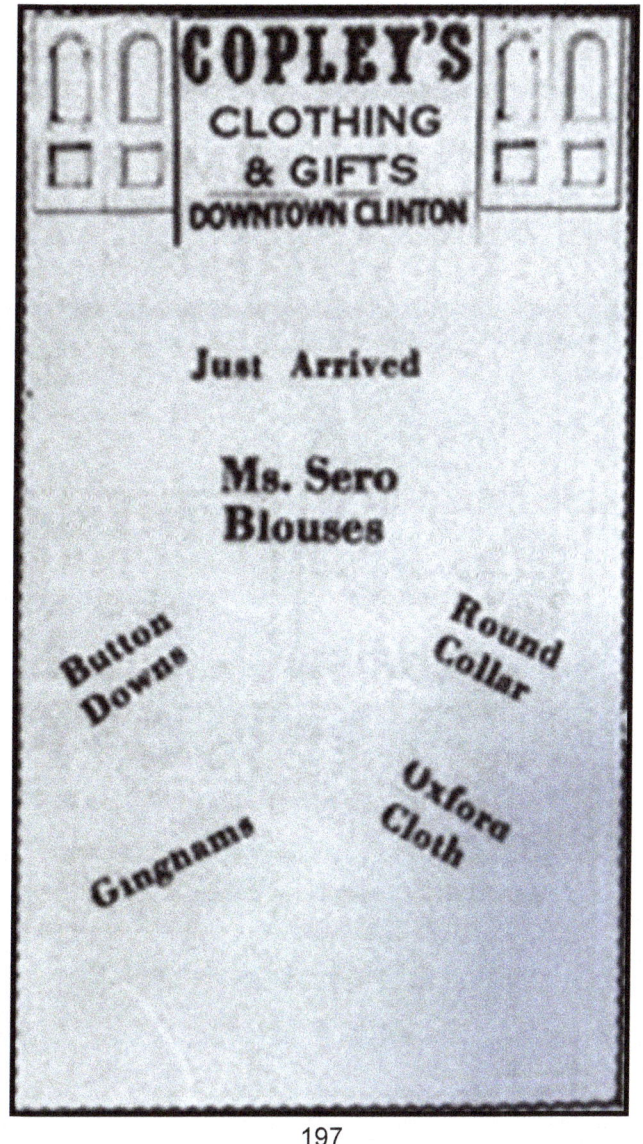

Presbyterian College Blue Hose
1979 NAIA Division 1 Ranking

		W/L	Score	Rank
September 8	The Citadel Bulldogs	W	21 - 13	9
September 15	Furman Paladins	W	17 - 10	6
September 22	Lenoir Rhyne Bears	W	28 - 14	2
September 29	Wofford Terriers	L	21 - 23	13
October 6	Catawba Indians	W	21 - 0	11
October 13	Elon Fightin' Christians	W	30 - 14	8
October 20	Mars Hill Lions	W	34 - 6	6
October 27	UCF Knights	W	48 - 0	6
November 3	Garner Webb Bulldogs	W	21 - 3	2
November 10	Carson Newman Eagles	W	34 - 28	1
November 22	Newberry Indians	W	16 - 14	1
December 1	Saginaw Valley Cardinals	W	38 - 6	1
December 8	Central State Bronchos	L	6 - 28	4

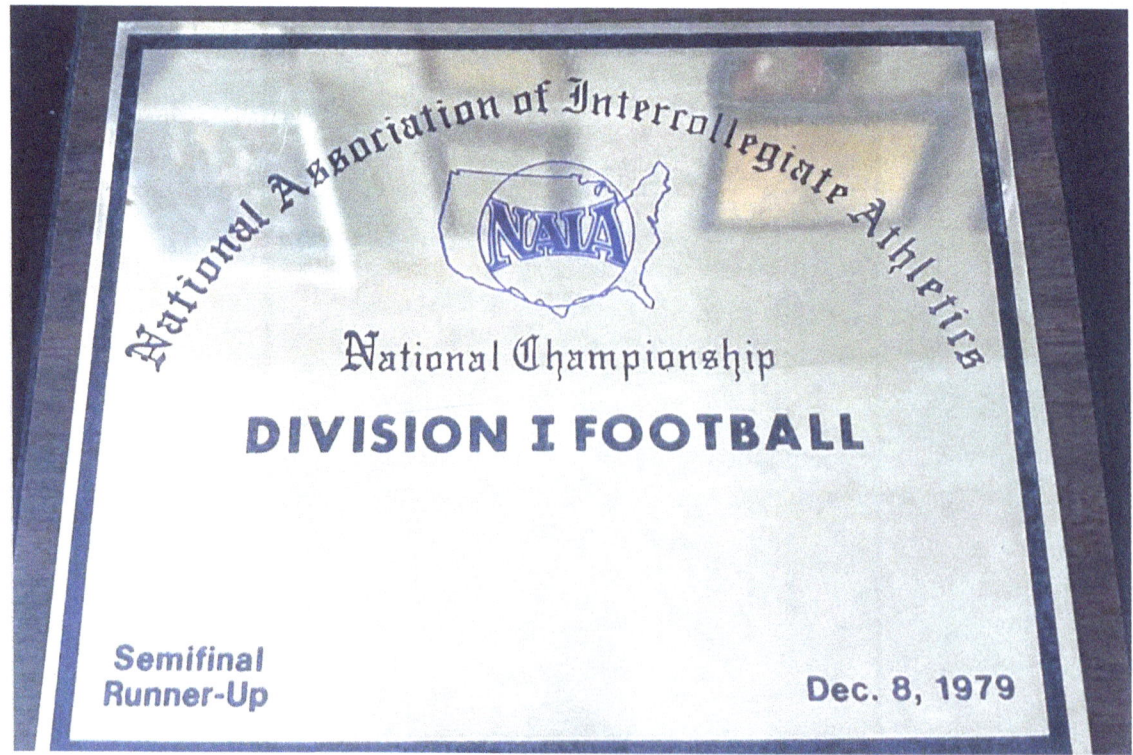

Notable Quotes Regarding National Rankings

"To be #1 in the national rankings was great. We had worked for four years to get to this point."
  - Roy Walker OT, 2023

"We didn't worry about the rankings. We played one game at a time."
  - Presbyterian College Assistant Coach Wayne Renwick, 2023

"When we look back, we were in something big. The rankings were nice, but we stayed focused on our team."
  - Jimmy Spence QB, 2023

"Our ranking was a culmination of what we achieved."
  - Jay Byars WR, 2023

"The ranking didn't change a thing."
  - Robbie Way OG, 2023

"We were excited about our results and did not get big headed."
  - Presbyterian College Assistant Football Coach John Perry, 2023

"The rankings were played down."
  - Leonard Howard MG, 2023

"The rankings were not a big deal. We never talked about chasing a Championship. We kept calm as a team and never got too big for our britches."
  - Joe Grant MG, 2023

"Coach Poss remained stoic. He had a grin on his face and kept the moment to himself."
  - Kathy Poss wife of Assistant Football Coach Elliot Poss, 2023

"The team took the rankings in stride. The team handled their business."
- Bruce Ollis OG, 2023

"The #1 ranking was a treat for the student body. Mr. Powell, Dining Hall manager prepared steaks for the whole campus!"
- Mitchell Poe Presbyterian College Cheerleader, 2023

"We didn't pay much attention to the rankings."
- Joe Mooneyham DB, 2023

"We were reminded that with one loss, we will go from the front page to the back page."
- Chris D'Andrea DE, 2023

"We had a fun time. We were enjoying the moment."
- Walt Atkins RB, 2023

"I was so excited to be on a nationally ranked team. I came from a high school that only won 4 games in 4 seasons. We knew we had work to do."
- Tom Steele TE, 2023

"I took great pride in the #1 ranking."
- Randy Morris WR, 2023

Presbyterian College Blue Hose Football and the 1979 Presbyterian College Blue Hose Football Team By The Numbers

0   Total wins and total points the University of Central Florida Knights have against the Presbyterian College Blue Hose in their 2 meetings in 1979 and 1980.

1   Presbyterian College had the first lighted college football field in the state of South Carolina. During the Cally Gault era, the lights were an integral part of scheduling home games. If Carolina and or Clemson played early on Saturday, PC would play late, resulting in the many night games at Johnson Field in Clinton, South Carolina. Spectators attending early college games could travel to Clinton, South Carolina for another college football game on Saturday evening.

2   1978 and 1979 Kodak All American awards received by Presbyterian College Blue Hose OT Roy Walker.

3   Interceptions by Presbyterian College Blue Hose DB Hal Brennen against Carson Newman on November 10, 1979.

4   Final NAIA Division 1 ranking of the 1979 Presbyterian College Blue Hose football team.

5   Presbyterian College Blue Hose total defensive interceptions against Furman University on September 15, 1979 and Carson Newman on November 10, 1979.

7   Total number of Conference wins on their way to a perfect 7-0 and a 1979 SAC-8 Championship.

8	Total individual interceptions by Presbyterian College Blue Hose DB Heyward Hinton in 1979.
11	In 1979, the most single season wins ever recorded by a Presbyterian College Blue Hose football team.
13	The lowest ranking in the 1979 NAIA Division 1 poll after the loss to Wofford on September 29, 1979. The Presbyterian College Blue Hose were in the top 13 every week of the 1979 season.
21	Length of field goal made by K Chuck Bishop in the closing minute to beat Newberry 16-14 in the Bronze Derby on Thanksgiving Day, November 22, 1979.
22	The total years Cally Gault was Head Coach at his alma mater Presbyterian College (1963-1984). Other Coaches who have been head coach at their alma maters for 20+ years include William Alexander, Georgia Tech (1920-1944); Shrug Jordan, Auburn (1951-1975); Terry Donahue, UCLA (1976-1995) and Frank Beamer, Virginia Tech (1987-2015).
25	Days the Presbyterian College Blue Hose football team was ranked #1 in NAIA Division 1 football in 1979.
31	Total interceptions by the 1979 Presbyterian College Blue Hose defense.
36	Unanswered points scored by the Presbyterian College Blue Hose football team after being down 6-0 to Saginaw Valley in the NAIA Quarterfinals on December 1, 1979.
47	Total individual tackles by Presbyterian College Blue Hose leader LB Steve Stalvey in 1979.

48	Total number of years Presbyterian College legendary Head Coaches Walter Johnson and Cally Gault have at PC for a combined record of 229-200-27.
50	Total number of players, by NAIA rules, that could dress and be eligible to play in Championship games.
59	Total receptions by Presbyterian College Blue Hose WR leader Jesse Cason in 1979.
61	1979 completion percentage that Presbyterian College Blue Hose QB Jimmy Spence threw for the season completing 122 of 203 for 1628 total yards.
66	1979 completion percentage that Presbyterian College Blue Hose QB Jimmy Spence threw for against Southern Conference completing 22 of 32 for 310 total yards.
72	Regular season roster positions for the 1979 Presbyterian College Blue Hose football team.
121	Average rushing yards per game by Presbyterian College Blue Hose RB Clayto Burke.
168	Total passing yardage by QB Paul Scott against Saginaw Valley. Paul went 14 for 15 leading the Blue Hose to a 36-6 win in the NAIA Division 1 Quarterfinals on December 1, 1979.
202	Single game season high rushing yardage by RB Clayto Burke against Catawba on October 6, 1979.
487	Total offensive yards gained against Saginaw Valley in 1979 NAIA quarterfinal game.

900 Total 1979 enrollment at Presbyterian College, compared to 2000 Cadets at The Citadel; 2700 students at Furman; 3700 students at Saginaw Valley and 12,800 students at Central State University in Oklahoma.

1575 Rushing yards gained in 1979 by Presbyterian College Blue Hose RB Clayo Burke.

1917 Coach Walter Johnson and his Presbyterian College football team was the first to beat both Citadel and Furman in the same year compiling a 8-1 record.

1948 The year that Presbyterian Head Coach Lonnie McMillan referred to Memorial Stadium as "Death Valley" as the Presbyterian College Blue Hose football team rarely won in Clemson. Years later, the name stuck with Clemson Head Coach Frank Howard.

1971 Coach Cally Gault beat both Citadel and Furman in the same season for the first time in his Presbyterian College coaching career. The Blue Hose went 8-3 in 1971.

1979 For the Presbyterian College Blue Hose football team, it was the year of the Southern (Conference) Massacre; Victory over SAC 8 1978 co-champion Elon; A NAIA Division 1 #1 ranking; A Bronze Derby win; A SAC 8 Conference Championship; A NAIA Division 1 quarter final winner and culminating with a NAIA Division 1 semi final loss.

The 1979 Presbyterian Blue Hose Football Team

Cally Gault
Head Coach

District 3 Coach of the Year
SAC 8 Coach of the Year
South Carolina Coach of the Year
Kodak Coach of the Year

Presbyterian College Record
Most Wins in Season: 11

from **Presbyterian College Fall Magazine 2019**

by **Presbyterian College**

A Coach of Life
Wayne Renwick '73 & Jimmy Spence '81
Remember Coach Cally Gault '48

"When I was 17 years old, I thought my parents were really dense; by the time I turned 21, I was amazed at how much mom and dad had learned those past four years" is a paraphrase of a quotation often attributed to Mark Twain.

Thinking about Coach Gault is like that saying: sometimes you just didn't understand what he said or why he did what he did until four or, in some cases, 40-plus years later. There have been many fond remembrances of Coach Gault's Yogi Berra-like sayings, all of which are true. But he was also a fierce competitor who realized college athletics was about more than winning and losing.

Wayne Renwick was an outstanding PC quarterback, team captain, and coach for Coach Gault in the 1970s. He has a unique perspective of

Coach Gault. He remembers: "My first opportunity to meet Coach was during recruiting. He had found out about me from his former PC roommate, who was coaching at Clemson. This coach also informed him that my brother had recently lost his life in Vietnam. I share this because our

first interaction centered on how our family was coping with the loss, not football. It was easy to see that he was truly concerned about the loss, and the importance of family was foremost in his life. When it came time to sign my scholarship, he wanted personally to come to meet my parents to offer his condolences and welcome us to the PC family -- truly a great expression of his kindness.

Fortunately, through his mentoring, I became a starter and team captain my senior year. During this time, I grew to understand his commitment to being a team player. Following my first starting effort against Furman, a game which we won, he called me into his office and stated that several news outlets wanted to interview me. He guided me through a few potential questions and asked for my responses. He made sure that the responses would include my teammates and their efforts in the win, not just what I had done. That made another big impression on me. He sat in on each interview and, after the first one, he congratulated me on how the questions were answered; I had passed another one of his life-coaching efforts.

As team captain my senior year, I learned another thing about Coach: He hated having to discipline his players. He stated to each team on many occasions: "When presented with a situation, think how you would respond if your mother was with you." He stated that the team captain was to be a help with discipline, acting as a buffer to handle a problem and present to him the things he needed to handle.

We were fortunate that we had very few problems that had to go to him. If we did, he wanted to know the circumstances and what efforts had been made to correct it. If he was satisfied that it was time for him to get involved, he did, but he took it very personally that the individual had failed to follow his lead -- another life-coaching event.

Three years following graduation, Coach offered me an opportunity to come back to PC to coach with him. What a dream come true! It was mid-summer, and I had let my hair grow longer and had a mustache. He had never seen me like this and stated: "You are hired, but your hair

The 1979 Presbyterian Blue Hose Football Team

growth is fired!" Another life-coaching point: Always look the part of a coach.

Football was changing offensively from the mostly power game that Coach knew so well, to the veer option game with which he was not familiar. It amazed me that he would turn the offense over to two young coaches to transition the offense into a new era at PC, an offense with which he was not familiar. Coach had been so successful with the power game and play-action passing that it could have been a difficult change, but it was not. Several times, he was questioned about why he would change, to which he stated: "I hire good coaches that I have confidence in and step out of their way to let them coach. If I need to step in, I do, but good coaches just need a little direction now and then just as players do! Hire the right people, and enjoy the ride." That brings in the good Coaches: Tiller, Jackson and Strock along with Coach Gault that I was fortunate to be associated with during my playing time.

1979 Football Team Reunion

The 1979 Presbyterian Blue Hose Football Team

Clayto Burke
RB

Single Season Records

Most Plays 360
Most Rushing Yardage 1575
347 Attempts for 4.54 Average
Rushing Yards per Game 121.2
90 Points Scored in 1979

1979 Awards

All District 6
All State
SAC 8 Offensive First Team
SAC 8 Player of the Year
NAIA Division 1 All American

Clayto looks for running room against Newberry

Southern Massacre

Did you know....

1979 Total Rushing Yardage

Charles White (USC, 1979 Heisman Trophy winner)	**2050**
George Rogers (University of South Carolina)	**1681**
Clayto Burke (Presbyterian College)	**1575**
Billy Simms (Oklahoma)	**1506**
Stump Mitchell (The Citadel)	**925**

Notable Quotes Regarding RB Clayto Burke

"I was honored to be part of Clayto's success. In high school, I played both offense and defense. I enjoyed the blocking role for Clayto by laying out those defensive linebackers to the ground."
   - Walt Atkins RB, 2023

"I had to learn a 3 step release. When Clayto's number was called, Clayto would outrun my arm with a five step release. Clayto was an athlete. He was both smart and talented. He was always under control in all good ways. He was my MVP."
   - Jimmy Spence QB, 2023

"Clayto was an animal. He pounded defenses."
   - Joe Mooneyham DB, 2023

"Clayto ran like Jim Brown. He acted so professional and was so coachable."
   - Ronnie Hollier WR, 2023

"Clayto was a tremendous athlete."
   - John Cann OG, 2023

"It was underestimated how good Clayto was."
   - Willie Cooper DB, 2023

"Clayto was both a helluva guy and running back."
   - John D'Andrea OG, 2023

"Clayto was smart. He could tote the mail. He had Earl Campbell thighs."
   - Mark Kay DT, 2023

"Clayto was good, Clayto was cocky, and Clayto was arrogant. Clayto was a great running back."
 - Roy Walker OT, 2023

"Clayto was a great running back. He was solid, strong and tough. He was a good guy."
 - Randy Randall Presbyterian College Women's Head Basketball Coach, 2023

"Clayto was a good leader on the team. He worked his ass off. He focused on his process."
 - Robbie Way OG, 2023

The Presbyterian College 1979 SAC-8 Championship Ring

Roy Walker
OT

**All SAC 8 Defensive Team
All District 6
All State
Kodak All American
Jacobs Blocking Trophy
NAIA Division 1 All American
American Football Coaches Association (AFCA) Honors**

Notable Quotes Regarding OT Roy Walker

"I was on the Cob team. Can you imagine during football season, I would wake up and think, "I have to be on the practice field at 3:00 PM. I had to face Roy every day!" Roy stuck to you like a magnet. He and others would beat the hell out of me every week! I am totally convinced Coach Poss enjoyed watching me get sacrificed daily!"
    - Eddie Addison DT, 2023

"Roy Walker was so mild-mannered off the field with his flip flops. However, once he put on the pads, he was King Kong on the field."
    - Ricky Kirkpatrick DB, 2023

"Roy Walker was a super athlete."
    - Presbyterian College Assistant Football Coach John Perry, 2023

"Roy Walker was a Superman freak. He carried himself so well. With his strength, you could not beat him. He was quick and fast."
    - Jo Nell RB, 2023

"Our gentle giant was Roy Walker."
    - Bentley Anderson Athletic Training Staff, 2023

"Roy had tremendous technique. He was a phenomenal player. The first game we played together at The Citadel I realized what a great player he was. He was my mentor!"
    - Robbie Way OG, 2023

"Roy Walker may have been the greatest offensive lineman to play at Presbyterian College."
    - Hunter Reid, Student PC Sports Information Director, 2023

"In a practice before the Elon game, I blindsided Roy and laid him out. I was afraid during or after practice that Roy may get confrontational. He later spoke to me, and simply said "Good hit!"
- Jeff South DB, 2023

"Roy was a natural player. On Friday nights during football season, we would watch the television show "Night Stalker" late at night. We did not watch the show together on Friday September 28, 1979 and Friday December 7, 1979. We lost to Wofford and Central State Oklahoma respectively on the next day."
- John Cann OG, 2023

"When I came into the huddle for the first time in the Saginaw Valley game after Jimmy went down, I looked up at Roy and he said "Paul, you got this."
- Paul Scott QB, 2023

Jimmy Spence
QB

**All District 6
All SAC 8 Offensive Team
All Conference First Team
NAIA Division 1 All American Honorable Mention**

Notable Quotes Regarding QB Jimmy Spence

"Spence was the difference in the game (Newberry). PC's not the same ballclub when he's not there. Even with the trouble he was having with his knee, he still came up with the big plays when PC needed him. That's something the really good players always do and Spence is one of the best."
- Newberry College Head Football Coach Reed Charpia, 1979

"Jimmy is a very smart man. Jimmy is a brilliant man and very kind hearted. His performance on the last drive of the Newberry game was incredible."
- Jay Byars WR, 2023

"Jimmy had an outstanding work ethic."
- Chip Cross OG, 2023

"Jimmy Spence is a heady, skilled quarterback."
- Furman University Head Football Coach Dick Sheridan, 1979

"Jimmy had great footwork. We were always on the same page."
- Jesse Cason WR, 2023

"Jimmy was a great player and special guy. He was my hero."
- Tom Steele TE, 2023

"Jimmy was an incredible player."
- John Cann OG, 2023

"Jimmy was the oldest 21 year old I ever met. He never lost his cool."
- Jeff South DB, 2023

"It was a tribute to him and the hard work he put in during his rehabilitation." (post The Citadel comment)
- Presbyterian College Head Football Coach Cally Gault, 1979

"Jimmy was a coach on the field. He was unbelievably talented."
- Hunter Reid, Student PC Sports Information Director, 2023

"Jimmy was a great leader that made great decisions."
- Paul Scott QB, 2023

"Jimmy was a brilliant man with an exceptional mind."
- Ronnie Hollier WR, 2023

"What Jimmy Spence did today (against Newberry) was the most courageous thing I've ever seen. A lot of people would have given up, but Jimmy didn't. That's the way everybody on the team is. Everyone is willing to do whatever is necessary to win. That's why we've won 10 games."
- Chuck Bishop K, 1979

"I played against Jimmy in a high school playoff game. Jimmy was an amazing talent."
- Roy Walker OT, 2023

The 1979 Presbyterian Blue Hose Football Team

Jim McCoun
DE

All District 6 Defensive Team
SAC 8 Conference First Team
NAIA Division 1 All American Honorable Mention

Jesse Cason
WR

All State
All SAC 8 Offensive Team
All Conference First Team

Most Career Recptions 122
1977-1979 1424 Total Receiving Yards

Blue Hose split end Jesse Cason battles
Furman's Jeff Burke for one of his six receptions.

The 1979 Presbyterian Blue Hose Football Team

Joe Grant
MG

All SAC 8 Defensive Team
All District 6

Erskine Reed
CB

All SAC 8 Defensive Team
All District 6

The 1979 Presbyterian Blue Hose Football Team

Chuck Bishop
K

All SAC 8 FG Kicker

Best % Field Goals Made
11/15   .733%

Chuck Bishop boots winning field goal to defeat Newberry.

Heyward Hinton
DB

All District 6
All State

Presbyterian's Hayward Hinton picks up a first down against Mars Hill ...after the Blue Hose faked a punt late in the game

Danny Thornton
DE

All District 6

Danny Thornton catches one against Furman.

Gene Harper
OT

All District 6

Paul Scott
QB

"The Saginaw Chainsaw" - Chris D'Andre DE, 2023

On 12/1/79, in the first round of the Division 1 NAIA quarterfinals, in a prepared backup role, Paul completed 14 of 15 passes for 168 yards versus Saginaw Valley. Midway through the first quarter, with the Blue Hose down 6-0, starting quarterback Jimmy Spence was injured. Paul guided the Blue Hose offense with 36 unanswered points against Saginaw Valley to lead the Blue Hose to a 36-6 victory. Prior to entering the game, Paul's collegiate career stats were 2 passing attempts with 1 interception and 4 rushing yards on 2 runs. Paul was recruited by The Citadel and transferred to Presbyterian College after his first semester at The Citadel.

Appalachian Pass versus Saginaw Valley.

Notable Quotes Regarding QB Paul Scott

"So proud of Paul Scott. He prepared and was ready to go when needed against Saginaw Valley."
    - Presbyterian College Assistant Coach Wayne Renwick, 2023

"What can you say? He completed 14 of 15 passes. You can't do much better than that. We knew that he was a good passer. He did a fine job of finding the open man. He didn't sit on it. He started throwing immediately and took advantage of things. He was well prepared."
    - Clayto Burke RB, 1979

"Paul had an incredible performance during the Saginaw Valley game. He displayed confidence and demonstrated it on the field."
    - Chip Cross OG, 2023

"Paul stepped up to the challenge."
    - Joe Mooneyham DB, 2023

"We were so excited about Paul's performance. We talked on the sidelines that he may not throw an incomplete pass. Looking back, Jimmy always looked like Joe Montana, but during the playoff game, Paul looked like Fran Tarkenton!"
    - Tom Steele TE, 2023

"(with a smile) Paul Scott!"
    - Presbyterian College Assistant Football Coach, Bob Strock 2023

"Paul was good! Paul for the Heisman!"
    - Randy Morris WR, 2023

"The most memorable pass I remember in the Saginaw Valley game we had worked on all week in practice prior to the game. It was the only incomplete pass I made. It was a bootleg to Ben Hood that I short-armed. In addition, I tossed a long touchdown pass to Jesse Cason in the game. I remember after the celebration Coach Renwick telling me I could have run!"
  - Paul Scott QB, 2023

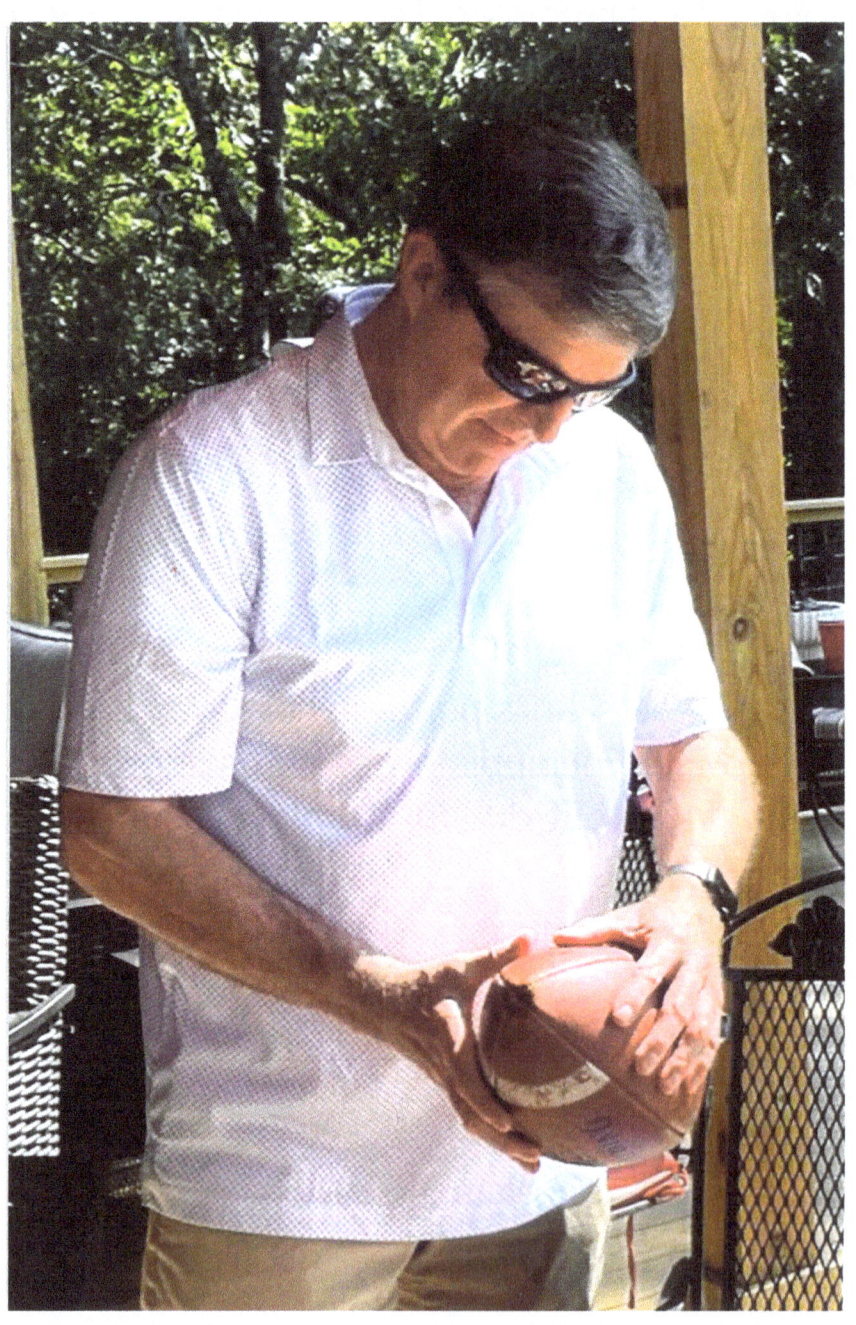

Paul Scott reunited with the 1979 Bronze Derby football.

"Paul was undersized and could run. Saginaw Valley was a good team. We just clicked that day."
 - John D'Andrea OG, 2023

"Paul Scott had poise. You couldn't rattle him. He was nice and easy going, but on the football field was as tough as nails."
 - Robbie Way OG, 2023

Willie Cooper CB sharing a memory of the 1979 season with Chip Porter.

Notable Quotes

"Jay Byars is the greatest blocker in the open field I have ever seen."
- Presbyterian College Assistant Coach Wayne Renwick, 2023

"Donald Porter was a tremendous athlete. We had to find a way to get him on the field."
- Presbyterian College Assistant Coach John Perry, 2023

"Elon was the team to beat in the SAC-8."
- Erskine Reed CB, 2023

"Joe Grant was quick as a cat. He was both a great nose guard and a great athlete."
- Leonard Howard MG, 2023

"Jesse Cason was really fast. He did not like practice, but on game day, when he got on the field, he was a tremendous athlete."
- Chris D'Andrea DE, 2023

"Danny Thornton was an intense player. He was a great ball player with great hands. Steve Stalvey was an amazing athlete. He seemed like he came from another planet. Finally there was Heyward Hinton. He would hit an opposing player and I would actually feel sorry for the guy he hit! When I look back, we had a few players that could have played Division 1 football. They were real special people."
- Tom Steele TE, 2023

"Joy Gault asked me if I could sew. I could, thus I joined Joy weekly and we would repair the jerseys each week for the team."
- Kathy Poss wife of Assistant Football Coach Elliot Poss, 2023

"Joe Grant was an excellent football player. At nose guard, he was like a stump in the mud."
    - Robbie Way OG, 2023

"Coach Perry convinced me to change positions. He told me "Bruce, it takes skill to play OG!"
    - Bruce Ollis OG, 2023

"We called Leonard Howard "Buffalo Big." He was a big guy with big hands and big hair."
    - Joe Nell RB, 2023

"Both Erskine Reed and Willie Cooper were not only great football players and great athletes, but were also good people!"
    - Joe Mooneyham DB, 2023

"I remember Jesse Cason's' Mom was coming up to see him play against the University of Central Florida. Jesse had injured his ankle and he was nervous about the game. I got him a high top shoe to support his ankle and he was most relieved and happy with the fit."
    - Presbyterian College Assistant Football Coach Bob Strock, 2023

"Joe Mooneyham was not only smart in college, but he may be the smartest guy I have ever met in life."
    - Andy Forrest, 2023

"Robbie Way had a great blocking technique."
    - Ronnie Hollier LB, 2023

"(With a smile) We referred to David Niesler as "Nasty!"
    - Presbyterian College Assistant Coach Bob Strock, 2023

"Willie Mason was a hard guy to bring down. Also, to this day, mistakes I made on the field still bother me."
    - Joe Mooneyham DB, 2023

"There were complaints from the nearby stadium neighbors after the UCF game. Remember that we shot a cannon after we scored. We scored 48 points!"
    - Bob Peterson DT, 2023

"Erskine Reed was a grown man playing a boys game!"
    - Andy Forrest OG, 2023

"At half time during the Elon game, I asked Coach Gault if I may address the team. I told them that both their cheeks and buttocks were tight. Before they left that locker room, they needed to get them flapping!"
    - Presbyterian College Assistant Football Coach Bob Strock, 2023

"Danny Thornton was the most underrated player on the team."
    - Hunter Reid, Student PC Sports Information Director, 2023

"Andy Forrest had a big heart. Although he was undersized, he was the first one out of the huddle and always gave it his all."
    - Eddie Addison DT, 2023

"In my era, the chop block was legal. I loved the chop block. I had a high school coach always tell us, "Take the wheels out! No car moves without any wheels!"
    - Roy Walker OT, 2023

Presbyterian College postseason well deserved honors.

The 1979 Presbyterian Blue Hose Football Team

Gault, players receive kudos

Presbyterian coach Cally Gault was named state coach of the year Tuesday by the South Carolina Sportswriter's Association.

Blue Hose offensive guard Roy Walker was elected winner of the Jacobs Blocking Trophy.

In 17 years of coaching, Gault has compiled a 100-75-6 record and this year's Presbyterian team attained a number one ranking in the NAIA. The Hose notched an 11-2 record and earned a trip to the NAIA playoffs where they were defeated in the semifinals.

The 6-4, 230 pound Walker, a Clinton native, is the 51st person to receive the trophy. He has also been named to the Kodak All-American team during the past two years.

Walker was earlier selected to the All-SAC-Eight and NAIA District Six teams. Gault was named the SAC-Eight and NAIA District Six coach of the year.

Five players from Presbyterian were named to the All-South Carolina football team Monday.

Quarterback Jimmy Spence was named on all 44 ballots along with South Carolina's George Rogers. Other Blue Hose named to the team were: receiver Jesse Cason, offensive tackle Roy Walker, running back Clayto Burke, and defensive back Heyward Hinton.

HOW 'BOUT THEM HOSE!

Frank Kube C reunited with the 1979 Bronze Derby football.

Presbyterian College Football
The Best of the Rest.....

1917 ..... 8-1 .... Coach Walter Johnson

1930 ..... 9-1 .... Coach Walter Johnson

1959 ..... 9-2 .... Coach Frank Jones

1978 ..... 8-2-1 ..... Coach Cally Gault

1987 ..... 8-5 .... Coach Elliot Poss

2005 ..... 10-2 .... Coach Tommy Spangler

Southern Massacre

In 1917, the Presbyterian Garnett and Blue boasted an 8-1 record under legendary coach Walter Johnson.

PC 0	Clemson 13
PC 55	Bailey Military Academy 0
PC 7	Citadel 0
PC 7	Wofford 6
PC 7	Guilford 0
PC 19	Erskine 0
PC 14	Furman 7
PC 20	USC 14
PC 20	Newberry 0

In 1917, at the end of the World War I era, Presbyterian managed wins over Furman, Citadel, Newberry and USC.

It was the first year PC had wins over Citadel and Furman.

To Coach Walter A. Johnson the Presbyterian College owes a great deal. He has placed P. C. on the map and given to her the position she holds in the spot light of the athletic stage. In 1915, when Mr. Johnson first came to take charge of athletics, the Presbyterian College was but little known in many parts of the state. In that year he built up a football machine that, for the first time, took the Denominational Championship of the state for P. C. In the same year enviable records were made in basketball and baseball. The next session, under his able guidance, P. C. again captured the Denominational Championship in football and was second in the state in baseball. In 1917, for the third time the Denominational Championship in football was won, as well as second place in the state, Coach Johnson's team being defeated but once while winning eight victories. We are glad that we have known him. As an athlete, as a gentleman, and as a friend he will be long remembered by those who know him.

The 1917 Presbyterian College Garnett and Blue

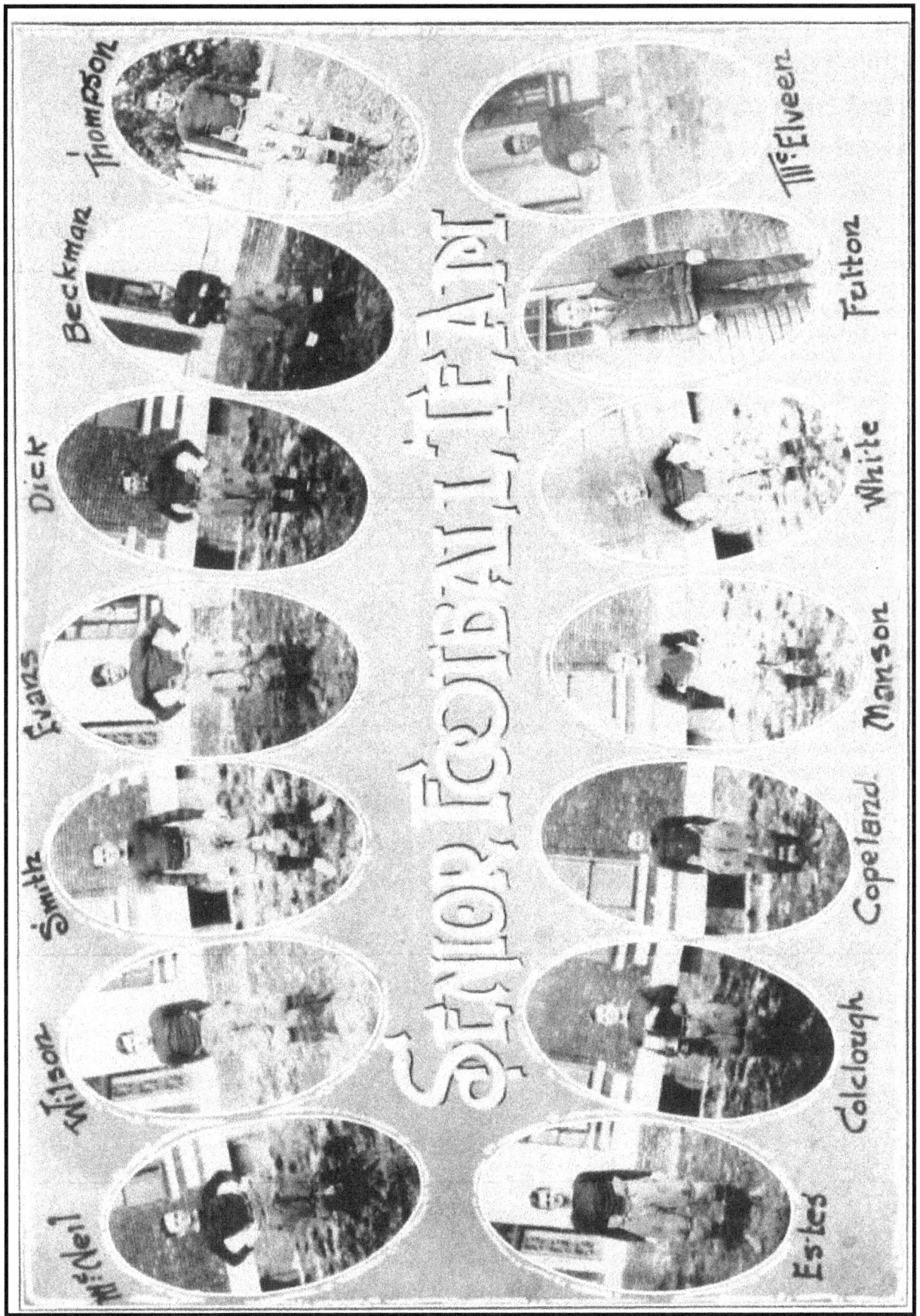

In 1930, Coach Walter Johnson posted a 9-1 record with key wins over NC State, Newberry and the Citadel. PC lost on their opening day to Clemson. PC went on to become the 1930 SIAA (Southern Intercollegiate Athletic Association) Champion. Of interest, during the last seven games of the year, the PC defense did not allow a point.

Coach Walter Johnson was not only a football coach at PC, he was also a basketball coach and administrator. He coached football for PC from 1915-1940. His career record at PC was 102-99-19.

Coach Walter Johnson

The 1979 Presbyterian Blue Hose Football Team

S.I.A.A. Champions 1930

SCORES 1930			SCHEDULE 1931	
P.C.	7	Clemson 28	Sept. 26	Clemson
P.C.	9	Mercer 7	Oct. 3	Lenoir Rhyne
P.C.	7	Chattanooga 6	Oct. 10	Mercer
P.C.	10	High Point 0	Oct. 17	Wofford
P.C.	14	Wofford 0	Oct. 24	Chattanooga
P.C.	6	Citadel 0	Oct. 30	Newberry
P.C.	2	N. C. State 0	Nov. 7	Wake Forest
P.C.	13	Wake Forest 0	Nov. 13	Erskine
P.C.	18	Erskine 0	Nov. 21	Citadel
P.C.	31	Newberry 0	Nov. 28	Pending

THE VARSITY

From The Papers

The Clemson Game

A smashing, crushing team of Clemson footballers vanquished a gallant Blue Stocking team here today by a 28 to 7 score.

Only once was the outlook doubtful, when, in the second period Jimmy Green scored a touchdown after his thirty-yard run to the ten-yard line, and kicked the point to tie the score.

—*Charleston News and Courier.*

The Mercer Game

A fumble in the final period by Walden, Mercer quarter, on his own twelve-yard line gave the game to the visitors. A P.C. player recovered the ball in a wild scramble and O. Dunlap rushed the line for the final yard. This with a safety made by Lobetti, Mercer end, in the third period, when he attempted to punt from his own end zone, counted for Presbyterian's victory.

—*The Greenville News.*

The Chattanooga Game

Presbyterian College from South Carolina, for the second successive Saturday flung a bombshell into the ranks of the S.I.A.A. by defeating Chattanooga here today 7 to 0.

Chattanooga has been champion of the association for two years or more and the light Presbyterians were not regarded as a difficult foe before the battle.

—*The Greenville News.*

The Wofford Game

The Wofford Terrier's big line failed to click in the first half of the Wofford-Presbyterian College game this afternoon and the Presbyterians ran across two touchdowns which with the two points after touchdown gave them the victory by a score of 14 to 0. The second half was a battle between two great lines and the backs on both teams had to take a back seat.

—*The State.*

The High Point Game

Driftwood on a storm churned ocean was no more helpless than the High Point Panthers before the raging Blue Wave of Presbyterian College here this afternoon, when, led by the shadowy Jimmy Green, the Calvinists piled up a 40 to 0 score.

—*The Greenville News.*

The Citadel Game

In the second period, Wilson, Citadel quarter, stepped back into the end zone and punted to his 35-yard line. In four plays, Presbyterian had scored. Three line plays carried the Clinton team to the 28-yard line. It was time to pass, and Dunlap did it, throwing to his right to Captain Lynn, the visitor's fine end, on the goal line.

Presbyterian thoroughly deserved the victory, even though it was unable to do much from scrimmage against a fine Citadel defense.

—*News and Courier.*

The N. C. State Game

Brilliant punting by Jimmy Green, field general of the P.C. eleven kept the Wolfpack backed into its own territory most of the game. Three times Green stepped back for quick kicks on the first down to catch the enemy out of position. It was a quick kick that rolled out of bounds on the 11-yard line that set the stage for the only score of the afternoon.

—*The Greenville News.*

The Wake Forest Game

A well drilled Presbyterian College football team continued its sweep through heavier opposition by handing a 13 to 0 lacing to Wake Forest's vaunted Demon Deacons. Two beautiful field goals from placement off the toe of J. B. Copeland, Presbyterian left end, and a touchdown by Jimmy Green on a short pass from O. Dunlap, provided the winners with their points.

—*The Greenville News.*

The Erskine Game

Both scores of the first half were made by Ritchie on end runs. The speedy P.C. half nearly ruined Erskine several times as he stepped around end for gains, once for the prettiest run of the game for 65 yards to be downed on his own 15-yard line. None of the P.C. interference could keep ahead of him and the Seceder safety man downed him.

—*The State.*

The Newberry Game

Presbyterian College established itself as champion of the S.I.A.A. here today by gaining an easy victory over Newberry 31 to 0.

In the second period, the Blue Stockings uncorked a passing attack which left the Indians gasping. The aerial bombardment netted two more touchdowns. O. Dunlap, P.C. fullback, went over for a marker and Pinson, substitute end, took a toss for another score.

—*The Greenville News.*

In 1959, Coach Frank Jones guided the PC Blue Hose to an overall 9-2 record. The team was crowned the Champion of the South Carolina Little Three Conference made up of PC, Wofford and Newberry. Key wins included East Carolina, Furman, Appalachian State and Newberry. The team was invited and played on January 1, 1960 in the Tangerine Bowl, losing to Ohio Valley Champion Middle Tennessee 21-12.

Coach Jones had a 24-22-3 record in five years at PC. He finished his coaching career at the University of Richmond, compiling an overall coaching record of 68-60-3.

Although Presbyterian Blue Hose lost the 1960 Tangerine Bowl game, Bob Waters of PC was named the games Most Valuable Player. Waters played for the San Francisco 49ers from 1960-1963. From 1966-1968, he was an assistant coach at Presbyterian and Stanford. He is best known for his leadership as Head Coach and Administrator at Western Carolina University from 1969-1988.

BOB WATERS - c-captain, Back-of-the-week in S. C., 1st Team Little Three, Most Valuable Player of Tangerine Bowl, Williamson's 1mid-bracket 1 All-American Honorable Mention, Drafted by San Francisco 49"ers.

In 1978, Coach Cally Gault guided the Presbyterian College Blue Hose to an 8-2-1 record. The team was led by QB Jimmy Spence and OT Roy Walker. Spence was named SAC-8 Player of the Year, and Walker was named as a Kodak All American. The defense only allowed an average of 12 points per game. A 26-0 victory over Newberry in the annual Thanksgiving Day Bronze Derby game highlighted the most successful season at PC since 1959.

PC 13	Mars Hill	10
PC 17	Citadel	28
PC 35	Guilford	0
PC 14	Lenoir Rhyne	7
PC 24	Fort Benning	12
PC 34	Catawba	14
PC 21	Elon	21
PC 12	Wofford	14
PC 10	Garner Webb	3
PC 41	Carson Newman	22
PC 26	Newberry	0

The 1979 Presbyterian Blue Hose Football Team

GAULT SAYS BEST EVER

Complementing a persistent offense with the stingiest defensive unit in the SAC-8 conference, the 1978 Battlin' Blue Hose rolled to an 8-2-1 record and the conference co-championship. Cally Gault's team opened the year with only four returning starters on offense, but, gaining momentum as the season progressed, the offensive unit, led by Kodak All-American tackle Roy Walker and SAC-8 conference "Player of the Year," Jimmy Spence, scored 247 points and piled up 3602 total yards. The defensive squad permitted less than 12 points a game and gave the offense good field position throughout the season.

The Hose opened the year with a contest against conference opponent Mars Hill. PC's victory was the first opening game win for a PC football team in six years. Placekicker Larry Bridges made the difference as his dramatic 32-yard field goal with only 14 seconds left sealed Lion's fate.

Warm sea breezes blew into Citadel's stadium along with nearly half of the PC student body, who had come to cheer the Blue Hose against the Bulldogs. Costly turnovers in the second half, however, spoiled the crowd's expectations and gave the Citadel the victory.

CONFERENCE CHAMPIONS

Back on Blue turf, the Mighty Hose ran rampant over the Catawba Indians to the pleasure of the Youth Day crowd. The next week the Blue Hose charged into Elon Stadium hot for Christian blood, but met with stiff competition from a fired-up Elon squad, but PC salvaged a dramatic tie in the game's closing minutes.

Following a narrow Homecoming victory over Gardner-Webb, PC's offense exploded for five touchdowns against the outmanned Carson Newman Eagles. Presbyterian's efforts were rewarded with a number 15 ranking in the NAIA poll, putting the Hose right on track for their annual clash with Newberry.

Holding a Turkey Day crowd of several thousand vocal rooters, Bailey Stadium provided the setting for the traditional Bronze Derby classic between PC and Newberry. Although the Indians held an emotional edge under first-year coach Reed Charpia, the Blue Hose dominated the contest in every aspect, salting away a share of the conference championship and an 8-2-1 season. Coaches Cally Gault, Bob Strock, John Perry, Elliott Poss, and Wayne Renwick deserved a maximum of praise from all PC fans for their excellent job of directing the Blue Hose to their best record in nearly 20 years.

In 1987, Coach Elliot Poss and the Blue Hose landed in the NAIA playoffs. It was the first year the NAIA playoffs included 16 teams in their format. Placing 2nd in the SAC-8, with a significant win over eventual NAIA national runner-up Carson Newman, the Blue Hose defeated Concord in the first round of the playoffs 41-0. PC lost to Pittsburgh State 42-24 in the NAIA quarterfinals. The 1987 team went 8-5 overall. Coach Elliot Poss compiled a 29-38-1 record as head Coach of the Blue Hose from 1985-1990.

The 1979 Presbyterian Blue Hose Football Team

The Season of Unity

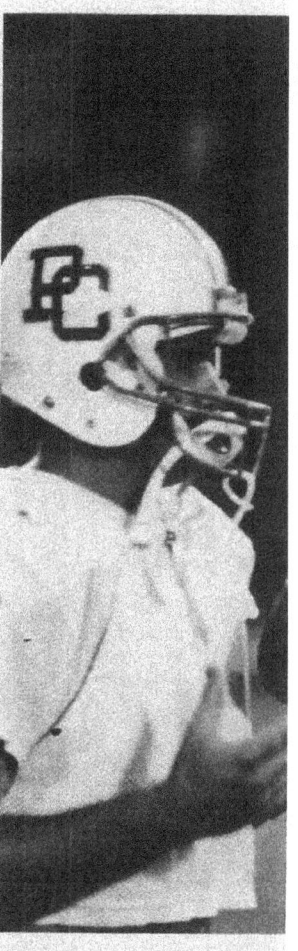

The 1987 Blue Hose football team had yet another successful season under the direction of Head Coach Elliott Poss and his talented coaching staff. As important as such coaches as Jeff Burke, Bruce Hill, Mike Lindley, Gary Nelson, and Bill Shaver were to the 8-5 overall season that Presbyterian had, there was not one person who did all the work. According to Coach Poss, "No individual has caused any of our success; it has all been a team effort." And it was this team unity, this ability to "hang together" that propelled the 1987 team to an NAIA postseason match-up against Pittsburgh State.

But before they played the Gorillas of Pittsburgh State, they had to manuever their way through a tough regular season against such teams as Newberry, Gardner-Webb, and Carson Newman. Two of the toughest games came early in the season with disappointing losses to Furman and Citadel. Coach Poss, however, clarified such losses by explaining that PC's schedule is "the toughest in the conference."

> "We play as a unit and not as individuals."

Their success-filled season did not, however, come naturally to the 95 players of the football squad: they had to put in long and exhausting practice hours to reach the playoffs. All members of the team practiced three hours a day for four days during the week. And then there was the developmental weight-training regimen that the Blue Hose coaches employed both in the fall and also earlier in the spring. Further methods to hone the players' conditionings and their speeds also included a running program during practice.

But above all else, the coaches and the players relied on their unity, their abilities to merge their unique talents to form a victorious team. Stevie Riggins summarized the attitudes of all the Blue Hose well when he said, "We play as a unit and not as individuals." Unity . . . PC's key to victory.

Southern Massacre

Men's Football: Front Row: **Wade Cooke, Scott Barefield, Richard Hilton, Billy Egan, Thomas Fair, Brad Moser, Kevin Calwile, Greg Kinsey, Lavern Reddick, Darren Murray, Jule Rembert, Chris Thompson.** Second Row: **Bobby Sheridan, Glenn Jackson, Tim Pitts, Andy Hamilton, David Kirkland, Eddie Gray, Nelson Jones, Benjie Crabtree, Bill Hiesl, Billy Kinard, Scotty Mozingo, Bobby Jones, Sam Picnkney.** Third Row: **Tommie Netting, Thomas Bates, Brian Thomas, Todd Wilder, David Smith, Gary Nelson, Jeff Burke, Elliott Poss, Bruce Hill, Mike Lindley, Bill Shaver, Todd Stanley, Robert Daughtry, Ron Hanrick, Doug Hinson.** Fourth Row: **Alan Rodemaker, Brett Garvin, Billy Cannon, Wrapper Kellett, Andy Smyth, Mike Bolchoz, Andy Crumpton, Derrick Smalls, Evander Gerald, Mike Leslie, Chuck Armstrong, Ed Healy, Kent Haltiwanger, Craig Segars, Mark Razzano.** Fifth Row: **Benny Allen, Chip Neal, Eddie Rogers, Howard McMichael, Eric Brown, Chris Wingo, Rod Fountain, Tyrone Lucas, Kevin Wade, Bobby Bentley, Telford Holmes, Andy King.** Sixth Row: **Todd Droze, Harold Nichols, Jason Alderman, Jeff Alligood, Steve Parsley, Rodney Williams, Stevie Riggins, Derrick Sessians, Jeff Benfield, Tommy Wells, Tommy Quinn, Jeff Shaffer, John Terrapin, Scott Segars.** Seventh Row: **Dean Richburg, Bill Chambers, Skipper Strickland, Will Duncan, Brad Roberts, Dean Balson, Keith McGriff, Stacey Shaw, Troy Stone, Marc Temples, Mike Herrington, Matthew Maxwell, Michael Speaks.** Back Row: **John Gentry, Johnny Clark, Michael Durant, Andrew Bishop, Christian Wolf, Kelly Andreucci, Brian Smith, DeNorris Heard, Andrew Lewis, Keith Bardolf, Bill Robb, Tony Messer, Lewis Burton, Darrin McGlamary.**

Men's Football		
Home	Game	Opponent
24	Davidson	7
3	Furman	23
12	Citadel	27
14	Lenoir-Rhyne	3
38	Wofford	15
31	Catawba	8
17	Elon	7
19	Mars Hill	7
26	Gardner Webb	27
28	Carson Newman	8
15	Newberry	17
41	Concord	0
21	Pittsburgh St.	42
Season record (8-5)		

In 2005, The Presbyterian College Blue Hose team led by Head Coach Tommy Spangler won the SAC-8 Championship with a 7-0 record. The only regular season loss came to longtime rival Elon. PC earned a first round bye in the NCAA Division II playoffs. In the quarter finals, the Blue Hose were defeated by Central Arkansas 52-28. Tommy Spangler, as a Head Coach for 10 years with Presbyterian College had an overall record of 54-52.

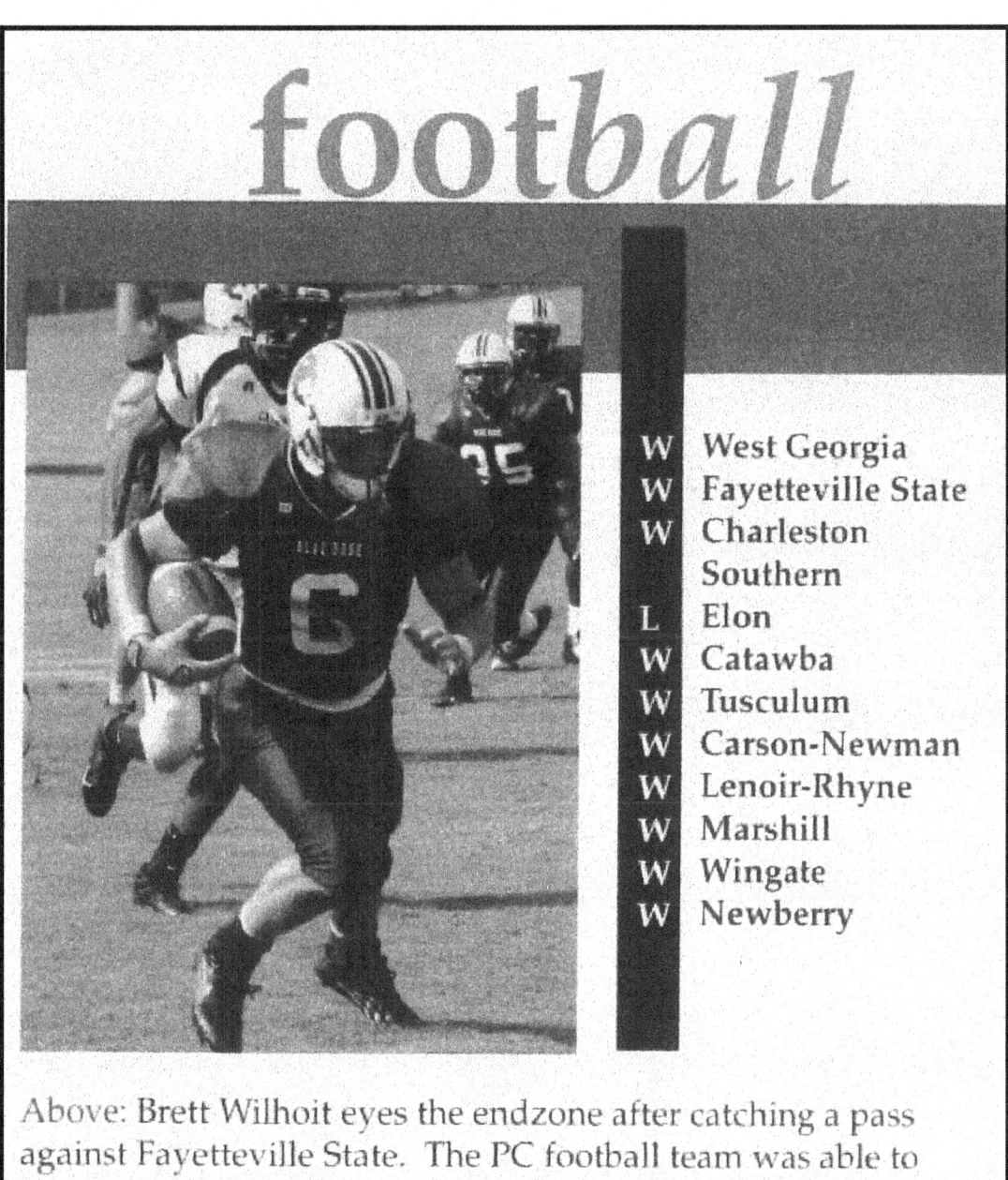

Above: Brett Wilhoit eyes the endzone after catching a pass against Fayetteville State. The PC football team was able to beat Fayetteville State en route to one of there best starts in school history.

ND
THE BLUE STOCKING
THE STUDENT NEWSPAPER OF PRESBYTERIAN COLLEGE

Thursday, November 10, 2005 — Volume 101, Issue 4

Congratulations PC Football!!!

PC Earns #1 Seed, First Round Bye in Division II Playoffs
By Stephen Speakman

When the announcement came across the television concerning the selection of teams for the Division II National Championship Playoffs this past Sunday, Presbyterian College had something to celebrate. After a stellar regular season (7-0 in the SAC, 10-1 overall), PC's football team enters into postseason play as the number one seed in the South East.

Playoff games begin this Saturday, November 12th. With its number one seed, Presbyterian College receives a first round bye and will host its opening playoff game the next weekend on November 16th against the winner of the game between University of Central Arkansas (9-2) and Albany State University (8-3).

The Blue Stocking staff would like to say congratulations to the Blue Hose for a job well done in the regular season. Best of luck in the weeks ahead! We'll certainly be there to root you on to victory! Go Blue Hose!

Photo by Andrew Howard

PC Crushes Newberry; Regains Bronze Derby
By Stephen Speakman

In what was a fitting end to a stellar regular season by the Blue Hose football team, Presbyterian College soundly defeated rival Newberry on Saturday night, November 5th, 2005 by the score of 38-7. Not only did the victory return the coveted "Bronze Derby" to its rightful home in Clinton, South Carolina, but with the victory, PC finished the regular season undefeated in the SAC with a record of 7-0. The team completed the regular season with a 10-1 record overall, and now will move into Division II playoffs next Saturday.

Presbyterian College quarterback Zach Ellis led the PC offense with 292 yards on 27 of 39 passing. Wide Receivers Chris Pope and Justin Durant led the receiving corps with 8 catches for 93 yards and 7 catches for 70 yards, respectively.

Chet'uane Reeder led the way on the ground attack for the Hose, taking 20 carries for 96 yards. Tailback Corey Fidler added 10 carries and 40 yards on the ground as well as made 6 receptions for 29 yards, acting as a potent double threat option for Ellis and the PC coaching staff.

Presbyterian led the way in every meaningful statistical category on offense, outpacing the Newberry Indians in first downs (24-13), rushing yards (108-80), passing yards (292-103), number of offensive plays (75-59), and time of possession (32:59-27:01).

The Blue Hose offense performed well in third-down situations, converting 10 of 16 third down attempts. They also capitalized on their red-zone opportunities, finishing drives with a score on 4 out of 5 trips to the red-zone.

Presbyterian College's defensive unit performed excellently for the Hose. Antwan Thomas led the team with 8 tackles, Justin Jones finished the night with 7, and Terrance Blake added 6 in what was a very strong defensive effort. Newberry's offense was limited to only 183 total yards and went the entire second-half without scoring. The only big play by Newberry came after a Zach Ellis fumble on the Newberry 5 yard-line which was returned all of the way to the Presbyterian College 20 yard-line. The ensuing drive resulted in the only Newberry score of the night.

When asked about the game, Senior defensive back Arthur Middleton said, "We were ready for them all week. We had a game plan that we talked about and the offense and defense were executing—going in and doing their jobs to make it a success.

"There wasn't anything outstanding. It's just been the same attitude: expecting to get it done; expecting to go in there and win."

The Blue Hose now move into Division II playoff action. Their first playoff game will be held at Presbyterian College's Bailey Stadium on Saturday, November 19th.

The 1979 Presbyterian Blue Hose Football Team

"A football season like no other, 1979 produced records galore, two All Americans, five All Staters and Coach of the Year honors for Calley Gault."

The year PC ranked Number One

A football season like no other, 1979 produced records galore, two All-Americans, five all-staters and coach-of-the-year honors for Cully Gault.

Blue Hose football took its highest bounce this past season in terms of national acclaim, team records and individual recognition.

Comparison among teams of different eras can be difficult, but even most longtime fans agree that 1979 is a prime candidate for the super season above all the rest.

After all, Presbyterian finished the regular season ranked Number 1 nationally in the NAIA and with a best-ever 10-1 record against strong opposition. This performance was only slightly tarnished by a loss in the semi-final round of the national playoffs, which brought a closing mark of 11 wins and 2 defeats.

At least two squads of past eras share special glory in the 66-year history of the sport at PC. The 1930 team of Coach Walter Johnson compiled a 9-1 record, losing only to Clemson while defeating the Citadel, North Carolina State and Wake Forest on successive weekends. And the 1959 Hose men of Frank Jones also went 9-1 before losing in the Tangerine Bowl.

Two PC players, offensive tackle Roy Walker and tailback Clayton Burke made the NAIA first team All-America, and Walker had the unusual distinction of being named for the second straight year to Kodak's college division All-America. Walker also received the Jacobs Blocking Trophy for the state—just the fourth PC

Not the least of the post-season honors have been the tributes paid to Coach Cally Gault. For the fifth time during his 17 years here, he was voted South Carolina "coach-of-the-year"—and, for a season when Carolina and Clemson coaches directed their teams to major bowl games, Gault also was cited as top coach in the SAC-8 and in NAIA District 6.

The dean of South Carolina college coaches in terms of tenure, Cally saw the 1979 season increase his overall PC record to 100 wins, 75 losses and 6 ties. He readily shares the coaching credit with assistants Bob Strock, John Perry '72, Elliott Poss '71 and Wayne Renwick '73.

Presbyterian produced its 1979 football magic with a well-balanced attack, sturdy defense and that extra dimension of "heart" necessary to sustain the winning momentum. The work of these ambitious young men with purpose in the classroom as well as on the field caught the imagination of the media and brought extensive coverage over a large area.

The regular season, dampened only by a close loss to Wofford, brought upset wins over the Citadel and Furman and a perfect SAC-8 campaign to claim that championship.

In the quarter-final playoff game against Saginaw State (Mich) in Clinton, injured quarterback Spence was replaced by Paul Scott, who completed 14 of 15 passes for 168 yards in directing the Blue Hose to victory. But the law of averages seemed finally to catch up with PC out at Central Oklahoma State. There, for the first time this season, numerous early turnovers gave that big opponent the opportunity to build a lead the injury-hampered Blue Hose offense could not overcome.

Central Oklahoma went on to lose narrowly in Texas A & I in the championship Palm Bowl game, and Presbyterian dropped to fourth place in the final national rankings, which followed.

In its 13 games last fall (11 regular-season, 2 playoff), PC accumulated 333 points and moved the ball a total of 4,805 yards from scrimmage for an average 370 per game. Quarterback Spence led the way with a record 2,064 yards running and passing. His aerial game also broke Blue Hose individual records in almost every category. 1,628 yards on 122 completions in 203 attempts for the remarkable accuracy of 61 percent and 12 touchdowns. His running added 436 yards and seven touchdowns.

The rushing sparks all belong to Clayton Burke, who finished among the national leaders. His 1,575 yards from scrimmage on 347 carries averaged 121 yards per game and 4.54 per run and produced the most touchdowns scored (16) amounting to the most points (98). This effort also gave him PC's career rushing record of 2,644. Other record performances:

Jesse Cason caught 50 passes for a new old season mark and set a new record of 127 (1,424 yards) over years.

Chuck Bishop's talented toe kicked 13 field goal attempts (73 percent accuracy) and 48 of 42 extra-point tries (95 percent) during 1979. His three field goals against Newberry represented the most ever kicked by a Blue Hose player in one game—the best-producing history with just 42 seconds left to play.

On defense, the secondary intercepted 31 passes for another team record—7 mainly to eight interceptions by Hal Hinton, seven by Hal Brannen and 5. Willie Cooper. Tackling honors went to Steve Stuby with 47 individual and assists, Jim McCraw with 46 and 72, Joe Grant with 37 and 76.

From every aspect, the 1979 season proved to be a great team effort by such fine individual performers. The final scores showed regular-season wins over the Citadel (21-13), Furman (17-10), Lenoir Rhyne (28-14), Catawba (21-0), Mars Hill (34-6), Univ. of Central Florida (48-0), Gardner-Webb (21-3), Carson-Newman (34-28) and Newberry (16-13), a loss to Wofford (27-24), a playoff win over Saginaw State (34-14) and loss to Central Oklahoma State (42-28).

Final Thoughts of the 1979 Presbyterian College Blue Hose Football Team

Jim McCoun simply stated that "The 1979 Presbyterian College football team was the best ever in school history."

I agree. Captain Jim McCoun DE was a leader who led by example. He and Captain Roy Walker OT and Captain Bruce Ollis OG learned from the best. There were numerous mentors. The 1979 Presbyterian College football team was a culmination of a three step blueprint for a winning program.

Presbyterian College Head Football Coach Cally Gault was in his 17th year at his alma mater. He had an incredible challenge in the mid 1970's as coaches needed to be added to his staff. He already had an outstanding DB Coach Bob Strock. The addition of Wayne Renwick (Offensive Backs), Elliott Poss (Defensive Line) and John Perry (Offensive Line) as Assistant Coaches was the first step to eventual success. Coach Renwick, Coach Poss and Coach Perry were all graduates of Presbyterian College. The three coaches were Captains of their respective Blue Hose teams. The three coaches stepped away from college football after they graduated, but came back together and knew exactly what Coach Gault expected, knew the Presbyterian College academic expectations, but most importantly, knew how to walk through a dorm on campus as a positive influence on a student athlete's life.

Recruiting duties were regionally distributed between the Coaches. They all knew the type of student athlete that needed to be on the Presbyterian College campus. "The team was full of personalities. They were good people. They were better people than football players," stated both Presbyterian College Assistant Football Coach John Perry and DB Joe Mooneyham. This was certainly the second ingredient for success in 1979.

The selection and character of the Captains in the mid 1970's was the third key for success. The 1977 Captains were such an influence on the 1978 and 1979 teams. In no particular order, a new culture was established with team rules, discipline and hard work. Players were held accountable for their play on the field, performance in the classroom and personal conduct. Was the system perfect? The answer is No. No organization is perfect, but problems were finally dealt with appropriately. Expectations were established and the culture was gaining momentum.

1978 put Presbyterian College football on the map. The Captains were leaders, but more importantly, other leaders appeared on and off the field. Relationships continued to build. The sense of camaraderie continued to form. A family atmosphere had been created. Dedicated work ethics on the field and in the classroom were paying off. An overall 8-2-1 record, which included both a Bronze Derby win and a tie with eventual NAIA National Championship runner up Elon. The defense allowed less than 12 points per game. The team was SAC-8 co-champions with Elon. The 1978 Blue Hose team was the best team since the 1959 Blue Hose team that went 9-2 and landed an invitation to the 1960 Tangerine Bowl.

The 1979 Presbyterian College Blue Hose football team has been chronicled in The Southern Massacre. Between the lines, an 11-2 record; Retention of the Bronze Derby; A victory over Elon; A #1 NAIA ranking; Victories over NCAA Division 1 Southern Conference teams The Citadel and Furman; An NAIA quarterfinal victory and an appearance in the NAIA semifinals.

While the 1979 Presbyterian College Blue Hose team was on the field, they could look around and see coaches, players, relatives, girlfriends, administrators, friends and fans. That crowd got bigger for obvious reasons as the season progressed. As we have progressed in life and because of the special bond created by their on field relationships, they still can see coaches, players, relatives, wives, administrators, friends and fans. The base has unfortunately decreased but the bond is greater than ever.

"Football is like life," said Jo Nell RB, "You get knocked down and then get up and do it again. Our bond doesn't break." On October 13, 1979, on a wet Johnson Field in Clinton, South Carolina the Presbyterian College Blue Hose lost, again, to those "Sons of Bitches" yet went on to become the NAIA #1 football team in the country. Did that happen because of a single coach or player? Absolutely not. The blueprint was in place. The blueprint worked.

Years later, the bond created in the late 1970's still exists. The players today still care and think about a mishandled punt return years ago. Cobs, who were most appreciated and were instrumental in a successful game plan for the week, were happy to be part of something special. Individual players were happy to see outstanding performances by their teammates. A once in a lifetime performance on the field in a NAIA Division 1 quarterfinal game was celebrated by all and they were elated to see it cherished by one. Preparation for the season was special. Wins were special. The players were special. The coaches were special. The season was special. The team was special. The blueprint was special and may never be replicated.

Mark Kay DT commented "Our football brotherhood resulted in familyhood later in life." Let that sink in.

Finally Hunter Reid, 1979 PC Student Sports Information Director and current Associate Athletic Director at Furman University told me,
"In 1979, Walker, Burke, Cason, Spence, Hinton, Grant, Atkins, McCoun, Stalvey, Ollis, Reed and Thornton may have been the best assembled group of football athletes ever at PC. They were part of the greatest football team ever at Presbyterian College."

I rest my case.

WR Jesse Cason and MG Joe Grant part of the bond created in 1979.

1979 Presbyterian College Blue Hose Defensive Game Plans

The Citadel, Furman, Wofford, Catawba
Elon, Carson Newman, Newberry
Artist: Coach Wayne Rewick

John Cann OG reunited with the 1979 Bronze Derby football.

Citadel Defenses 1979

6-2 Base defense
G's read → will slant & play different techniques

Tite 6 – LB'rs move around, will try to run through – will fire over the center! Linemen will slant – Don't let them fire through your head!

½ tite – ½ wide
Watch for slanting guards & stunting LB'rs

50 look – Usually slant back to six – Block with 50 blocking schemes – be ready for slant.

Goaline – T's & E's must block area!

Fist

Use on short yardage Linemen will slant!

Southern Massacre

#81 Mike Adams-DE
6-11 180 Sr.

#35 Kevin Curry
5-11 185 Sr.

#80 David Wardlaw-DT
6-5 235 Sr.   or   Gerry Bique-#8?
               5-3 225 Jr.
               Will Probably Start

Bill Salley-LB
6-2 215 Jr.

#69 Tony Purkett-DG
6-0 220 Sr.   or   Sedrick Brown-#67
               6-2 235 So.
               Will Probably Start

#46 Paul Gillis
5-11 185 Sr.

#65 Scott Wages-DG
6-0 230 Jr.

Mike Ashains-DB
6-0 200 So.   or   Kelly Curry-#32
Will Probably Start   6-0 210 So.

#60 Chuck Strong-DT
6-0 235 Sr.

#33 Joe Harvey
6-1 175 Jr.
or
#7 Bruce Alexander
5-11 170 So.
Will Probably Start

#48 Dale McBerty-DE
6-2 205 Jr.

6-2

```
              B       B
        E  T  G  G  T  E
     O     O  O  ⊠  O  O
                              O
                3     2
          15Load 15  13    12   14  14Load
  19(Only To Twins)                          18(Only To Twins)
            27D  25   BF  BF   24  26D
            39         31  30       38
          F-31 Opt  F-27  F-31T  F-30T  F-26  F-30 Opt
                        91  90
                        F   F
            F-15 G              F-14 G
```

39R 19R (Best Run To Wing Set)   18R 38R

Q.B. Note - If Play F-30T or F-31T Is Called And They Stay In The 6-2 But Move A LB over The Center, Check To F-26 or F-27 To The Side The LB Moved From.

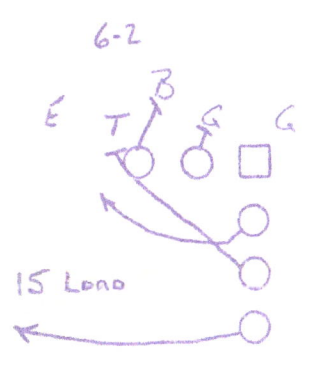

15 Load

Load The 1st Man Outside The Tackle - QB Must Read DE's Play

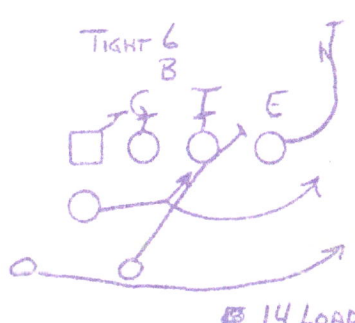

14 Load
Aim Point. Tackles Crack

Southern Massacre

The 1979 Presbyterian Blue Hose Football Team

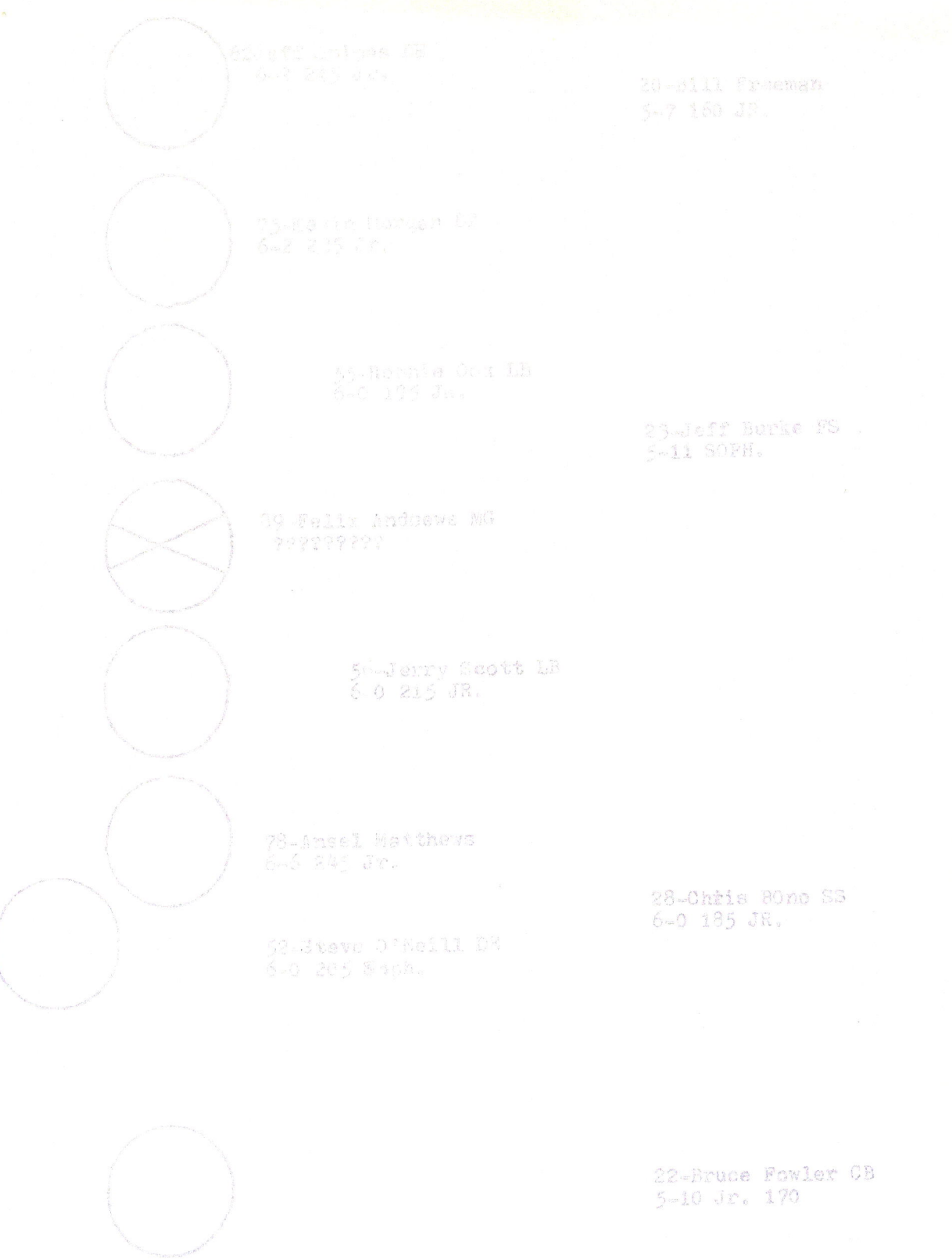

Southern Massacre

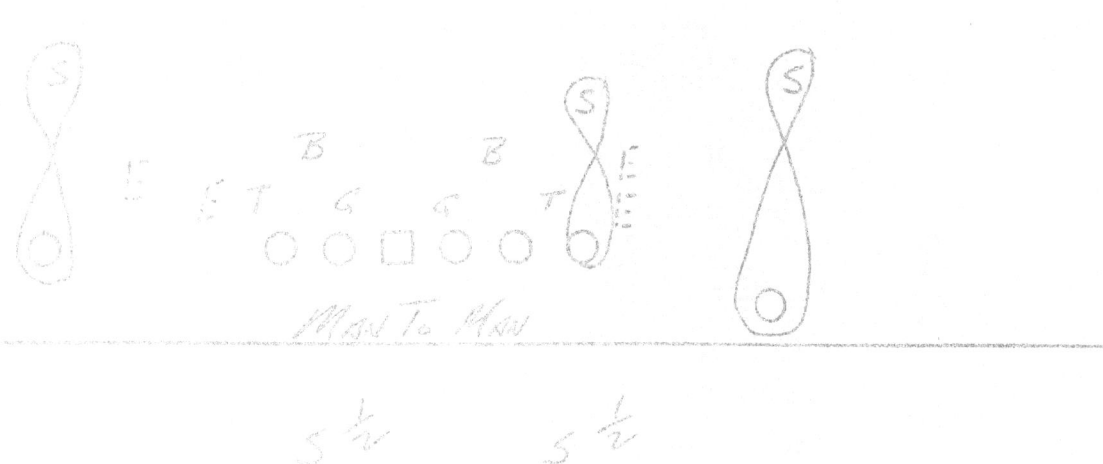

Southern Massacre

The 1979 Presbyterian Blue Hose Football Team

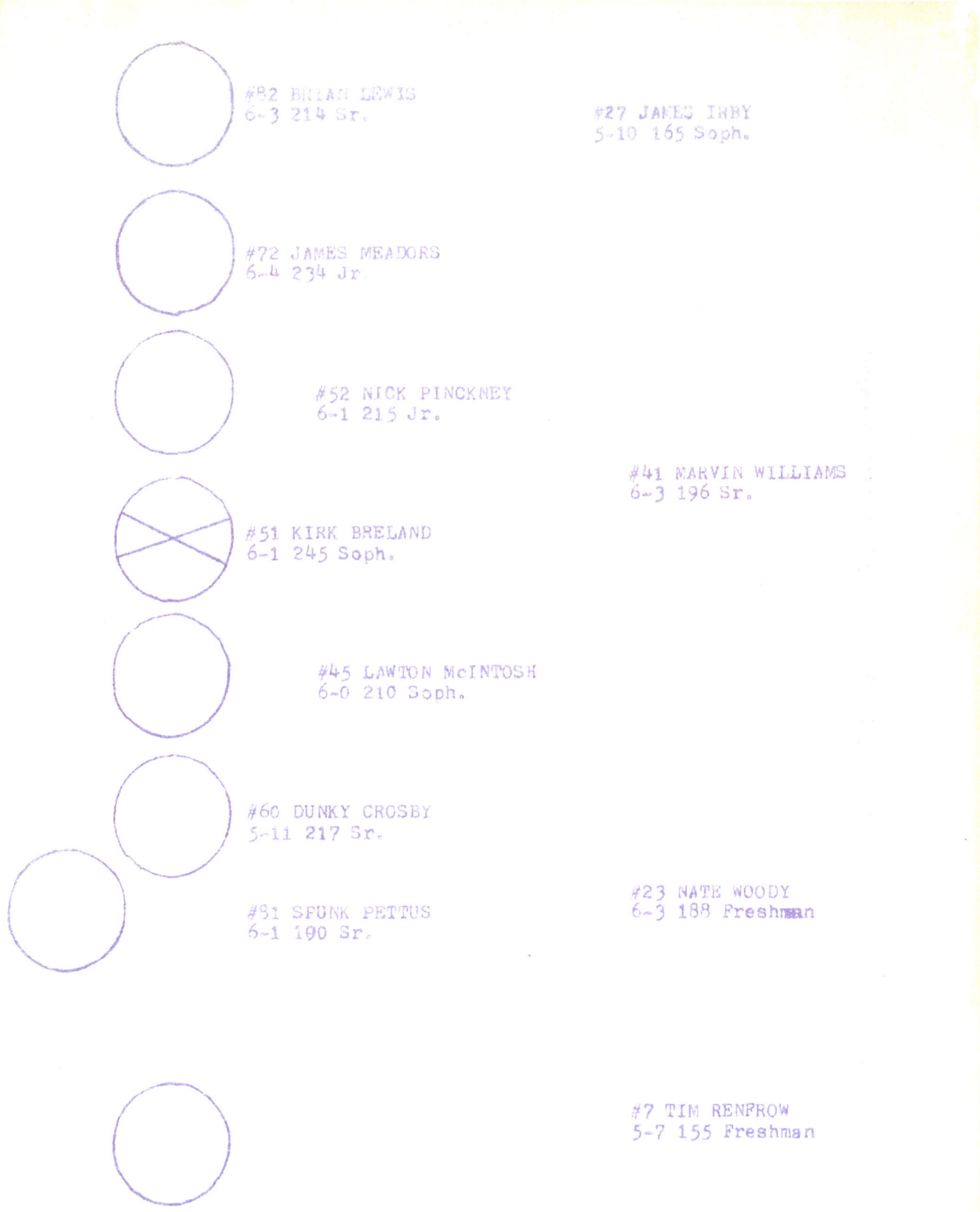

#82 BRIAN LEWIS
6-3 214 Sr.

#27 JAMES IRBY
5-10 165 Soph.

#72 JAMES MEADORS
6-4 234 Jr.

#52 NICK PINCKNEY
6-1 215 Jr.

#41 MARVIN WILLIAMS
6-3 196 Sr.

#51 KIRK BRELAND
6-1 245 Soph.

#45 LAWTON McINTOSH
6-0 210 Soph.

#60 DUNKY CROSBY
5-11 217 Sr.

#23 NATE WOODY
6-3 188 Freshman

#81 SPUNK PETTUS
6-1 190 Sr.

#7 TIM RENFROW
5-7 155 Freshman

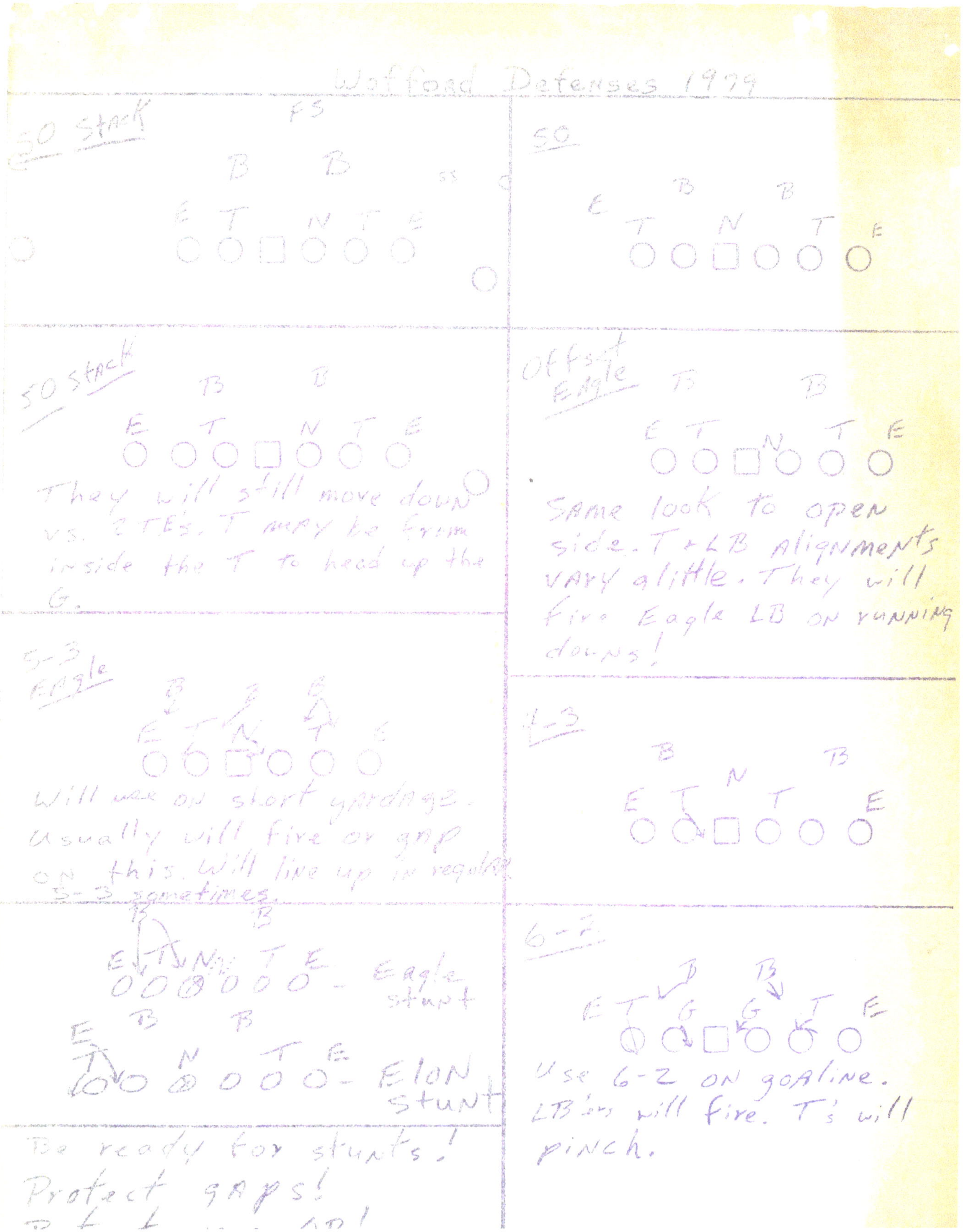

Wofford Defenses 1979

50 stack

(diagram: FS, B B, SS; E T N T E)

50

(diagram: B B; E T N T E)

50 stack

(diagram: B B; E T N T E)

They will still move down vs. 2 TE's. T may be from inside the T to head up the G.

Offset Eagle

(diagram: TS B; E T N T E)

Same look to open side. T & LB alignments vary a little. They will fire Eagle LB on running downs!

5-3 Eagle

(diagram: B B; E T N T E)

Will use on short yardage. Usually will fire or gap on this. Will line up in regular 5-3 sometimes.

4-3

(diagram: B B; E T N T E)

(Eagle stunt)

(diagram: E T N T E; B B)

(Elon stunt)

(diagram: E T N T E)

Be ready for stunts! Protect gaps!

6-2

(diagram: B B; E T G G T E)

Use 6-2 on goaline. LB's will fire. T's will pinch.

The 1979 Presbyterian Blue Hose Football Team

269

Catawba Defenses 1979

50

```
          S
C    B   B      S
  E T  N  T E
O  O O □ O O  O
```

- Played in a 50 front against us last year.
- T's and Nose play off about 1 yard.
- Nose takes a side most of the time.
- Run these 50 stunts
- Slant
- Fist
- Change
- Pinch tackles
- Elon stunt

(Free safety)

50 Stack

```
       B   B
        S
C   E T N T E   S C
O   O O □ O O   O
                  O
```

Used this defense more this year and stunt more.

```
       B    B
   E T   N   T E S
   O O   □   O O
```

Strong safety on weak corner blitz — they fist on that side.

6-2

```
B       B    B     B
 E T G   G T E
 O O □  O O O
                   O
```

Goalline — they will pinch G's and T's some

On short yardage they will stack, fist, or 6-2.

DEFENSE	1st-10	2nd Long	2nd Med	2nd Short	3rd Long	3rd Med	3rd Short
50 (37)	21	16	2	—	4	5	3
50 STACK (42)	21 (5) STUNTS	4 (1)-STUNT	3 (1) STUNT	1	3 (1) STUNT	—	3
50 END OFF (26)	5	5	—	—	14	2	—
50 FIST (31)	15	7	1	—	1	1	6
50 SLANT (14)	3	6	1	—	2	2	—
SS BLITZ (6)	2	1	2	—	—	(1)	—
ELON STUNT S/F P.R. (4)	3	—	—	—	—	1	—
FS BLITZ (2)	1	—	1	—	—	—	—
WEAK CORNER BLITZ (5)	3	1	1	—	—	—	—
50 CHANGE (5)	2	3	—	—	—	—	—
EAGLE (1)	—	—	1	—	—	—	—
6-2 GL	—	—	2-G-6yd 2-G-5yd	—	3-G-11yd	3-G-4yd	4-G-1yd
6-5 GL vs NEWBERRY	1-G-1yd	—	—	—	—	3-G-6yd	4-G-1yd

The FS #22 has always been the one that lines up as the weak corner on the line and blitzes. The FS Blitz as listed means he is coming up the middle. #41 the SS has always come on the SS Blitz.

Southern Massacre

The 1979 Presbyterian Blue Hose Football Team

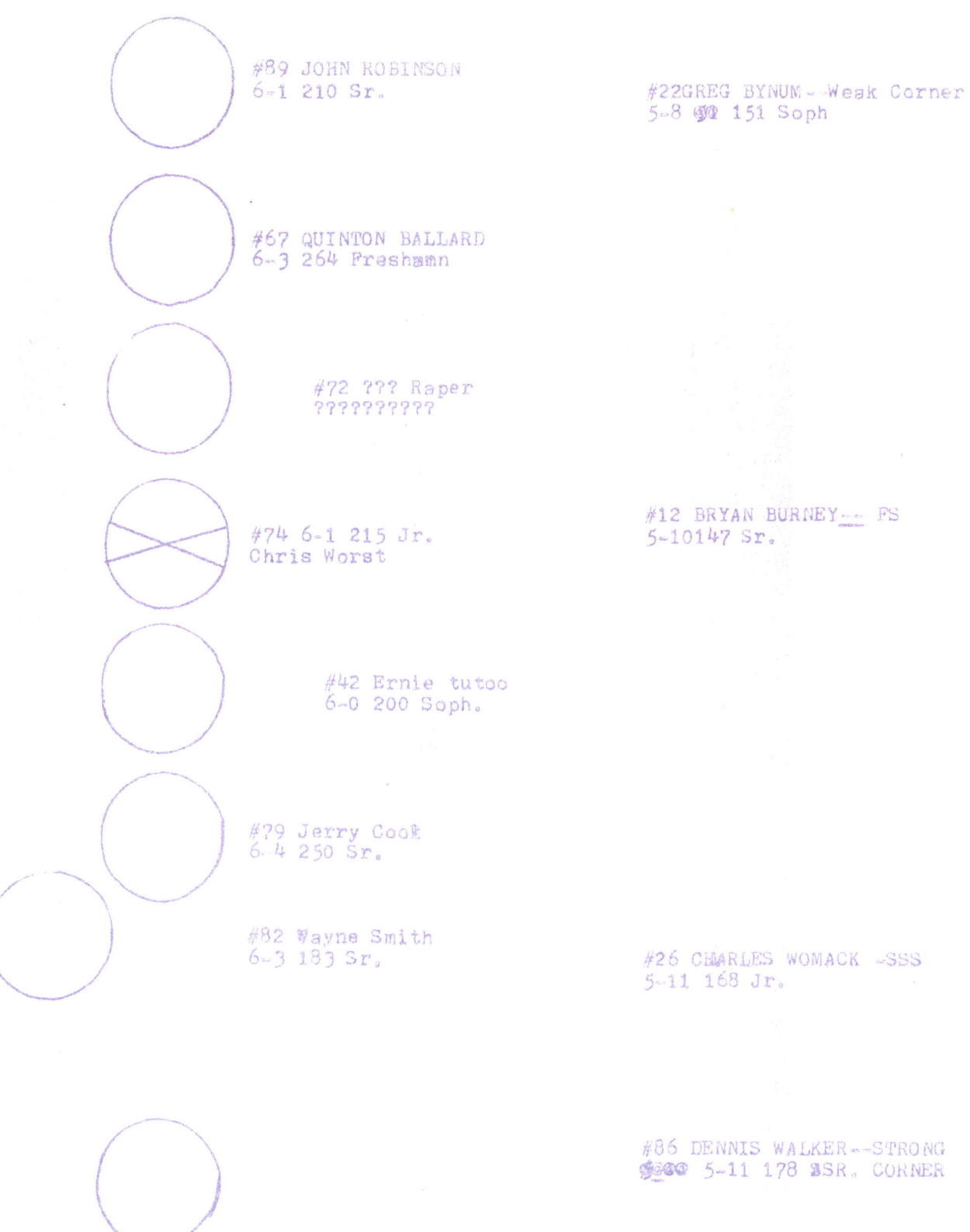

#89 JOHN ROBINSON
6-1 210 Sr.

#22 GREG BYNUM - Weak Corner
5-8 151 Soph

#67 QUINTON BALLARD
6-3 264 Freshamn

#72 ??? Raper
?????????

#74 6-1 215 Jr.
Chris Worst

#12 BRYAN BURNEY - FS
5-10 147 Sr.

#42 Ernie tutoo
6-0 200 Soph.

#79 Jerry Cook
6-4 250 Sr.

#82 Wayne Smith
6-3 183 Sr.

#26 CHARLES WOMACK - SSS
5-11 168 Jr.

#86 DENNIS WALKER -- STRONG
5-11 178 SR. CORNER

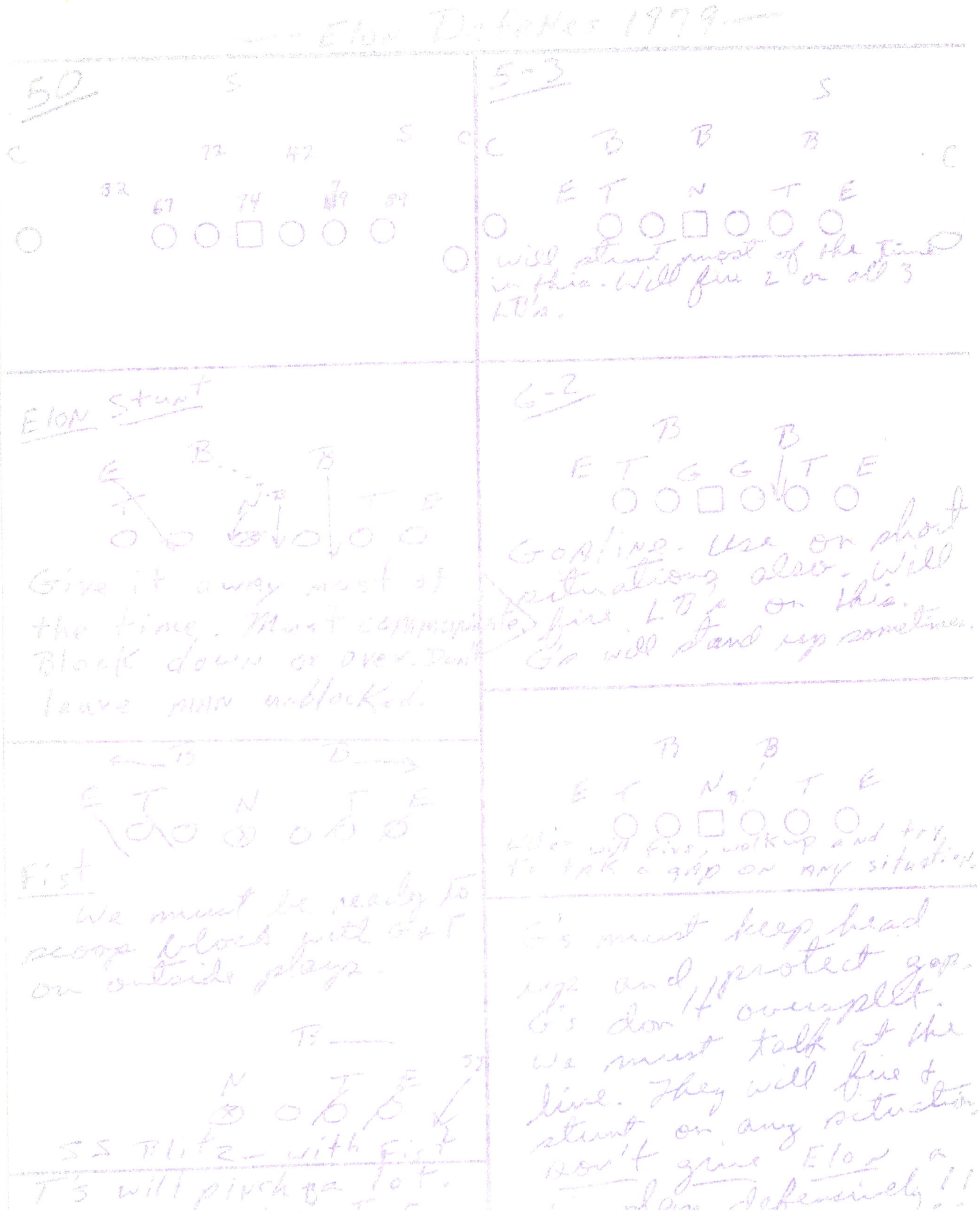

Elon October 1979

50

C 72 S 47 S C
   52 67 74 79 59
O   O O □ O O   O

5-3

C B B B C
   E T N T E
O O O □ O O O

Will stunt most of the time in this. Will fire 2 or all 3 LB's.

Elon Stunt

E B B
   T N T E
O O O □ O O O

Give it away most of the time. Must communicate. Block down or over. Don't leave man unblocked.

6-2

B B
E T G G T E
O O □ O O O

Goaline. Use on short situations also. Will fire LB's on this. G's will stand up sometime.

Fist

←B   B→
E T N T E
O O O O O O

We must be ready to scoop block with G+T on outside plays.

B→
N T E
O O O

SS Blitz - with fist T's will pinch ga. to E.

B B

E T N T E
O O □ O O O

LB's will fire, look up and try to take a gap on any situation.

G's must keep head up and protect gap. G's don't overplay. We must talk at the line. They will fire & stunt on any situation. Don't give Elon anything defensively!!

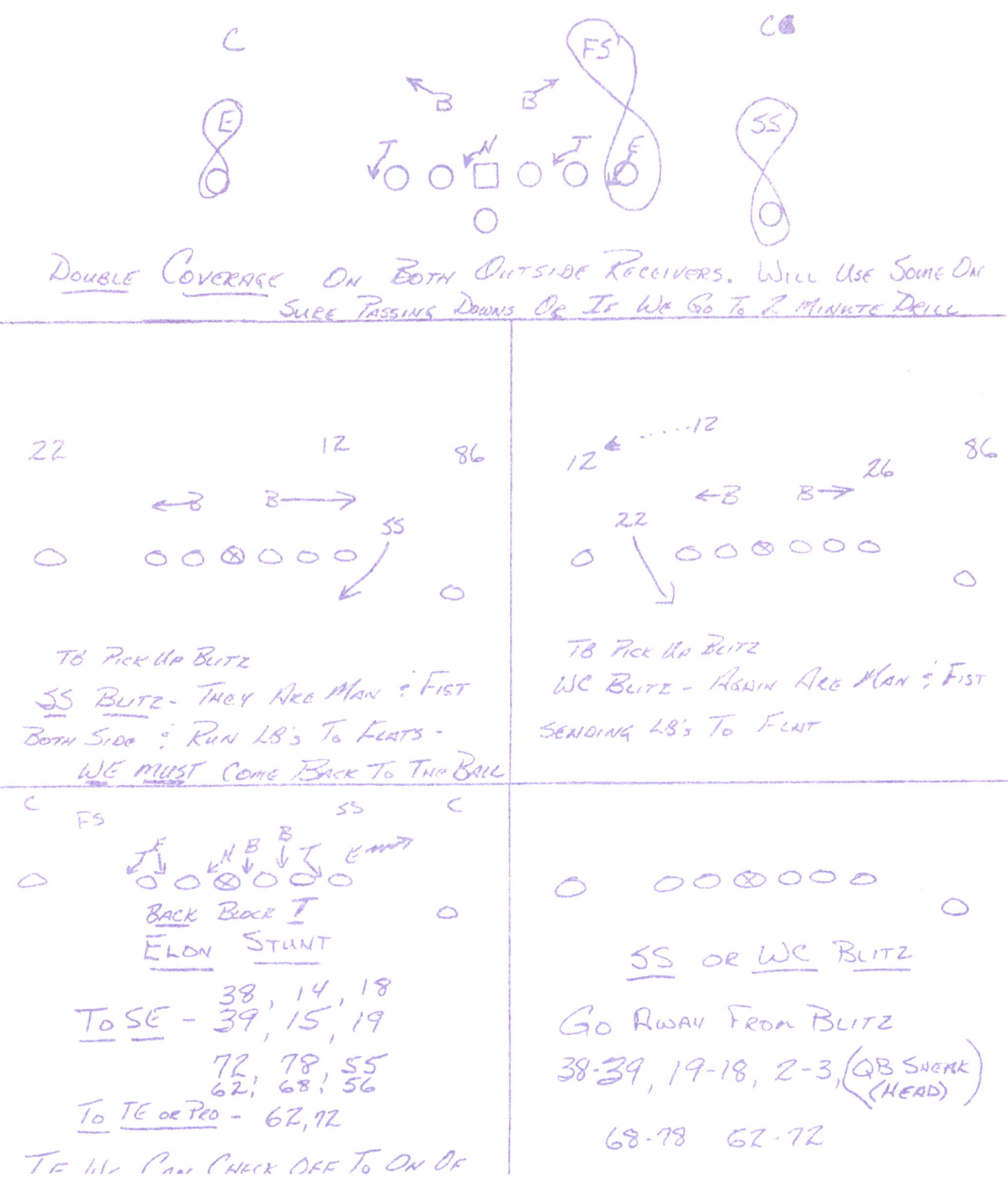

Southern Massacre

Defense	1-10	2-way	2-man	2/skull	3/man	3/man	3/skull	Total
50	29	10	5	2	7	?	3	68
50 Eagle	5	4	5	2	3	2	1	23
80/4	—	1	—	1	—	3	—	5
4-3	8/3	5		1	—	?	3	17 (3-stunts)
80/4 c	9	3	—	3		1	2	20
3-4 Stunt	5	5	1				1	17
Stunt	3						—	8
51 st	2	3					—	7
Stunt	2						—	2
4-3	—	—	—		2	1	—	3
6-2	1	—	1	—	—	—		8 (all Goal line)

The 1979 Presbyterian Blue Hose Football Team

Southern Massacre

The 1979 Presbyterian Blue Hose Football Team

The 1979 Presbyterian Blue Hose Football Team

Southern Massacre

Anatomy of Defenses 1979

50

```
        B    S    B
    E  T   N   T   E
    O  O   □   O   O   O
O                           O
```
T's read – LB's react and move quickly on flow

50 Stack

```
          B       B
    E  T     N    T   E
    O  O   □   O   O   O
```
Will stunt from this. They like to stunt more on long yardage.

Eagle Stunt

```
    B          B
    E  T   N   T   E
    O (O) (□)  O   O   O
         B    B
    T        K
    O  O   □  O   O
```
Cont. pinch with one or both LB's

Flow Stunt

```
         B    B
    E  T    N    T   E
    O (O) (□)(O) O   O
```

7 Crash

```
    E  T  LB   N  LB   T   E
    O  O      □      O   O
```
G/L or short

50 Eagle

```
        B         B
    E  T   N   T   E
    O  O   □   O   O   O
                              O
```

50 Offset

```
          B        B
    E  T    N    T   E
    O  O   □   O   O   O
```

6-2 Goalline

```
         B        B
    E  T  G   G   T   E
    O  O  □   O   O   O
```
G's come hard. They will fist from this or five LB'ers.

Fist

```
        B        B
    E  T   N   T   E
   (O) O  □   O  (O)
```

T's pinch

```
        B        B
    E  T   N   T   E
    O (O)  □  (O) O
```

SS Blitz

```
        B        B                SS
    E  T   N   T   E /
    O  O   □   O  (O)
                        O
```

Defensive Tendencies

Defenses (185)	1-10 (64)	2-long (58)	2-Med (43)	2-Short (5)	3-long (24)	3-Med (12)	3-Short (0)
50 (71)	35	10	7	5	7	4	3
50 Eagle (23)	4	9	1	—	6	1	2
50 Offset (11)	5	4	1	—	—	—	1
50 E off (10)	—	2	—	—	5	3	—
50 T Pinch (7)	4	1	1	—	—	—	1
50 Eagle Stunt (6)	1	1	—	—	2	2	—
50 Peck (22)	10	6	2	—	3	1	—
S/F Pass (5)	1	4	—	—	—	—	—
Centerfire (6)	2	1	1	—	—	1	1
Riot (4)	4	—	—	—	—	—	—
S S Blitz (3)	2	1	—	—	—	—	—
Slot Blitz (2)	1	—	—	—	1	—	—
7 Card (2)	—	—	—	—	—	—	2
6-2 (14)	(14 Regular, 3 long, 3 med 10% or 3 down)						

Acknowledgements

A special thank you to the players, coaches and all that participated in the success of the 1979 Presbyterian Blue Hose football team. Many of you were classmates and part of the administration while I was at Presbyterian College. It was wonderful to reconnect. In particular, a huge thank you to Sarah Leckie, Presbyterian College Librarian in charge of Archives and Technical Services at the Presbyterian College James H. Thomason Library. Sarah went above and beyond in helping me obtain the resources I needed for this project. Finally, thank you, in no particular order, to the following for your special contributions to the success of documenting <u>The Southern Massacre</u>.

Rene Wertz, Presbyterian College Athletic Department
Brent Stastiny, Presbyterian College Athletic Department
Keith Jude, Presbyterian College Class of 1982
Mitchell Mercer, Editor, "Presbyterian College Blue Stocking"
Randy Randall, Mayor, Clinton, South Carolina
Ginger Crocker, Director of Community Relations at South Carolina Public Service Commission
Stump Mitchell, Running Backs Coach, Cleveland Browns
Kim Porter, Wife, Best Friend and Motivator
Hank Mason, Athletic Trainer, 1979 Presbyterian College football team
Randy Morris, Player, 1979 Presbyterian College football team
Erskine Reed, Player, 1979 Presbyterian College football team
John Cann, Player, 1979 Presbyterian College football team
Jim McCoun, Player, 1979 Presbyterian College football team
Andy Forrest, Player, 1979 Presbyterian College football team
Jay Byars, Player, 1979 Presbyterian College football team
Tom Steele, Player, 1979 Presbyterian College football team
Bruce Ollis, Player, 1979 Presbyterian College football team

Bibliography

Page 23 .... Baker, "Greenville News and Piedmont," September 9, 1979
Page 23 ....Gault, "Greenville News and Piedmont," September 9, 1979
Page 24 ....Gault, "Greenville News and Piedmont," September 9, 1979
Page 25 .... Sheridan, "Greenville News and Piedmont," September 13, 1979
Page 36 ....Gault, "Greenville News and Piedmont," September 16, 1979
Page 36 ....Gault, "Greenville News and Piedmont," September 16, 1979
Page 36 ....Gault, "Greenville News and Piedmont," September 16, 1979
Page 36 ....Gault, "Greenville News and Piedmont," September 16, 1979
Page 37 ....Gault, "Greenville News and Piedmont," September 16, 1979
Page 37 ....Gault, "Greenville News and Piedmont," September 20, 1979
Page 101 .... Bishop, "Greenville News and Piedmont," November 23, 1979
Page 101 ....Charpia, "Greenville News and Piedmont," November 23, 1979
Page 101 .... White, "Greenville News and Piedmont," November 23, 1979
Page 102 ....Gault, "Greenville News and Piedmont," November 23, 1979
Page 135 .... Waters, "Greenville News and Piedmont," November 30, 1979
Page 136 .... Waters, "Greenville News and Piedmont," November 30, 1979
Page 161 ....Gault, "Greenville News and Piedmont," December 9, 1979
Page 175 ....Spangler, "The Presbyterian College Report," 2019
Page 188 ....Gault, "The Laurens Advertiser," August 29, 1979
Page 219 ....Charpia, "Greenville News and Piedmont," November 23, 1979
Page 219 ......Sheridan, "Greenville News and Piedmont," September 16, 1979
Page 219 ....Gault, "Greenville News and Piedmont," September 13, 1979
Page 220 .... Bishop, "Greenville News and Piedmont," November 23, 1979
Page 229 .... Burke, "Greenville News and Piedmont," November 23, 1979

The 1979 Presbyterian Blue Hose Football Team

Photo and Periodical Credits

Title page	Courtesy of Presbyterian College Pac Sac
Dedication	Photo by Chip Porter
Page 1	Courtesy of "Presbyterian College Report"
Page 4	Courtesy of Presbyterian College "Blue Stocking"
Page 11	Used with permission from "The Laurens County Advertiser"
Page 12	Used with permission from "The Laurens County Advertiser"
Page 13	Courtesy of "Presbyterian College Report"
Page 14-15	Courtesy of Presbyterian College archives
Page 16	Used with permission from "The Laurens County Advertiser"
Page 17	Used with permission from The Citadel archives
Page 18	Used with permission from The Citadel archives
Page 19	Used with permission from The Citadel archives
Page 22	Used with permission from "The Laurens County Advertiser"
Page 22	Photo courtesy of Walter Atkins
Page 26	Courtesy of Presbyterian College "Blue Stocking"
Page 26	Photo courtesy of Hank Mason
Page 27	Used with permission from Furman University archives
Page 28	Used with permission from "The Laurens County Advertiser"
Page 29	Used with permission from Furman University archives
Page 32	Courtesy of Presbyterian College Pac Sac
Page 33	Used with permission from "The Laurens County Advertiser"
Page 34	Courtesy of Presbyterian College "Blue Stocking"
Page 35	Courtesy of Presbyterian College "Blue Stocking"
Page 37	Photo courtesy of Hank Mason
Page 39	Used with permission from "The Laurens County Advertiser"
Page 42	Courtesy of Presbyterian College "Blue Stocking"
Page 43	Photo courtesy of Randy Randall
Page 44	Used with permission from "The Laurens County Advertiser"
Page 45	Courtesy of Presbyterian College archives

Page 48 .... Used with permission from "The Laurens County Advertiser"
Page 48 ....Courtesy of Presbyterian College "Blue Stocking"
Page 50 ....Photo by Kimberly Porter
Page 51 ....Itinerary by Coach Wayne Renwick
Page 54 ....Courtesy of Presbyterian College "Blue Stocking"
Page 56 .... Used with permission from "The Laurens County Advertiser"
Page 57 ....Courtesy of Presbyterian College archives
Page 60 ....Courtesy of Presbyterian College "Blue Stocking"
Page 61 .... Used with permission from "The Laurens County Advertiser"
Page 62 ....Courtesy of Presbyterian College Pac Sac
Page 63 ....Courtesy of Presbyterian College archives
Page 66 .... Used with permission from "The Laurens County Advertiser"
Page 67 ....Itinerary by Coach Wayne Renwick
Page 68 ....Courtesy of Presbyterian College "Blue Stocking"
Page 69 ....Courtesy of Presbyterian College archives
Page 72 ....Courtesy of Presbyterian College "Blue Stocking"
Page 73 .... Used with permission from "The Laurens County Advertiser"
Page 74 ....Itinerary by Coach Wayne Renwick
Page 75 .... Used with permission from "The Laurens County Advertiser"
Page 76 ....Courtesy of Gardner Webb archives and used with permission
Page 79 ....Courtesy of Presbyterian College "Blue Stocking"
Page 80 .... Used with permission from "The Laurens County Advertiser"
Page 82 ....Itinerary by Coach Wayne Renwick
Page 83 ....Courtesy of Presbyterian College archives
Page 86 .... Used with permission from "The Laurens County Advertiser"
Page 87 .... Used with permission from Newberry College archives
Page 88 .... Used with permission from "The Laurens County Advertiser"
Page 89-93 ....Courtesy of Jay Byars from the "Sandlapper"
Page 94 .... Used with permission from Newberry College archives
Page 97 ....Courtesy of Presbyterian College "Blue Stocking"
Page 98-99 .... Used with permission from "The Laurens County Advertiser"
Page 100 ....Coaches photo courtesy of Hank Mason

Page 100 .... Football photo by Chip Porter
Page 102 .... Courtesy of Presbyterian College Pac Sac
Page 103 .... Derby photo courtesy of Joe Grant
Page 103 .... Sticker photo courtesy of Bruce Ollis
Page 104 .... Used with permission from "The Laurens County Advertiser"
Page 105 .... Courtesy of Presbyterian College "Blue Stocking"
Page 108-122 .... Courtesy of Jay Byars with permission from the NAIA
Page 128 .... Courtesy of Andy Forrest
Page 132 .... Used with permission from "The Laurens County Advertiser"
Page 133 .... Football photo by Chip Porter
Page 133 .... Football reception photo courtesy of Jay Byars taken by Vic Tutte.
Page 134 .... Used with permission from "The Atlanta Journal Constitution"
Page 137 .... Photo courtesy of Bruce Ollis
Page 138-152 .... Courtesy of Jay Byars with permission from the NAIA
Page 153 .... Used with permission from "The Laurens County Advertiser"
Page 154 .... Courtesy of "The Vista"
Page 158 .... Courtesy of and used with permission from "The Oklahoman"
Page 159 .... Courtesy of and used with permission from "The Oklahoman"
Page 160 .... Used with permission from "The Laurens County Advertiser"
Page 163 .... Photo courtesy of Bruce Ollis
Page 164 .... Sticker courtesy of Bruce Ollis
Page 166 .... Courtesy of Presbyterian College Pac Sac
Page 167 .... Courtesy of Presbyterian College Pac Sac
Page 169 .... Photo by Kimberly Porter
Page 170-172 .... Courtesy of Presbyterian College archives
Page 178 .... Courtesy of Presbyterian College archives
Page 179 .... Captains photo courtesy of Presbyterian College archives
Page 179 .... Team photo courtesy of Hank Mason
Page 183 .... Photo by Kimberly Porter
Page 184-186 .... Courtesy of Presbyterian College archives
Page 190 .... Photo by Kimberly Porter
Page 191 .... Courtesy of Presbyterian College archives

Page 194 ....Courtesy Presbyterian College archives
Page 195 ....Furman scoreboard photo courtesy of Hank Mason
Page 195 ....CSU scoreboard Courtesy of Presbyterian College Pac Sac
Page 198 ....Photo courtesy of Hank Mason
Page 205 ....Courtesy of Presbyterian College Pac Sac
Page 206 ....Photo courtesy of Presbyterian College archives
Page 206-210................................ Courtesy of Presbyterian College Magazine
Page 210 .... Photo courtesy of Presbyterian archives
Page 211 ....Courtesy of Presbyterian College Pac Sac
Page 212 ....Courtesy of Presbyterian College Pac Sac
Page 214 .... Photo courtesy of Bruce Ollis
Page 215 ....Courtesy of Presbyterian College Pac Sac
Page 218 ....Courtesy of Presbyterian College Pac Sac
Page 221 ....Courtesy of Presbyterian College Pac Sac
Page 222 .... Used with permission from "The Laurens County Advertiser"
Page 223 .... Photo courtesy of Joe Grant
Page 224 .... Photo courtesy of Erskine Reed
Page 225 ....Courtesy of Presbyterian College Pac Sac
Page 226 .... Used with permission from "The Laurens County Advertiser"
Page 227 ....Courtesy of Presbyterian College Pac Sac
Page 228 ....Photo courtesy of Paul Scott taken by Vic Tutte.
Page 230 ....Photo by Kimberly Porter
Page 232 ....Photo by Kimberly Porter
Page 235 .... Used with permission from "The Laurens County Advertiser"
Page 236 ....Photo by Kimberly Porter
Page 238-245 ....Courtesy of Presbyterian College Pac Sac
Page 247-251 ....Courtesy of Presbyterian College Pac Sac
Page 252 ....Courtesy of Presbyterian College "Blue Stocking"
Page 257 .... Photo courtesy of Joe Grant
Page 258 .... Photo by Chip Porter

Advertisements courtesy of Presbyterian College archives